THE REUNIONS

TAMMY MELLOWS TRILOGY BOOK 3

TINA HOGAN GRANT

Autographed by Author

To Lisa,
Love
Tina Hogan Grant

Tina Hogan Grant

Edited by Crystal Santoro Editorial Services: https://chrissyseditorialservices.org/

Cover Design by T.E.Black Designs – http://www.teblackdesigns.com

Visit The Author's Website

www.tinahogangrant.com

❀ Created with Vellum

To my sisters
Jane & Debbie

Miles apart
but
close at heart

***Don't put off until tomorrow
what you can do today**** - Benjamin Franklin*

PROLOGUE

Two years ago, not only had Tammy met her calling as a commercial fisherwoman, but she had also unexpectedly fallen in love with Dwayne. A man who showed her the beauty and freedom of the open ocean and lobster fishing skills.

He tolerated her stubbornness and hardheaded attitude as she slowly learned to trust again after being in an abusive relationship that left scars unhealed. She had become dependent on alcohol to numb her wounds, and he was there for her throughout her sobriety. Dwayne believed in her and saw beyond her tattered shell. He was determined to help her rise beyond her troubles and to believe in herself like he did.

He admired her strength, her beauty, and the determination she held to prove herself worthy and rise above her troubled past.

Tammy entered the fishing industry, feeling intimidated and fearful of the unknown. She feared the ocean and its power. Men dominated the fleet, and the opinions they voiced of her had her on edge. They questioned if she would be capable of keeping up with the enduring intense labor expected of her during the six months of the season. But just as Dwayne had expected, she faced every challenge that came her way with an attitude of steel and refused to be defeated. The bigger the challenge, the more she pushed herself to succeed, and she never gave up.

Tammy's love for the ocean was instant, and so was the respect she had for those that worked it. It's one of the toughest ways to make a living, but it drew Tammy to it like a magnet. Dwayne saw her eagerness to learn and taught her everything she knew about commercial fishing and living a life at sea.

Dwayne saw what Tammy couldn't, and because of his patience, he brought the best out in her. She finally had a sense of belonging and a passion that drove her to keep pushing herself and work hard. At the end of each day, her body ached to the core, her muscles were sore, and she could barely move, but she still had a smile on her face because the work, as grueling as it was, gave her a feeling of satisfaction.

After her first year, Tammy earned the respect of the other fishermen. Like Dwayne, they admired her strength and stamina, and let's not forget her homemade chicken dinner, which she had cooked for them one night while they were all anchored in the harbor. By the end of the season, she was considered part of the fleet.

Tammy's son, Matt, was four years old when she met Dwayne, and for the first time in his life, he finally had a father figure. Matt took to the boats, fishing, and ocean as quickly as his mother did. He fished off the back of Dwayne's boat, the *Baywitch,* most nights with Dwayne after he and his mom had moved onto the boat with him shortly after they had met. And even though the boat's living quarters were small, especially when Dwayne's son, Justin, visited, they were content and happy and most of all a family.

But all good things came with a price, and Tammy allowed herself to become estranged from her close friends and immediate family. Once she left her job at the restaurant where she worked for most of Matt's life and moved out of the home in Pasadena, she shared with her best friend Judy; Tammy never looked back. Sadly, she and Judy never kept in touch, and she no longer knows where she is.

Tammy last saw her mother, Rose, five years ago. She rarely writes or calls because of the times she spends on the ocean. She is even more estranged from her sister Jenny, who also lives in England with her husband, Stuart, and their two children, Tommy and Kate. It saddens Tammy that she had a niece and nephew that she has never met, and Jenny has never met her nephew Matt.

Tammy was seventeen when she last saw Jenny. That was ten years ago. They were sisters by blood but knew nothing about each other. Calls between them were non-existent. They only shared letters and photos over the holidays. Tammy had often wondered if they were to pass each other on the street, would they recognize each other?

Her father, John, and his second wife, Joanne, still lived in Florida, and Tammy called them often. Ever since her big move to the states, she had remained close to her father and continued to seek his approval. Finally, after numerous embarrassing mistakes, Tammy heard the pride in his voice when she called after returning from the island with adventurous tales of their fishing trip.

Before Tammy took up a life as a commercial fisherwoman, she remained close and saw her other sister Donna often, who was Jenny's identical twin. She lived only an hour away from the house Tammy shared with Judy. But once Tammy moved in with Dwayne on the boat, her regular visits stopped. Tammy was either out at sea or on the mainland for just a few days to sell the lobsters and pick up more supplies before heading back out. There wasn't enough time to make the two-hour drive from the Marina to Donna's place. It's been over a year since she last saw her.

Her mother's only wish was to have her daughters all in the same room one more time, and she reminded Tammy every time they spoke on the phone. It was how she always ended her calls, and each time Tammy's heart tore just a little more. She realized her mother wasn't getting any younger, and she saw the signs of aging were showing on the rare occasions she made it to the States. Tammy wanted to make her mother's wish come true. But how and when?

CHAPTER 1

*I*n a panic, Tammy dropped the Pepsi can she held, ignoring the soda explosion that spilled over the deck of the *Baywitch.* With her heart racing, she ran to the stern of the boat, where her son screamed. Blood poured from his mouth. She predicted the accident before it occurred and couldn't move fast enough. It happened so quickly.

They were at San Clemente Island, anchored in the harbor after dumping a load of lobster traps to prepare for the upcoming season. It was Tammy's third season fishing with Dwayne, and it was the second time they had taken Matt. Last year she refused to send Matt to Florida to stay with her dad and Joanne for three months like she'd done the year before. Being separated from him was just too unbearable.

Somehow, they juggled care for him between the wives of the workers at the boatyard and the mothers of Matt's friends at school. This year they were more organized and hoped things would go smoother.

They knew from experience that dropping off the lobster traps before the season's opening wasn't as intense as pulling the gear, so they took Matt with them for these short turnaround trips.

Last year, Tammy and Dwayne stayed at the island for five to seven days at a time. This year it will be different. They would only be gone weekdays Monday thru Friday.

Tammy became good friends with Louise-a mother from Matt's school and one of Matt's friends. She agreed to watch Matt at her house for the five days they would be gone with the promise that they'd return Friday night. This arrangement would give Tammy weekends with Matt. Even though she knew they would spend the time getting ready for the next trip, Matt would at least be with her and not thousands of miles away in Florida, where she couldn't see him at all.

It was only an eight-week arrangement with Louise, depending on the weather. After that, just like the previous years, Dwayne and Tammy would move all their gear to Malibu and fish every three days. Because Malibu was closer, and they would be home every night, they planned on taking Matt on some trips when he didn't have school.

The first trip to San Clemente Island with Matt on board went great. He was a burst of energy in his orange life vest and took everything in as his mother had on her first trip. He never got seasick and walked around the boat like it was second nature. When the time came to drop the traps, Dwayne sent Matt down to the cabin where it was safe. Periodically Tammy made it a point to check on him. She laughed at how entertained he was with Matchbox cars that moved by themselves across the table inside the rocking boat.

"Look, mom, no batteries," he would say, making Tammy laugh.

Because last year went so well, they took Matt again this year. Everything went according to plan. They had all their gear in the water, waiting to be fished the following week when Tammy and Dwayne would return. Tammy just removed her slickers and rested her tired body while sipping on a Pepsi. Dwayne worked on the *Little Boat*, ensuring everything was cleaned up and secured for the crossing home.

Matt stood at the back of the *Baywitch*, watching an airplane take off from the island.

"Look at the plane, mommy," he yelled as he pointed his finger up to the sky and then quickly covered his ears from the roaring sounds as it took off. The loud sound scared Matt. Tammy knew he was about to run toward her. She saw the puddle of water on the deck and screamed.

"No, Matt, don't run!" But it was too late.

Tammy watched with horror as Matt slipped on the water, and his body crashed onto the deck facedown, and his face slammed into the non-skid finish of the deck. She immediately saw the pool of blood, and his blood-curdling screams tore at her heart.

"Oh, my god!" Tammy screamed as she raced over to her son. "Dwayne! Dwayne! Come quick!" She hollered above Matt's piercing screams, who was still face-down, kicking his legs while his head remained still.

Tammy didn't know how severely Matt was hurt. It scared her. She trembled as she knelt beside him and gently lifted him into her arms. She gasped when she saw his face covered in blood.

The boat suddenly rocked from the force of Dwayne leaping onto it from the Little Boat. Tammy steadied her feet until the rocking subsided and noticed her shirt sleeve saturated with blood.

Dwayne saw the panic on Tammy's face and heard the screams from Matt, who coughed from the blood trickling down his throat. He couldn't see Matt's face from where he stood, but he could read the fear in Tammy's eyes.

"What happened? Is he okay?"

Tammy shook her head hysterically as the tears she had been holding back streamed down her face. "No, he fell, and he is bleeding badly," she cried.

Dwayne went to Tammy's side and gently touched Matt's head

as he inspected his face. "Jesus! We may have to call the coast guard."

Tammy held Matt tighter, who was still screaming at the top of his lungs, "Is it that bad?" She tried to comfort him with rubs to his back. "Shh, it's okay, baby," she whispered. Guilt was flooding through her. "There was a pool of water on the deck, and he got scared of the planes taking off. I knew he was going to run over to me. I couldn't stop him in time."

Dwayne tried to inspect Matt's face to see where the bleeding was coming from, but it was impossible to tell with all the blood smeared across his skin. "Hey hon, it's not your fault. Let's get him down below and clean him up. I think he may have knocked some teeth out."

Tammy gasped. "What, oh, no!" She rubbed Matt's back some more. "Come on, buddy. We're going to clean you up and see where you are hurting." "Okay," she said over Matt's heart-wrenching tears that weren't subsiding at all.

Dwayne went down into the cabin first. "Here, sit on the edge of the bed with him and turn him around so I can see his face. I don't want him lying down in case he has a loose tooth that may become dislodged. He could choke on it."

Tammy gently lifted Matt's head off her shoulder and, with care, turned him around and placed him on her lap with the back of his head against her chest.

"No!" Matt protested as Tammy folded his arms in front of him and held them tight.

"Jesus, that's a lot of blood," Dwayne whispered, not wanting to scare Matt. He rubbed Matt's knee. "It's okay, buddy. We're going to help you, okay. Now sit still with mommy while I go find a towel to clean you up with."

Matt nodded and hiccuped some tears back.

"It looks like most of the blood is coming from his mouth. I'll be right back with some fresh water and towels."

Tammy nodded and kissed the top of Matt's head as she rocked him on her knees. His crying continued, but not at the screeching level it had been.

A few minutes later, Dwayne returned with a saucepan of water and towels and kneeled before Matt and surveyed his face. It was hard to tell where the injuring originated from. Dwayne moistened the towel. "I'm going to clean your face, okay, buddy."

Matt darted his head away from Dwayne's hand. "No!" He screamed.

Dwayne looked at Tammy. "Hold on to him while I do this."

Tammy nodded and tightened her grip. "It's okay. Dwayne is going to make you feel better. Relax, sweetie."

After a few shakes of his head, Matt finally allowed Dwayne to gentle dab his face. Dwayne wanted to get his mouth clean where most of the blood was coming from. The blood smeared on his cheeks, and his forehead had no cuts. He could clean those parts up later after determining how severe the wound was around the mouth. Little by little, with care, Dwayne wiped away the blood. Matt was still bleeding, and it seemed to come from his lower lip. His crying now subsided to hiccups and sniffs.

Dwayne wanted Matt to trust him and spoke softly, "Can you open your mouth?"

Matt nodded and slowly separated his lips.

Dwayne was pleased to see all his teeth were in place and felt them with his fingers. "None of his teeth seem to be loose. That's good," he said as he dabbed more blood that was oozing out of his lip. "Bite softly on the towel," he told Matt, which he did.

"I'm going to leave it there for a few minutes to stop the bleeding. Okay, buddy."

Matt nodded.

"It looks like it's just his bottom lip that's cut."

Tammy released an enormous sigh of relief before kissing Matt tenderly on his head. "Thank god! So, he's going to be okay?" Tammy pleaded.

Dwayne crouched down and removed the towel from Matt's

lips, looking at it closely. "Yeah, I think so. There's no need to call the coast guard. It looks like when he fell; his upper teeth bit down onto his lower lip. I see at least three teeth marks."

"I saw him. He hit the deck hard, and his face slammed into it." Tammy said as she lifted Matt from her lap and looked at his lip. She looked at Dwayne with pity in her eyes. "We can't bring Matt out here until he's older. I thought he'd be okay on these quick turnaround trips, but look what a bit of water on the deck did, and most of the time when we are fishing, this deck is drenched." She shook her head with frustration. "We have to figure something out for next year when we have to dump the gear. You realize that, don't you?" she said as she laid Matt down on the bed.

Dwayne gave her a loving smile, and she couldn't help but notice the sudden sparkle in his eye.

Tammy narrowed her eyes and gave him a suspicious grin. "What?" She turned her head and watched Matt as he crawled onto the bed and laid down.

"Well, I have an idea, and we have an entire year to plan it."

Tammy's eyes became wide. "Well, are you going to share it with me?"

Dwayne sat on the bench at the table and turned his body to face Tammy, who was still sitting on the edge of the bed, rubbing Matt's tummy as he drifted off to sleep.

"Didn't you tell me that the last time you had talked to your mom, she had said she could come visit us next year?"

Tammy shrugged her shoulders. "Well, yeah, but where is she going to stay? She can't stay on the boat with us. There's no room, and besides, when we go fishing, the boats go with us."

Dwayne laughed at her logic. "Well, what if we look into renting a house?"

Tammy leaped up from the bed and into Dwayne's arms. "Really? Are you serious? I love living on the boat, but Matt is growing by the minute, and I think it's time he had his own room. By the time next season rolls around, we'd have lived on the

Baywitch for almost four years." Tammy chuckled. "I'm not sure if Matt will like the idea, though."

Dwayne creased his brow. "You don't? I thought he'd be happy to have his own room and a yard to play in."

Tammy laughed again. "A backyard is no comparison to an entire boatyard to play in and docks to fish off and not to mention a dinghy to go row-about, as Matt calls it. He loves the water and fishing just like we do."

Dwayne nodded. "You have a point, but we would still have to go to the boatyard every day to work on gear, and we'd have the option to spend the night on the boat if we wanted to."

"Don't get me wrong, I enjoy living on the boat, but it would be nice to have a house to go to after spending a week on the ocean." Tammy gave him a dreamy smile. "I could soak in a bubble bath and sleep in a king-size bed where there are no dangers of me banging my head," she laughed, "and besides, Matt is seven now, and I think it's time he had his own room."

Dwayne pulled her in tight and wrapped his arms around her waist, giving her a long lingering kiss on the lips. "Yes, I agree. Living on the same boat that we also use for fishing is not getting any easier. Even for me, who has been around boats all my life," he laughed. "If we rent a house, your mom, who I still have not met, could stay there with Matt while we went fishing."

Tammy squeezed Dwayne's waist and kissed him hard on his lips. "That's a brilliant idea! I know she's going to love you as much as I do, and It's been over five years since she last saw Matt, or me for that matter." Tammy did some calculations in her head. Wow, Matt was only two when she last saw him. That's sad. We miss her so much. I'm sure she would love the idea of watching Matt. It would give her a sense of feeling needed. I know she hasn't felt important since her girls have all grown up and now have their own families. I'm not sure if she watches Jenny's kids in England. I've never asked her." She turned and looked at Matt. "Oh good, he finally fell asleep. I'm going to put a clean shirt on him while he's sleeping." She turned to face Dwayne again. "Are we all ready to shove off and head home?"

"We sure are. The *Little Boat* is all secured. I'm going to fire up the boat and head out of here. Why don't you stay down here with Matt for the first few hours and get some rest, and I'll let you drive once we've passed the west end of Catalina?"

"Sounds good! I can't wait to get back and call mom." Tammy said with a beaming smile. "We're getting a house! I'm so excited."

CHAPTER 2

*N*ight-time came quickly, and they did the rest of the crossing to the mainland, guided by the stars. Tammy and Dwayne took turns driving while one of them hunkered down in the cabin with Matt. His lip was healing nicely, and he didn't seem to be in any pain.

By the time they tied up to the Marina dock, it was nearing 4:00 am, Sunday Morning. There would be no time to rest. They wanted to be back at the Island by tomorrow morning, which meant they would have to leave that afternoon.

With the eight-hour time difference between America and England, Tammy knew it was a good time to call her mom. She checked on Matt and saw he was still sleeping. Dwayne was on the deck. "I'm going to call my mom," she said.

Dwayne smiled from the back of the boat while tying fenders to the stern. "Oh, good. I'm eager to hear if she likes my idea."

"I'm sure she will," Tammy said as she stepped off the boat and headed to the phone booth.

After feeding the coin box a ton of quarters, she finally heard the foreign ringtone of an English phone. After three rings, her mom picked up.

"Hello." She said in her thick British accent.

"Hey, mom. It's Tammy."

Tammy instantly picked up on the smile in her voice. "Tammy! What a pleasant surprise. Is everything okay? How's my grandson?"

Like always, she answered the call with many questions but never gave Tammy a chance to answer any of them. Tammy couldn't blame her. Months passed since she last talked to her.

"Everything's fine, mom. We just got back from fishing. Matt is fine too."

"You're still fishing, eh? Are you sure you like it, Tammy?" her mom asked.

Tammy laughed. It was another favorite question of hers. "I love it, mom. I wouldn't do it if I didn't. Listen, I need to make this quick. I only have a few more quarters. After the season ends, we're going to look for a house to rent."

Her mother's tone turned sharp. "Well, it's about time. I don't know how you can all live on a boat. And doesn't your boyfriend have a son too?"

"Yes, he does, but he doesn't live with us. Anyway, mom, listen," she said, rushing her words.

Suddenly a recorded voice interrupted her. "Please deposit $1.75 to continue this call."

"God damn it," Tammy barked as she fed more quarters into the phone. "Mom, are you there?"

"Yes, I'm here."

"Listen, mom." Tammy couldn't help but smile as she spoke her next words. "How would you like to come over next year and watch Matt at the house we plan on getting while Dwayne and I go fishing?"

Her mom didn't hesitate to answer and squealed into the phone.

"Oh, Tammy, I would love that. Are you serious?"

Tammy laughed. Her mom's reaction was all that she had hoped for. "Yes, mom, I'm serious. You would help us out a lot, and I love the idea of you and Matt bonding while we are away."

"Will I get to see Donna too?" her mom questioned.

"I'll make sure of it, okay. Look, I'm out of quarters. We are heading back out later today. I'll call you when we get back in, and I'll also write to you and explain all the details. I love you, mom."

"I love you too, Tammy. Be careful out there on the ocean."

"I will, mom, bye."

Tammy hung up the phone and skipped back down to the boat to find Matt awake and eating cereal at the table. The engine hatch on the deck was open, and Dwayne stood at the edge, wiping his hands on a towel.

"Everything okay?" she asked while looking down at the engines.

"Yeah. Just checking everything before we leave again."

Tammy inched closer to him and gave him a peck on the cheek. "You are so thorough. I always feel safe with you. Even sixty miles out at sea," she told him, followed by a loving smile.

"Gotta take care of my sweetheart," Dwayne said before climbing down between the two engines.

Tammy leaned over to talk to him, "I called my mom, and she is super excited about watching Matt. I knew she would be."

Dwayne looked up and wiped his forehead, leaving a smear of oil on his brow. "That's great! I think it will all work out."

"I do too. It's a brilliant idea you had." Tammy glanced over at the cabin and saw Matt was still eating. "After Matt has finished his breakfast, I'm going to pack his clothes and backpack for school and drop him off at Louise's in your truck. That way, I can go down to Los Angeles and get the bait."

"Sounds good. I'll take the *Baywitch* over to the fuel dock and fill her up, and then I'll take the *Little Boat* over and fill her up too.

When you get back, we'll go grocery shopping. I want to be out of here no later than two this afternoon if we can."

"Okay, I'll be back as soon as I can. I'll see you later. Love you."

"Love you too." Dwayne hollered with his head buried next to an engine.

An hour later, Tammy was on the freeway heading to Los Angeles, where she would hit up the fish markets for their fish scraps, which made excellent bait. She would also buy a thousand pounds of frozen mackerel. All the guys at the markets knew her and made it a habit to save her scraps. Tammy was pleased that it didn't take her much time to collect eight barrels of fresh bait.

After making her last stop where she purchased the mackerel, she noticed she was low on gas and pulled into the next gas station before getting on the freeway. After paying for the gas and a cup of much-needed coffee, she headed back to the truck to pump the gas. She looked over at her truck and saw a middle-aged man, wearing jeans, a black jacket, and a black baseball hat walking around her truck and looking under the rear bumper.

Tammy hesitated before approaching the stranger, knowing she was not in the best part of town. As she drew closer, she made her presence known.

"Hey. Can I help you?" she said with an edge to her voice.

Startled by her sudden appearance, the man quickly stepped away from her truck. Tammy looked at his hands for any weapons. There was none, but she noticed he was wearing a wedding ring and felt less threatened by him. His eyes were wide when he spoke, and there was a slight tremble to his voice.

"Yeah. Did you know there is blood dripping from the back of your truck?"

Tammy sensed the uncertainty in his voice and chuckled to herself. Feeling a little mischievous, she messed with the guy and bent down to look under the truck. "Oh, dear, there sure is." She said with narrowed eyes and a straight face.

The guy took another step back and glanced at a silver SUV at a nearby pump. Tammy assumed it was his "So, what do you have in there?" the guy asked, with his eyes still wide.

Tammy folded her arms and leaned back against her truck, giving him a devious smile. "Wouldn't you like to know?"

The guy's jaw dropped, and his eyes grew to twice their size. Fear masked his face. "Never mind. I have to get to work. Have a nice day." He said in a rushed voice as he raced over to his car without looking back.

Tammy laughed to herself. The poor guy probably thought she was some wife that had just killed off her husband. Then she had a troublesome thought. Shit, I hope he doesn't call the cops and give them my license plate number. She wondered if she went a little too far, making a joke about the barrels' fish blood leaking. But the look on his face was well worth it. Tammy chuckled; he'll probably be talking about the crazy lady at the gas station for years to come. She didn't see him write anything down and assumed he probably just wanted to get away from her as quickly as possible.

Tammy still had a smirk on her face when she arrived back at the boat. She found Dwayne on the deck of the *Baywitch*, making room for the bait.

"Well, you look happy," Dwayne said as he picked up some tools and set them on the dash. "How did it go with the bait? Any problems? I worry about you going down there by yourself. It's a pretty rough neighborhood."

"Oh, I'm fine. I can take care of myself. I told you I wanted to go on my own last time we came in. That way, we can get every thing done quicker. But I think I scared the crap out of a poor guy at the gas station."

Dwayne laughed before he even heard the story. "Oh, crap. What did you do?"

Tammy walked up to him, wrapped her arms around his waist, and gave him a peck on the lips. Dwayne pulled her in and swayed her from side to side as she spoke.

"Well, he asked me why there was blood dripping from the

back of the truck. I knew it was the bait, but to him, it probably looked pretty suspicious. He looked scared too." Tammy laughed.

"So, what did you tell him?"

"Well, I didn't tell him what it was. I just asked him with a devious smile, wouldn't you like to know?" Tammy cracked a laugh and tossed back her head. "Oh, you should have seen the look on his face. He looked petrified."

Dwayne gasped. "No, you didn't. Oh, that poor guy."

"I know. But I couldn't resist. It's the devil in me. What can I say?"

After sharing her story and having a few more laughs, Dwayne and Tammy spent the next hour and a half unloading the bait from the truck, carting it through the boatyard on a dolly, and stacking it on the *Baywitch*. Out of breath and winded, they took a thirty-minute break before going to the market to buy their groceries for their five-day trip to the island. By two-thirty, they untied the boat from the dock, and they were heading back out to sea.

If all goes to plan, they should reach the island early Monday morning when it is still dark, which would give them time to rest for a few hours. They would spend Monday and Tuesday moving and baiting the gear before the first day of the season begins on Wednesday, and because it was the opener, Louise had agreed to watch Matt an extra day. But Tammy had her doubts things would go so smoothly. Something always happens that derails their plans. She just wondered what it would be this time?

CHAPTER 3

*W*hat felt like a tornado came out of nowhere? Buckets, slickers, and anything else that was not tied down had been thrown across the deck from the force of the pounding winds. Before the chaos erupted, Tammy had spent the morning pulling traps with Dwayne.

It was their third day of fishing at San Clemente Island and a day after the opener. They had left the mainland like many times before, with no sleep, and took turns driving the *Baywitch* with the *Little Boat* in tow so they could each try to get some sleep. But the boat's noise and rocking made it hard for Tammy to fall into a deep sleep, and she failed to get enough rest.

On this day, fatigue had caught up with her. Her body hurt to the core, her muscles hurt down to her bones, and her hands were chapped and raw to where she couldn't bend her fingers without expressing the piercing pain she was feeling.

They left the harbor in the Little Boat before sunrise to begin their day of pulling one-hundred-fifty traps. But by noon, Dwayne grew concerned when he looked over and saw Tammy's face tight, and her eyes scrunched closed from the agony she felt when she heaved a trap across the deck to be stacked and dumped at a better fishing spot.

When she finally voiced her pain with a loud, piercing scream, Dwayne immediately turned off the motor. "Okay, that's it. I'm taking you back to the *Baywitch*," he said as he precariously walked over to Tammy while trying not to lose his balance as the *Little Boat* bobbed around in the vast ocean. "You need to get some rest."

Tammy gripped her hips and tried to stretch her back, but it hurt too much. "I'm fine," she protested. "My body is just a little stiff. I'll loosen up soon," she said as she continued to rub her sides.

Dwayne shook his head. "I'm not taking no for an answer. You've been pushing yourself hard lately, and I want you to take the rest of the day off." He gave her a playful grin. "Captain's orders."

Tammy rolled her eyes and grunted. "Oh, I hate it when you pull rank on me." She knew she didn't stand a chance. When Dwayne made up his mind, he took the authority; there was no arguing with him.

Still keeping his balance as the boat rocked, he approached Tammy, who was now leaning against the stacked traps for support, and started rubbing her shoulders. Tammy closed her eyes and moaned from the sudden pleasures she was feeling. "Oh god, that feels so good," she moaned with her eyes still closed.

Dwayne chuckled from the relief his hands were giving her. "Now, I'm going to take you back to the *Baywitch*, and you're going to rest for the remainder of the day," he insisted.

Tammy tilted her head from side to side to loosen her sore neck as Dwayne continued to massage her, "But you can't pull all the traps by yourself," she protested.

"I'll pull what I can today, and tomorrow when you are feeling better, we will play catch up."

Tammy pouted her lips and folded her arms across her chest, knowing she had lost the argument. "Fine. Take me back to the boat."

They weren't far from the harbor and were at the *Baywitch* within thirty minutes. Dwayne put the boat in idle and approached Tammy, who was still dressed in her yellow slickers and boots. He smiled and took her in his arms.

Tammy giggled as she tried to push him away playfully. "What are you doing? I'm covered in fish goo," she laughed.

Dwayne, also dressed in slickers, moved his hips from side to side and rubbed his belly with hers, smearing the goo some more across their slickers. "Oh, but you look so sexy and smell like money." He said before planting a hard kiss on her lips.

Tammy laughed out loud and pressed the palms of her hands on his chest. "You're nuts. You've been out at sea too long." She changed her tone to a more serious one. "Are you sure you'll be okay by yourself?"

"Yeah, I'll be fine. We will be in radio contact." He scanned the harbor. "And look, you have the whole harbor to yourself. All the boats are out fishing. You could go skinny dipping and wash up if you wanted to," he said, followed by a wink.

Tammy checked the other moorings and saw they were all empty. "Huh. I just might. I smell like bait."

Dwayne held her hand as she stepped onto the *Baywitch*. She turned and watched as he put the boat in gear. "I'll see you just before sunset." he hollered over the roar of the motor. "Get some rest. I may have my way with you tonight," he laughed, followed by a sexy smile and a wink that never ceased to make Tammy's heart flutter.

Tammy continued to watch as he sped off, feeling a little envious that she wouldn't be reaping in the fruits of their labor and feeling the rewards. But it was just for today. She had been pushing herself hard to meet the deadline of the opener. She was grateful for what would be an afternoon of rest.

Tammy watched Dwayne as he disappeared around the point and, for a moment, enjoyed the sudden silence that surrounded her. She only heard the gentle splash of the ocean against the hull.

She took in a deep breath, closed her eyes, and filled her lungs with fresh air. She tilted her head back slightly so the slight breeze could brush against her face. It was exhilarating and immediately made her feel a little better.

Tammy looked down at her slickers and saw the fish goo was already drying. She needed to wash them before the goo became too hard to clean and stepped out of her boots. After sliding the straps off her shoulders and stepping out of the slickers, Tammy removed her socks, threw them down into the cabin, and went barefoot for the rest of the afternoon. It was a favorite of hers and one she couldn't do too often on the drenched decks of the boat. She wasn't going anywhere, and the deck was clean. It felt good to give her feet a chance to breathe and not be scrunched in the rubber boots.

Underneath the slickers, Tammy wore jeans and a sweatshirt. They were still dry, and she left them on. She walked over to the stern with her slickers in hand and stepped over the side onto the swim step. Steadying herself with one hand on the rail, Tammy knelt and dipped the slickers into the ocean and pulled them up and down in a fast motion to wash off the grime. The water felt good on her hands. It was refreshing. Maybe I should go for a quick dip? Tammy thought as she scanned the harbor. No one's here. She put her arm deeper into the water and smiled. Yeah, she was going for a swim; Tammy decided and hastily stepped back on to the boat carrying the slickers and headed to the cabin to undress.

After hanging up the slickers to dry on a hook by the helm, Tammy went down into the cabin to disrobe and returned to the deck a few minutes later, wrapped in a white towel. She checked the harbor one more time and saw it was still empty. She looked out to sea to make sure no boats were coming in. There were none.

Satisfied it was safe to go for a quick dip, Tammy unwrapped herself from the towel and let it fall to her feet. The warmth of the sun felt good against her naked skin. After soaking up the rays for a moment, she headed back to the swim step and dove into the water. It felt better than she had imagined. After coming back up to the surface, she shook her head vigorously and enjoyed being immersed in the cool crispness of the water.

Tammy swam around for a good fifteen minutes before heading back to the boat. She felt rejuvenated and refreshed. Her body no longer ached, and it relaxed her muscles. If Dwayne had shown up at that very moment, Tammy would have insisted she'd go back out with him and help pull the rest of the gear. But she knew the route, and at this time of day, he was probably over at the backside of the island.

The harbor was still empty, but she soaked up some rays on the deck of the boat. A surge of guilt hit her, knowing Dwayne was hard at work, but hey, she's just following the captain's order, right?

After laying out the towel, she laid naked on her back and released an enormous sigh as her body soaked up the heat from the sun. In no time at all, she drifted off to sleep until the tornado winds blasted above the boat.

CHAPTER 4

$\mathcal{T}$ammy released a high-pitched scream and jolted her body up to an upright position. She hollered, "What the hell!" Afraid to move and the fact that she was naked, Tammy remained frozen in place and watched in horror as a white bucket, one of the deck chairs, and her slickers flew across the deck in a fury. Tammy was relieved that they didn't land in the water.

She covered her eyes as sprays of water hit her face and stung her sunburnt cheeks. Tammy heard the motor's loud noise from above, but the powerful winds prevented her from looking up. "What the hell is going on?" she yelled again. The strong winds lasted for maybe a minute until they subsided. They were still present, but not as harsh. Finally, she was able to open her eyes and look up, which is when she broke out into a roaring voracious laugh.

Tammy hollered, "Really?" Even though she knew she couldn't be heard over the loud noise of the helicopter that hovered above the boat. Then she saw the heads of six navy seals hanging out of the doorway, waving their arms.

There was nothing Tammy could do but laugh and wave back. *I guess they haven't seen a naked girl in a while.* Their intrusion flat-tered her on what should have been a peaceful afternoon of rest. She laughed again and gave them a friendly wave and smile. They'd already seen her naked, so she thought it senseless to cover up. As the helicopter ascended, it took the wind with it. Tammy watched and waved as the helicopter and the happy navy seals flew off in the distance, leaving Tammy once again in the harbor's calm waters and the glorious warm sunshine.

Tammy waited until they were off in the distance before she stood up and wrapped her body in the towel. She giggled and shook her head at the boldness of the men that had just surprised her with their grand presence. "Well damn, that's one for the books. Wait till I tell Dwayne about this." She snickered and thought it would be a good idea to get dressed in case she had any more unannounced visitors.

Feeling more energized and some-what guilty for not helping Dwayne pull traps, Tammy wanted to be more productive for the rest of the day and spent the next few hours chopping mackerel for tomorrow's pull. She also surprised Dwayne with a hearty fried chicken dinner, a rarity on the island. After fishing all day, they usually only had enough energy to open a can of soup and butter a bread roll.

It was almost dark when Tammy spotted Dwayne entering the harbor. He was the last boat to come in, and being later than usual, Tammy smiled and released a sigh of relief when she saw him.

She beamed him an enormous smile when he slowed down the *Little Boat* and, with caution, eased it alongside the *Baywitch*.

"How did it go?" Tammy hollered over the roar of the motor before tossing him a line.

Dwayne caught the rope and quickly tied off the boat before shutting off the engine. "Great! We did well." He turned and pointed to two large grey barrels full of circulating ocean water and filled with lobsters. "Both barrels are full," he said with a satisfactory smile. "Wanna help me get them into the receivers?" he asked.

Still feeling a tad guilty, Tammy was eager to help. "Sure. How many receivers do you need?"

"I'd say three," Dwayne replied.

Tammy headed over to the stern of the boat where they were stacked and handed one at a time to Dwayne, who set them on the deck of the *Little Boat*. She then jumped down, grabbed a pair of rubber gloves off the dash, and began pulling the lobsters out of the barrels to give to Dwayne.

"So, how was your afternoon? Did you get plenty of rest?" Dwayne asked as he took a lobster from Tammy's hand and placed it in a receiver.

Tammy gave him a smirk, "Oh, I guess you could say it was interesting,"

"How can hanging out on a boat in an empty harbor be interesting?" he said with a creased brow. He looked at her with wide eyes and beamed her a huge smile. "Wait! Did you go skinny dipping?"

Tammy felt her cheeks blush. "I did. But that's not what I'm talking about," she said while handing him another lobster.

Dwayne's eyes lit up. "Ooh, you went skinny dipping, and I missed it. Darn it. So, did someone see you? Is that it?"

"No, it was after my swim when I was lying naked on the deck."

Dwayne's jaw dropped. His eyes remained wide. "You sunbathed naked too? Damn, I should have taken the afternoon off with you. I really missed out," he laughed. "So, tell me what happened?"

"Let's put it this way, I and everything on the boat almost got blown out to sea by the helicopter hovering super low above me with a bunch of navy seals straining their necks over the side to get a good view of me sunbathing naked."

Dwayne cracked a loud laugh. "You're kidding me? What did you do? Run down to the cabin?"

"No, I couldn't move because of the force of the wind coming from the helicopter. I figured, screw it. They were harmless and twenty feet above me in a bloody helicopter. What could they do? And I'm sure I made their day."

"Well, shoot, I missed it all. Do you know how many navy seals are going to be jacking off in their bunks tonight while visions of you naked crowd their brain?"

"Dwayne!" Tammy shrieked as she handed him the last lobster.

"What? You know I'm right." He leaned in and gave her a smooch. "I think it's pretty cool that my hot girlfriend diverted the US government's navy seal from their training exercise."

Tammy gave him a friendly slap on the arm. "Oh, stop. They probably hadn't seen a naked woman in months. Now come on, let's get cleaned up. With all the free time I've had this afternoon, I made us a chicken dinner."

Dwayne's eyes bulged. "No way! Really? Oh, wait till I get on the radio and ask the other captains what they are having for dinner. They're going to wish they bought their other halves with them too." He released another loud, cocky laugh. "Oh, I love showing you off and bragging about you. Come here and kiss me," he said before they put the last receiver in the water and stepped onto the *Baywitch*.

By the time Tammy exited the cabin with two plates of chicken and instant mashed potatoes, the sun had set, and a full moon appeared on the horizon. It was a glorious evening with very little wind. "God, what a beautiful night," Tammy said as she sat in one of the deck chairs and gazed up to the darkened skies.

Dwayne joined her. "Thanks for cutting all the bait today. Now we get to watch the other guys prep for tomorrow while we eat." He chuckled.

All the familiar captains and boats had returned this year. Dwayne's good friend Mitch on the *Sea-Life*. Patrick on the *Patience* and Tom on the *Lobster-Fest*. Lester was also back on his boat, *Out to Sea*. Tammy remembered him well. He was the one who doubted she would make it through the season. But he had surprised her this year with a friendly wave and smile when they first arrived. Dale on the boat, *Dreaming* was still his grumpy self but had warmed up to Dwayne and Tammy after receiving a home-cooked meal from Tammy at the end of her first season.

When Tammy returned for a second season, the captains couldn't hide their look of surprise. She made it through her first year with endurance, and more strength than other fishermen held and had earned their respect with flying colors.

This year, there was no rank; they considered her one of them. They treated and spoke to her like they would any other member of the fleet. They'd wave and smile at her as they drove by and included her in the conversations when they pulled up to the *Baywitch* at the end of the day for a quick chit-chat before heading over to their moorings.

Dwayne and Tammy had two more days of pulling traps before they would have to head back to the mainland. They wasted no time and left the harbor before the sun was up and before any other boat. Feeling rested, Tammy was eager to pull the first trap and, like a pro, gaffed it on her first try. She rarely missed a trap now.

They had the system down and made a good team. Dwayne pulled out the legal lobsters and tossed them into a barrel of water while Tammy replenished the bait compartment with mackerel and fish scraps she had gotten from the fish markets.

"Ready?" Dwayne asked. He pushed down on the fish in the bait compartment so he could close the door.

"Yep, ready to dump, captain," Tammy said with a smile.

Dwayne pushed the bait down one more time and then suddenly jumped back. "Ow! That friggin' hurt," he said, ripping off his glove. He let it fall to the deck, so he could inspect his hand, which was now throbbing.

Tammy pulled off her gloves and walked over to Dwayne's side. "What happened?"

"Something poked me in the bait compartment. It stings like hell." He brought his palm closer to his face. "But I don't see anything."

Tammy took his hand. "Let me look." She rubbed over his skin with her fingertips. "Where does it hurt?"

"Right in the middle. That's where I was pressing down on the bait. Damn, it still hurts." He said as he scrunched his eyes and shook his hand.

Tammy looked closer. "I see a little pinprick with a spot of blood. Is that it?"

"That's where it hurts, but now my whole hand hurts. It must have been a fishbone or something. But why the hell is it hurting so much?"

"What do you want to do? Are you going to be able to drive the boat, or do you want me to?"

"I'll be fine. I'll just keep an eye on it," he said as he continued to shake the pain away.

When they pulled up to the next trap a few minutes later, Dwayne looked worried. "I can't feel my arm and look. It's all swollen."

Tammy raced to the helm where he stood. "What!" She gasped when she saw his fingers had swelled to double their size. "Oh, my god! Let me see your arm. Hold it up."

Dwayne tried to raise his arm. "I can't; it's dead." Using his other hand to support it, he pulled it up just enough so Tammy could see it. His wrist disappeared from the swelling, and his arm was twice its size all the way up to his elbow.

"Holy shit! That doesn't look good. What the hell poked you?"

"I have no idea, but I can't feel my arm at all. What the hell are we going to do?"

CHAPTER 5

*T*ammy's face turned pale, and her jaw tightened from the fear she felt. She didn't like it, and it scared her.

With a look of despair, Dwayne looked down at his arm that continued to swell. "I can't have my arm flopping around on the boat like this. It's too dangerous, and we have to pull traps today and tomorrow; otherwise, we won't make enough money to come back out." Dwayne twisted his body in an awkward position so he could turn off the motor. "Let me think for a minute."

Tammy spoke in a stern voice, "Think! What's there to think about? We're going home. You can't fish with one arm, and we need to get that looked at. Look how much it's swollen, Dwayne." Tammy shook her head in frustration. "Why is it every time we come out here something happens? Last year we drove over a line, and it got tangled in the prop. Do you remember?"

Dwayne nodded. "Oh yeah, the water was freezing."

"Yes, you had to jump into a frigid cold and cut off the line. The next day, the navy seals decided they would do underwater explosion practices in the harbor and only gave us an hour to vacant with our two boats and the lobster receivers. We had to spend the next two nights anchored out at sea in a rocky ocean." Tammy stomped her feet. "Every year, there is a challenge of some kind. And now this. You can't fish with that arm, Dwayne. It's dead," Tammy insisted.

Dwayne refused to listen to her reasoning. He could be stubborn when he wants to be. "Going home is not an option, Tammy. We won't have any money to come back out. You know how broke we are the first week of the season."

Tammy stomped her feet again in protest. "Goddamn it, Dwayne. This could be serious." She looked around at the vast emptiness of the ocean. "We are in the middle of nowhere. Do you see any hospitals? What if you get sick?"

"I don't feel sick. It's just my arm; that's all."

Tammy raised her voice. "We need to go home, Dwayne. The swelling is growing while we are sitting here arguing."

Dwayne stood up and brushed by her without speaking. He reached over to the far end of the dash and grabbed a rope with his good hand. Using his teeth, he unraveled the line.

"What are you doing?" Tammy said abruptly and with an edge to her tone.

He held out one end on the line to her. "Here, take this and tie my arm to my waist so it won't flop around."

Tammy placed her hands on her hips and creased her brow. "What? Are you crazy? What good is that going to do?"

Dwayne raised his voice, which startled Tammy. "Just do it!"

Tammy grabbed the rope and placed his arm behind it as she wrapped it around his waist. "Fine," she said, feeling defeated.

"Make sure you tie it tight. I don't want my arm slipping out because I'll never know if it does, and I could knock it against something and break it."

Tammy wasn't happy with his solution and let him know by giving the rope an extra hard tug.

"Ouch!" Dwayne yelled.

"Well, you said to make it tight." She tugged again. "So now that you are the one arm fisherman, what are your plans?" she snarled at him, still not happy with his ridiculous plan.

"We're going to keep fishing."

Tammy shook her head. "Seriously! That's the craziest thing I've ever heard. It's obvious that something poisonous poked you, and we need to get it checked. I think it's affected your brain too. I can't believe you want to continue fishing. It might travel through your entire body and kill you."

Dwayne released a slight chuckle while trying to adjust his dead arm. "It won't kill me." He said with a smirk.

Tammy flared her nostrils. "This is not funny, Dwayne. It could be serious. I mean, look at your bloody arm now. It's twice its normal size. You can't fish like that."

"Tammy, we don't have a choice. I'll keep an eye on it, and if I start feeling sick, I'll let you know."

"No, you won't. I know you. Fine, we'll fish, but I'm taking your temperature as soon as we get back to the *Baywitch,* and if you have a fever, we're heading home. Even if I have to lock you in the cabin and get us out of here on my own," She shook her head again. "This is fucking unbelievable, and you call me stubborn." She folded her arms in front of her. "So how are we going to do this, Captain Dwayne?"

Dwayne gave her another smirk, but Tammy wasn't amused and rolled her eyes.

"Look, we only have two more days, and then we head home. I can stick it out until then. I can drive the boat with my good arm and reach over to work the throttle, and you'll be in charge of everything else, including measuring the lobsters. We can do this, Tammy. We fished without steering in the *Little Boat* for five days; we can sure as hell do this."

Tammy grunted. She worried about Dwayne's arm but knew there was no sense arguing with him. Yet again, he had pulled rank, and she had no choice but to go along with his absurd plan no matter what her opinion was.

While they had been drifting, the swell had increased, and Tammy grabbed the handrail on the trap table to get her balance. "Fine, let's do this. The sooner we get back to the *Baywitch*, the sooner I can take your temperature."

Tammy watched as Dwayne started the boat with his right arm. Being left-handed, she could tell it was awkward for him. He then twisted his body so he could work the throttle and put the boat in gear.

"I'm not sure about this, Dwayne." Tammy hollered above the sound of the motor as Dwayne headed to the next trap.

It took a few traps to get the system down, but they were a good team, and Tammy knew what was expected from her to get the job done. Periodically she insisted that Dwayne let her check his arm. It remained swollen for the entire day, but it seemed to hold twice its normal size and not swell anymore.

By the end of the day, much to Tammy's surprise, they pulled the rest of the gear, and the catch was plentiful.

Dwayne didn't complain of any pain, just that his hand and arm were completely dead, and he couldn't feel anything. Tammy was at least thankful that he wasn't experiencing any pain, but she still didn't like it.

On their way back to the harbor, Tammy discovered she was hurting more than the usual aches and pains she experienced. Her body ached down to her bones, her hands were chapped, and she could barely bend her fingers. Her hair was a matted mess, and she could hardly bend her knees. She took on a lot more tasks and would be for the next two days. She wasn't sure if she'd be able to handle the extra workload.

Once Dwayne had the *Little Boat* alongside the *Baywitch*, Tammy quickly grabbed a line and tied off the boat, but not before letting out a scream of pain.

"Are you okay?" Dwayne yelled after he turned off the motor."

Tammy shook her hand. "Yeah, my hands are so sore, and grabbing that rope didn't help. Even with gloves on."

Once they secured the boats, Tammy attempted to jump up on the *Baywitch* to grab some receivers for today's catch, but the leap was more than her body could handle. With one foot on the *Baywitch,* her knee buckled, and she lost her balance. Before she could save herself, she fell backward and crashed to the deck of the *Little Boat,* slamming her back hard on the rough non-skid finish. "Ouch! Goddamn it!" She screamed as she winced her body from the sudden burst of pain she was experiencing.

Dwayne faced away from her, looking through his binoculars with his good arm at a strange boat on the horizon. He had not seen Tammy fall but heard her scream. In a flash, he turned to find her curled up in pain. "Shit! Are you okay? What the hell happened?"

He set down his binoculars on the dash and knelt beside her, steadying himself with his working arm.

"I lost my frigging balance while trying to step on the *Baywitch.* My knee buckled." She screeched with her eyes closed and a tight jaw. "My bloody back is killing me. God, I'm sick of this shit!" She grunted through gritted teeth.

Dwayne rested his hand on her shoulder. "Are you able to get up?"

"Yeah, just give me a minute."

For the next few minutes, Tammy laid on her back, waiting for the sharp pains that were shooting down her back to disappear. She had her eyes closed and a hand over her brow. She was on the brink of crying but refused to give in to the forces that were continually trying to knock her down. Commercial fishing was dangerous and a constant battle with the ocean, the weather, and the intense labor that would break you if you didn't have the stammer to fight it off. This, too, would pass, she told herself as the pain subsided.

For the first time since she fell, she moved her legs until they were straight and rubbed her back.

Using his good arm, Dwayne supported her shoulder. "Are you

able to sit up?"

"I'm going to try," Tammy grunted while holding out her hand. "Give me your hand and try to pull me up," she moaned.

Dwayne did as she asked and tried not to winch when she squeezed his hand hard and was thankful her fingernails were short.

Tammy braced herself, and with her other hand, she pushed on the deck as she dragged herself up. "Argh," she screamed at the top of her lungs, trying to fight off the burning pain she was feeling.

Dwayne held her hand tight. "You're almost there! Come on, babe, you can do it." He encouraged her.

Tammy released another cry from the unbearable pain she was experiencing before she could eventually sit upright. Panting and out of breath, she rubbed her side. "Oh, fuck, this really hurts. You are going to have to help me get to my feet."

Dwayne stood and held out his hand. "Take my hand."

Tammy continued to rub her side. "Give me another minute," and then she chuckled.

"Well, I'm glad you're able to see the humor in all this," Dwayne said and joined her in her laughter.

Tammy laughed again, but this time a little louder. "Will you look at us? You with your dead arm, and me with a bad back. We're quite the fishing team, don't you think?"

Dwayne had to agree and laughed again. "Come on, let me help you up. Are you ready?" He asked with his good arm extended.

Tammy reached for his hand and let out another "Argh." She dragged herself up and steadied her feet. "Okay, I'm going to try this again. We need to get these lobsters in the water. I'll be right back," she said, giving her back one last rub and worked through the pain. After her second attempt to jump on the *Baywitch* was successful, she grabbed three receivers and handed one at a time to Dwayne, who lined them up on the deck. It was then up to Tammy to load up the receivers, and using his functioning hand, they both lowered them into the water, and Tammy tied them off.

"Okay, I'm going to take your temperature now." Tammy insisted. Go sit in the cabin while I look for the thermometer.'"

"I'm sure it's fine," Dwayne contested. "It's been hours since it happened."

Tammy was in no mood to hear Dwayne's protests. She was tired, her back was killing her, and she still had quite a few chores to do before the day was over. "Just do it!" She bellowed.

Dwayne didn't argue and went down into the cabin to wait for nurse Tammy. After taking his temperature, she was relieved to see he didn't have a fever. "Let me see your arm." She said.

Unable to lift it, Dwayne stood up away from the table so Tammy could take a closer look.

"Wow, it's still swollen. Your hand and arm are still twice their sizes."

Dwayne seemed surprised it hadn't gone down at all. "I still can't feel anything either."

"I wonder what the hell poked you."

"I have no idea, but we're not getting any more fish scraps. We'll only be using mackerel from now on. If we still have some scraps, dump them in the water. The fish will love them."

"Good idea," Tammy said, taking hold of the rope that tied around his waist to keep his arm secured. "Okay, let me help you get out of these slickers, and then I need to go cut up some bait. Why don't you call Mitch on the *Sea-Life* and ask him if anything like this ever happened to him?"

It took a good ten minutes to get Dwayne comfortable and retie his arm to his waist.

"I'm going to have to call you the one-armed bandit," Tammy laughed.

Dwayne cut her off and spiked his ear. "Shh, I hear a boat in the harbor. It sounds like they are coming this way."

"I hear it too," Tammy said as she headed up the steps to the deck. Dwayne was right behind her.

Dwayne looked out into the harbor; none of the other fishing boats had returned yet—so who were those guys? Dwayne questioned as he watched the vessel head their way. He soon realized it must be the boat he saw earlier through his binoculars.

"Shit, it's Fish and Game," Dwayne said as the boat drew closer. "What do they want? I've never been boarded before."

Dwayne explained to Tammy that Fish and Game would board your boat unannounced to check that the fishermen were abiding by the fishing laws and had no short lobsters on board.

"Well, we're not doing anything wrong. Let them do their thing, and then they'll leave." Tammy tried to reason after she noticed how upset Dwayne had become.

"That could take hours. Especially if they want to go through all eight of our receivers and measure every lobster."

"What! They would do that?"

"Sure. It happened to Mitch a few years ago. They were on his boat for five hours. They checked everything."

"Well, that's bloody ridiculous. Don't they realize we are tired, and we still have to get ready for tomorrow's pull?" Tammy watched the warden's pull up alongside the *Baywitch* on the other side from where the *Little Boat* was tied. "A warden at the helm leaned out and yelled. "How's it going today? Can I throw you my line?"

With her nerves now peaked, worried that they might find something, Tammy rushed to the other side of the boat and braced herself to catch the line. "Sure."

She caught it on the first throw and quickly tied off the boat, and then ignoring the shooting pains in her back, she rushed to the bow to tie the other line.

Dwayne saw two wardens on the boat and waited until the one driving had shut off the motor before he spoke. "Hey, how's it going?" He said with a forced smile.

Having never dealt with Fish and Game before, Tammy remained quiet and let Dwayne handle the conversation.

"May I come aboard, sir?" a warden asked.

Tammy was impressed that they had asked first.

"Sure," Dwayne replied as he leaned against the dash.

Tammy nodded as they boarded their boat and watched as they held out a hand to Dwayne. "Are you the Captain? I'm officer Peaks, and my partner here is officer Kinsley. Would you mind if we look around your vessel?"

"Sorry, my arm is bound; otherwise, I'd shake your hand," Dwayne said, followed by a nervous smile.

Office Peaks looked down at Dwayne's arm and took a step back. "Good lord. What happened to you? Do you need medical assistance?"

Dwayne shook his head. "No. I'll be fine. I pushed down on some bait in the traps earlier today, and something poked me. I think it was a poisonous fish of some sort. It should be fine in a day or two."

The officer looked alarmed and glanced over at Tammy and then back at Dwayne. "And you're still fishing?" the officer asked.

"I have no choice." Dwayne looked over at Tammy and nodded. "My girlfriend, who is also my deckhand, is carrying most of the load. We only have two more days to fish. We should be able to do it."

The officer looked stunned that Tammy and Dwayne were still fishing despite Dwayne's injury. "Well, listen. Keep an eye on it, and if anything changes, we'll be anchored in the harbor for a few days. Call us on the radio if you need anything."

Dwayne nodded. "I will. Thanks."

Officer Peaks scanned the boat. "Well, everything looks in order here. You take care of that arm, okay."

Dwayne didn't want to question their brief visit and assumed they thought it would be too difficult for him to retrieve the lobsters from the water with only one arm. "Okay, thanks again. Enjoy the rest of your night," Dwayne said with a polite smile.

Tammy helped untie their boat and waited until they were far enough away before she spoke. "Well, that went well." she chuckled.

Dwayne stood across the deck. "Too well, I'd say. That must have been their shortest inspection ever. So, I guess they'll be boarding all the other boats as they come back into the harbor."

Tammy walked over to where he stood and nuzzled herself into his space. He draped his good arm around her neck and gave her an affectionate smooch.

Tammy smiled. "We sure have fun together, don't we?"

Dwayne jerked back his head and laughed. "If this is your idea of fun, then you are easy to please." He laughed again when Tammy gave him a playful slap on his chest.

"Hey, how is your back doing?" he asked in a more serious tone.

Tammy rubbed it. "It's still really sore, but much better than a half-hour ago. I'm going to take it easy for an hour before I cut the bait."

"Good Idea." He kissed her again. "Hey, thanks for taking on most of the work today. You did an outstanding job. Are you going to be okay tomorrow?"

"I'll be fine as long as I don't fall again." She rubbed his chest and smiled. "I got this okay. We're in this together. If it were me, you'd be doing the same thing."

Dwayne nodded. "I sure do love you. How did I ever get so lucky?"

"I love you too, babe. Hey, are you going to call the other boats on the radio and let them know Fish and Game are in the harbor?"

"Nah. It's an open channel, and Fish and Game are probably on the same channel. They'll find out soon enough."

Tammy pulled away and grabbed one of the folded deck chairs stored on the side of the boat and unfolded it. "Okay, then. Well, why don't you have a seat, and I will make us two cups of hot chocolate, and we can kick back for a while before I toss the fish scraps over the side and cut up more bait."

"Sounds good," he said with a loving smile.

CHAPTER 6

*D*wayne and Tammy pushed through the next two days and got a decent catch before planning their trip home. Dwayne talked to the other captains about his arm, and none of them had ever seen or heard of a fisherman getting injured that way. Curious by what Dwayne had told them over the radio, each captain swung by the *Baywitch* to see it for themselves.

The swelling didn't go down until their last day, and Dwayne finally experienced some feeling in his fingertips. It was a good sign and a tremendous relief for them both. Dwayne was going to be okay, and they were heading home with a good catch, which will pay their bills and pay for their next trip to the island. Tammy hated to admit it, but Dwayne's stubbornness had paid off.

Tammy never liked the grueling ten-hour crossing home. Unlike the journey to the island where they were excited to fish and couldn't wait to get there. The trip back to the mainland always seemed much longer. After fishing for a week, she was exhausted, and it was still a struggle. They took turns at the wheel, but she could never get enough rest as tired as she was. The constant loud sounds of the motors and the boat's continuous rocking made it impossible to sleep. And then there was the worry of the *Little Boat,* which they towed behind them.

They pulled into the Marina in the wee hours of the morning, and even though Tammy was eager to see Matt, it was too early to call Louise. She would have to wait at least another three hours until seven when the sun would be up.

"I can't wait to see Matt," Tammy yelled to Dwayne from the dock. "I love fishing, but I hate being away from him," she added as she cleated off the *Baywitch.*

"I know, babe. I miss him too." Dwayne shut off the boat. Tammy embraced the peacefulness of the dock. She closed her eyes, released a heavy sigh, and smiled. "Oh, it's so quiet. I just friggin love it." Tammy tickled her ear with her finger. "But, there is always a ringing sound in my ear after listening to the loud sounds of the engines for the last ten hours." But the ringing was soon forgotten when she looked up to the night skies and smiled at the stars.

Dwayne jumped off the boat and took her in his arms. He looked up to the skies with her. "Yeah. It can't get any better than this. Let me take care of the *Little Boat.* I'll be right back."

"Not before you give me a kiss," Tammy laughed, covering her lips with his and then broke away to inspect his arm. "How's your arm?" She rubbed his skin with her fingertips. "It looks like the swelling has almost gone."

Dwayne ran his hand down his arm. "It's much better. It has most of its feeling back. That was the weirdest damn thing."

Tammy chuckled. "It sure was. No more fresh bait from now on."

When Dwayne returned from tying up the *Little Boat,* Tammy helped him get the lobsters into the water. The receivers were heavy, and it took all their strength to ease them beneath the surface slowly.

"I'm going to go call the fish buyer," Dwayne said while still trying to catch his breath.

Tammy heaved her chest. Lifting the receivers took all her strength. "Okay. I'm going to take a shower and then go pick up Matt."

The highlight of Tammy's return home was holding Matt in her arms and smothering him with kisses. He may be almost eight, but he was still her baby, and he always welcomed her and held her tight every time she picked him up.

Today was no different. She saw Matt looking out the window before she even pulled up in front of the apartment building where Louise lived. Louise must have told him she was on her way. He beamed her a big smile that melted Tammy's heart and waved both his arms. In a flash, she saw the front door swing wide open, and Matt raced down the pathway before she stepped out of the truck. "Mom!" he screamed.

Tears pooled in Tammy's eyes. "Oh, there's my boy," she cried as she met him half-way down the path with her arms wide open.

Matt came to a sudden halt in the embrace of his mother's arms and wrapped his arms around her. "Mom. I've missed you. Did you get a lot of lobsters?"

That was always his first question. Tammy kissed the top of his head and ran her fingers through his hair. "I've missed you too, buddy. We did good, and we got a lot of lobsters," she said with a huge grin.

Tammy held Matt in her arms for a little while longer and thought of Dwayne's idea about renting a house. The idea of Matt being with his grandmother in his own home and bedroom while she was out fishing warmed her heart. The thought excited her, and soon, she would write her mom a detailed letter about their plans.

"Hey, do you want to go out for breakfast? You can have your favorite. Chocolate chip pancakes." Tammy asked Matt as she smiled.

Matt leaped from her arms and spun around. "Yes. Let's go."

After grabbing Matt's bag, they went to a nearby Denny's,

where Tammy shared stories with him about their trip. It was a time where they reconnected. Matt listened as his mom told him about Dwayne's arm and the poisonous fish with bright eyes and pinned ears. He laughed when she joked about always banging her head in the v-berth, and her hands were covered in poke holes from the lobsters poking her.

After breakfast, she took him with her to downtown LA to pick up bait for their next trip. The guys all knew Matt and gave him a high-five. Tammy told the owner about Dwayne's arm, and he, too, had never heard it happening to anyone before either. They processed so many varieties of fish he had no idea what kind it could have been.

By the time they got back to the dock, the lobsters were sold and picked up by the buyer. Dwayne had called his son, Justin, and smelt fresh from his shower.

He smiled at Matt when he spotted him running through the boatyard towards him.

"Dwayne!" Matt yelled.

"Hey, buddy. It's so good to see you. We've missed you," he said, giving him a high-five. Dwayne waited for Tammy to catch up, who was still walking through the yard.

"Hey," Tammy said with a smile, followed by a kiss on Dwayne's cheek. "I've got the bait in the truck."

"Great. Let's take Matt fishing at the dock for a little while, and then we can all go shopping for our next trip."

"Sounds like a good idea, but I'll only stay on the docks with you guys for a little while. I need to call Donna. I've not called her in over two months."

While Dwayne and Matt had fun fishing, Tammy snuck away to call Donna. She was excited at the possibility of their mom coming out and couldn't wait to tell Donna, who also hadn't seen their mom in over five years. Tammy's thought was that their mom would have two of her daughters in the same room if she took their mom on a road trip to visit Donna. But it still wouldn't fulfill her mom's one wish of having all three daughters together. Tammy was determined to make it happen someday.

After two rings, Donna answered the phone.

"Hello."

"Hey Donna, It's Tammy. How's it going?"

"Tammy! God, I've been trying to call you for the past month. I hate not being able to get a hold of you."

Guilt suddenly swept through Tammy. "I'm sorry. We've been so busy. Lobster season has started, and we're only in the marina for the weekend, and then we head right back out again for a week. We have to make a quick turnaround trip because, after a few months, the seas are too rough to fish the island."

"Who's watching Matt while you're gone?" Donna asked.

"Oh, the mother of one of Matt's friends from school. It's working out great."

"If I knew how to drive and lived closer to you, I'd probably watch him again. But when he got hurt while he was with me, it freaked me. I felt terrible."

"It's okay, Donna. Don't feel bad. So how is everything with you?"

"Well, I have some news for you, which is why I've been trying to call you. It sucks that you don't have a phone, Tammy."

"Yeah, I know. I'll try to call you more often. I promise." It was a promise Tammy had made before but failed. "So, what's this news you have for me?" Tammy asked. "I have some news for you too." She suddenly had a thought. "Wait! Are you pregnant? Am I going to be an aunt?" she gasped.

Donna laughed. "No, I'm not pregnant." She took a deep breath. "Jason and I have sold our house, and we are moving."

Tammy's heart sank. "What? Where are you moving to?"

Tammy sensed Donna's hesitation. "Colorado."

"Colorado!" Tammy shrieked. "What the hell is in Colorado?"

"More work for Jason. He's a tree trimmer, and the work is endless out there. He already has jobs lined up that will carry him through to next year. Once we get settled, he plans on hiring a crew."

Tammy shook her head. "This is all so sudden. When are you leaving?"

"It's sudden to you, but we put the house on the market over six weeks ago and took a drive out to Colorado and bought a house. Like I said, I've been trying to call you. We leave this Wednesday."

"What! You're leaving in three days." It crushed Tammy's heart. A few minutes ago, she couldn't wait to tell her about their mom coming over. Now she didn't want to upset her by sharing the news. "So, when I get back from fishing next week, you'll be gone."

"I'm afraid so. Any chance I can see you before we leave?" Donna asked.

"No. We leave tomorrow night and won't be back for five days. We have just enough time to load up the boat before we head out," Tammy said with a tinge of guilt.

"Wow! You spend a lot of time on the ocean, Tammy. Do you ever see anyone anymore? How does Matt handle it?"

"It's only for the first couple of months of the season. We don't fish the island all year. It gets too rough out there. Matt is much better now that I see him on weekends. I'll never send him to Florida again. That was bloody awful."

"So, what news do you have for me?" Donna asked.

Tammy hesitated. "Well, it doesn't matter now because you won't be here, but mom is coming over next year, hopefully."

"Hopefully? What does that mean?"

"Well, Dwayne and I are going to look for a house to rent, and if we do, then mom is going to stay with Matt while we are fishing."

"Really!" Donna squealed. "That's a brilliant idea. Who thought of that?"

"Dwayne did. But it's not definite. We need to find a house first. And I'd have to arrange for someone to take Matt to school and bring him home. Mom doesn't drive, as you know."

"Well, it's about time you guys got a house. I don't know how you can live on a boat. There's no room. Don't you get cabin fever?" Donna laughed.

It was a question she got asked a lot, and for the most part, she never complained. She and Dwayne spend most of their time outdoors. The only time she remembers having a hard time living on the boat was when they had twelve days of non-stop rain, and they were confined to the cabin. Tempers flared, and harsh words were said between her and Dwayne. But Tammy has no recollection of what the trivial arguments were about. "I actually enjoy living on the boat, but Matt is getting bigger, and it's about time he had his own room. Anyway, I was hoping mom, and I could visit you if she comes over, but now that you're moving to Colorado, that's not going to happen. I know Mom won't be happy. She asked me if she was going to see you, and I told her yes."

"Yeah, I know. I write to her every so often, but I've never been good at writing letters. You know that, Tammy."

"Do you call her?" Tammy asked. "Every time I talk to her, she always tells me she wants to see all three of her daughters in the same room. I could hear the excitement in her voice when I told her we would visit you. God, now I have to tell her you're moving. That's not going to be a fun phone call."

"I've called her a few times, but she always sounds so pissed off because we are all spread apart. We always argue, so now I just write, so I don't have to listen to her. I know she wants to see us all together, but I don't see that happening anytime soon, and that's all she talks about. She doesn't understand that I can't travel to England because I'm still trying to sort out my status even after all these years in this country. It got all screwed up when I ran away from home."

"What about Jenny? Do you talk or write to her?"

Donna cracked a sarcastic laugh. "Hell no. I've not spoken to her in years. The last time I spoke to her was when I lived with you at the motel. Yeah, she sends me photos of her kids at Christmas time, and I send her a Christmas card every year, but I don't know her, Tammy."

Tammy had to agree with her. "Yeah, I know what you mean. I don't know her either. It's pretty sad, don't you think?"

Suddenly a voice interrupted their conversation. *"Please deposit seventy-five cents to continue this call."*

"God damn it. I'm out of quarters, Donna. I have to go. I love you, and I'm really sorry I won't get to see you before you leave." Tammy said in a rushed voice, afraid the call might end.

"Yeah, me too. I love you too, sis. Call this number when you get in from fishing. It will forward the call to our new one, and the recording will give you the new number. It will only forward for thirty days, so make sure you call."

"I will. I love you. Bye." And then the phone went dead.

Feeling numb from Donna's sudden news, Tammy turned around and lost herself in the view of the hundreds of boats sitting calmly in the docks. There was a slight breeze, and the sound of the rigging rattling on the sailboats always seemed to soothe her.

Regret filled Tammy. She should have called and visited Donna more often when in from fishing. If she had, she would have known about her move to Colorado and could have made plans to see her before she left. Now Tammy didn't know when she would see her, and the idea of fulfilling her mom's wishes to have all three of her girls together just became much more challenging.

CHAPTER 7

ammy kept her promise and called Donna when they returned to the mainland after fishing a week at the island. She wasn't about to let another sister slip away and was tired of not having a phone and keeping a jar of quarters just to make phone calls. It saddened her that she lost contact with so many friends because of not having a phone and was unreachable while on the ocean. Tammy realized that getting a house held another advantage. They could finally get a phone.

The more Dwayne and Tammy thought about getting a house, the more confined they felt on the boat. Dwayne's son, Justin, visited less frequently because, like Matt, he was growing, and the boat wasn't big enough for all four of them. When he visited, it was just for the day, and they took him home by nightfall. But months would go by between each visit. Justin was now a preteen and would much rather hang with his buddies from school than in a boatyard.

As soon as their third season at the island had ended and they were now fishing, Malibu, Dwayne and Tammy began the grueling task of looking for a house to rent that was close to the Marina, but they soon discovered everything was out of their price range.

"How do people afford these places? The cheapest we have found is $1,800, and that's without coming up with the first and last month's rent and whatever else they require. There's no way we can afford that," Tammy said, feeling discouraged. They looked at dozens of houses and even a few apartments, which they realized would never work for them. They needed a yard for Matt to play in and space to store their fishing gear. Also on the list was a garage for Dwayne. Tammy couldn't hide the frustration in her voice. "My God, we only pay $300 a month for our boat slip. We'd still have to pay that on top of the rent." Tammy leaned against Dwayne's truck outside the last house they looked at and folded her arms. "What are we going to do? I can't tell my mom to buy her tickets until we have a house, and she's hoping to come out here in September, which is just eight months away."

Dwayne approached her and rubbed her shoulders before giving her a loving kiss. "We still have time. Quit worrying so much. We can look some more tomorrow or later today after we've picked up Matt from school."

Tammy shook her head and raised her hands. "I'm done for today. I don't want to take Matt to different houses and have him ask a bunch of questions. He loves the boatyard, and I'm sure if he could, he would ask for a house in the boatyard." Tammy laughed, checking her watch. "Speaking of which, we should get going. School gets out in ten minutes."

Dwayne nodded and walked around the truck to get in on his side. Tammy hesitated and took one last look at the overpriced home that would have been perfect before getting in herself.

They arrived at the school just as the bell went. Tammy leaned over and gave Dwayne a peck on the cheek. "I'll be right back," she said as she stepped out of the truck. A few minutes later, she spotted Matt exiting from the double doors and waved. He smiled and waved back while adjusting his backpack with a wiggle of his shoulders.

"Hey, buddy. How did school go?" Tammy asked as they walked back to the truck, where Matt gave Dwayne his usual high-five through the open window.

"We're having a career day," Matt said as he got in the back seat. "Can you come, mom?"

Tammy, who was already in the front seat, glanced over her shoulder at Matt and then at Dwayne. "You want me to come to career day? Matt, I'm a fisherwoman," she said with a creased brow.

Dwayne threw her a devious smile. "You should do it. I bet you'd be the only parent that is a commercial fisherwoman." He gave her an encouraging nudge. "Come on, Tammy. the kids would love it."

"Yeah, come on, mom. It would be cool," Matt echoed from the back seat.

Tammy laughed. "Yeah, I could show up in my slickers, carrying a gaff, and I'd also bring a lobster trap."

Dwayne gave her a grin. "There you go. Now you're talking."

"That would be awesome, mom," Matt shrieked.

"So, are you going to do it?" Dwayne asked while giving her another nudge.

Tammy took another look at her son, who beamed at her with hope in his eyes. "Yeah, I'll do. I'll talk to your teacher about it."

Matt shouted out a victory, "Yes!" He gave Dwayne another high-five.

Now that they settled it, Tammy would do career day; Dwayne fired up the truck and took the side streets back to the Marina to avoid the crowds of parents picking up their kids from school. When they were just a few minutes away from the boatyard, Tammy's outburst startled Dwayne. "Stop the truck!" She yelled while looking out her window. "I see a house for rent."

Dwayne slowed down and peered over Tammy's shoulder. "I

thought you were done looking at houses for the day. Don't forget; we also have Matt with us."

"Oh, but this one looks so cute, and it's so close to the Marina," Tammy said, sounding hopeful.

"Which means it will be expensive," Dwayne reminded her.

Tammy wasn't listening. "There's a parking space. Pull in over there," she said as she pointed out the window.

"Okay, but I'm telling you right now, it's probably going to be too expensive."

"I just want to take a look," Tammy said as she stepped out of the truck and opened the back door for Matt.

Tammy couldn't help but feel a little excited as they approached the front gate. It had a for rent sign on it. It was a one-story house just off the main road on a quiet street and only a few minutes from Matt's school and the boatyard.

"Look, it has a fenced front yard with grass," Tammy said as they all walked through the gate. "And the front door is open," she whispered.

Dwayne knocked on the door. "Hello."

Tammy held Matt's hand as they waited patiently.

"Are we getting a house?" Matt asked.

She squeezed his hand. "No, we're just looking," Tammy told him.

Dwayne called again. This time a little louder. "Hello."

They heard a woman's voice come from inside the house. "Coming."

Tammy and Dwayne smiled at each other and held hands while they waited patiently. A few minutes later, they were greeted by an older woman, probably in her sixties.

"Hello. Can I help you?" the lady asked.

"Yes, we saw the for rent sign on the gate and wanted to ask how much it was," Dwayne replied.

"Eight-hundred." The woman said firmly. It's non-negotiable.

Tammy's eyes grew wide. "Only eight hundred." she gasped.

She beamed Dwayne with an enormous smile. "Can we look? I'm Tammy; this is my boyfriend, Dwayne, and my son Matt."

The lady held out her hand to Tammy and smiled when she shook it. "I'm Sherry. Sure, you can come in and look round, but if it's for all three of you, I don't think it will be big enough. It only has one bedroom."

Tammy laughed, "We've been living on a boat for three years. It's like a bloody mansion."

Sherry stood back to let them in where they stood in a pretty good size living room.

"Oh, look, it has a fireplace," Tammy beamed.

"I'm not sure how often we'll use that," Dwayne chuckled. "We live at the beach in southern California."

Sherry led them through to the kitchen. It was also a good size, and it looked out onto a large backyard and a garage.

"Wow, look at the garden, Dwayne. It's massive, and there's a garage too," Tammy said from the window where she stood.

"Can I go outside, mom?" Matt asked.

Tammy looked over at Sherry. "Would that be okay?"

"Yes, that's fine."

Matt immediately left Tammy's side and ran out the open back door to check out the yard.

Dwayne stood and talked to Sherry in the kitchen while Tammy was too eager to see the rest of the house. There wasn't much left to check out. It disappointed her. At the end of the hallway, she only found a large bathroom and one bedroom with a small closet off from the kitchen. She returned to the kitchen, and Dwayne threw her a smile.

"Sherry knew my dad when he had the yacht brokerage in town," Dwayne told her.

"Really! Wow, small world. He was there for many years, right?"

Dwayne nodded. "Yep. I grew up on boats, just like Matt is doing," he said with pride.

Tammy took to Dwayne's parents, Cathy and Charlie, immediately when she first met them just over three years ago. They were the perfect role model parents, married more years than Tammy had lived on this earth. She first met the entire family, which was huge on her first Christmas with Dwayne. There were his two brothers and one sister and a lot of his other relatives, all of whom welcomed and treated her like family. Tammy hadn't been to a family gathering in years, but every time they went to Dwayne's parents, it reminded her of the family get-togethers at her auntie Maddie's house in England.

Dwayne wrapped his arm around Tammy's waist and pulled her in close. "So, how do you like the house?"

"It's cute, but yes, it's small with only one bedroom," Tammy said, wearing a frown.

"That's why it's only eight hundred," Sherry said. "I told you it would be too small for the three of you."

Tammy glanced out the window to check on Matt and saw he had found a soccer ball and was kicking it around the yard.

"Now hang on a second, Tammy," Dwayne said. "Right now, we don't even have one bedroom, so this is a vast improvement. We can let Matt have the bedroom, and we can put a hide-a-away bed or a futon in the living room."

Tammy's frown soon turned into a smile. "I never thought about that."

"Are you saying you would like to fill out an application? I should tell you, though, I have forty applicants already."

"Forty!" Tammy shrieked, sounding discouraged.

Dwayne ignored her. "Yes, we do. Can I do it here and leave it with you?"

Sherry walked over to the counter and handed Dwayne a pen and the application. "Yes, that will be fine. After running your credit check, which will take a day or so, I'll arrange a meeting with you at my house. I like to interview all of my prospective tenants. I'll leave you to it. I'll be out in the garage when you're finished; just bring it out there."

Dwayne nodded while taking the form and throwing Tammy a smile.

"Really! You're going to apply for the house?" Tammy said as she cuddled up to Dwayne and gave him a peck on the cheek.

"Why not? We can afford this place and compared to the boat, it's huge."

Tammy did a little skip through the kitchen, "Oh, I'm so excited. I'm going to take another look while you fill that stuff out."

Dwayne used the counter for a desk and began writing. "Don't get your hopes up too much. There are forty other people after this place, remember."

CHAPTER 8

Dwayne and Tammy didn't hear from Sherry for four days, and Tammy couldn't stop thinking about the house. Dwayne was afraid that she was setting herself up for a hard fall. There were many applicants, and Dwayne knew their chances of getting it were slim. He tried to get her to look at other houses while they waited, but Tammy refused. She had her heart set on that house.

"But what if we don't get it? Don't you want to have some others to fall back on?" Dwayne had said the next day.

Tammy had shaken her head defiantly. "Nope, I don't want to jinx this one. It's the perfect house for us, and the location is ideal. Suppose we don't get it, then we can start looking again." She crossed her fingers and closed her eyes. "Please let us get this one."

Dwayne knew from past debates that when Tammy's mind was made up, he never tried to change it. "Okay, then. I guess we will have to wait and see."

On day four, Dwayne's beeper went off when he and Tammy were in downtown LA selling the lobsters they had caught the day before at Malibu. Dwayne recognized it to be Sherry's number.

"Shit, we have to find a phone booth after we are finished here. That was Sherry beeping me."

"Oh, crap. I think there's one at the gas station right before the on-ramp of the freeway." Tammy said, sounding alarmed.

After settling the sale with the lobster buyers and with a decent size check in hand, they headed for the gas station and spotted the phone booth straight away.

Tammy waited in the truck while Dwayne made the call. She didn't take her eyes off him, trying desperately to read his body language. But he gave off no clues.

"What did she say?" Tammy asked anxiously when he returned to the truck.

"She wants us to go for an interview this afternoon after we've picked up Matt from school."

Tammy shifted in her seat. "Oh, now I'm nervous,"

Dwayne rested his hand on her thigh. "It will be fine. Points for us, she knew my dad," he said with a laugh. "He was well known and highly respected in the Marina."

"Okay. Well, I hope Matt will be on his best behavior."

Tammy and Dwayne thought the interview went well. Sherry was friendly towards Matt and asked if he liked the house. Dwayne's dad was the highlight of the conversation. They must have talked a good fifteen minutes about his yacht brokerage business, and Sherry mentioned her brother might have bought a boat from him. Their fishing careers fascinated Sherry, and she had tons of questions for Tammy and how she ever became a fisherwoman. So, of course, Tammy had to tell her the story from the beginning when she had first met Dwayne.

The interview lasted about an hour, and Sherry told them she would get back to them in a day or so with her decision.

"God, I'm tired of waiting. Why can't she just tell us today?" Tammy whined as they headed back to the truck.

"She probably has more interviews to do," Dwayne said as he took her hand and glanced over at Matt, who was trailing behind. "Come on, let's have a barbecue on the dock and do some fishing."

"Yes!" Matt yelled as he picked up his pace and raced to the truck.

Tammy's hopes of getting the house dwindled as more days went by. Three days had passed, and they were getting ready to head out to Malibu to pull their gear. That was one thing nice about fishing Malibu—the lobsters were not in danger of being eaten by other critters, and they didn't have to pull the traps every day like at San Clemente Island. It was safe to pull them every two or three days.

Tammy had just dropped Matt off at school and arranged for Louise to pick him up if they were late coming back in. She found Dwayne on the *Little Boat* with the motor already running. He was anxious to go.

"Untie me and jump on," he yelled as she approached the boat.

Tammy flicked him a salute. "Aye aye, Captain." And set the boat free from the cleats before jumping on board.

They only had a couple of months left of the season before it closed for six months in March. They would then pull all one-hundred-fifty traps out of the water and stack them in the boat-yard until next season. The summers would be spent making any repairs and building new traps if needed. Tammy was amazed at how many traps they lost each year. And they weren't cheap. Each trap costs roughly sixty dollars to make.

After the season had ended and the traps were stacked, they would fish crabs for the rest of the year, which meant many trips out to Malibu to dump the one hundred crab traps they had made over the years. These were bigger and heavier traps and more of a toll on Tammy's body.

Dwayne knew how much Tammy loved to drive the *Little Boat* and stepped aside when she jumped on board. Tammy happily took the wheel and headed for the main channel. For January, the water was calm, and the sun was out. It looked like the weather would be on their side for the day. Half-way down the channel, Dwayne's beeper went off. Tammy slowed down the boat a notch so Dwayne could steady himself as he reached into his front pocket for his beeper.

"It's Sherry," he said after glancing at his beeper.

Tammy gasped and quickly put the boat in neutral, so they were drifting in the main channel.

"What are you doing?" Dwayne asked with a creased brow.

"We have to go back and call her. What if we got the house? If we don't call her back right away, she may give it to someone else." Tammy put the boat back in gear. "I'm turning around."

"Seriously!" Dwayne said with an edge.

"Yes. I don't want to wait until tonight to call her. We can always head back out after you've called. What's another thirty minutes?"

Dwayne knew there was no sense in arguing with her and nodded in defeat as she headed back to their slip.

With the motor still running, Tammy practically pushed Dwayne off the boat. "Hurry, go call her. I'll wait here."

Dwayne laughed at her urgency and hoped the news would be good. "Okay, okay, I'm going," he said with a smirk.

Tammy turned off the boat and watched as Dwayne walked up the ramp and across the boatyard to the telephone booth. To kill time, she paced back and forth on the dock, waving at boaters as they went by. Ten minutes later, Dwayne returned, but he didn't look happy. Tammy's heart sank, and she felt her dream slipping away.

Dwayne approached and placed a hand on her shoulder. Tammy tried to see a glimpse of a smile, but there wasn't one.

"Well?" Tammy asked and held her breath for his reply.

Dwayne took a deep breath. "Do you still have the newspapers with the rent classifieds in them?"

Tammy felt the wave of disappointment. "Yes, damn it."

Suddenly Dwayne burst into laughter. "Good! Because you can throw them away. We don't need them anymore. We got the house!"

Tammy gasped and shrieked, "What!" She raced into Dwayne's arms. Dwayne pulled her in tight and spun her around before kissing her hard on the lips.

"We got it, babe! We can move in today if we want to. The keys are ready for us to pick up."

"Oh, my god! I want to move in today. Can we?" She begged. "We can fish tomorrow."

Dwayne set her back down on the dock but continued to hold her close. "I was going to suggest the same thing," he said with a loving smile.

CHAPTER 9

*W*hen Tammy found out the house was theirs, she was beside herself. They spent the next five minutes cheering, crying, and pacing up and down the dock. Tammy couldn't believe it, and tonight, if she wanted to, she could cook dinner in a full-size kitchen and not on a tiny counter. Tammy smiled, knowing the house came with a full-size oven. For the last three years, they had only a small toaster oven. Her head swelled with meals she hadn't cooked in years and new recipes she'd been wanting to try but didn't have space: roast beef and Yorkshire pudding, a whole chicken with roasted potatoes. The list was growing by the minute. Tammy giggled when it suddenly dawned on her that she could boil potatoes, carrots, and gravy all at the same time and not have any sitting cold.

The house also came with a full-size fridge and a washer and dryer. "Ow wow! No more laundromat." Tammy squealed. "Oh, my god. I'm so friggin excited. I can't wait to tell Matt when I pick him up from school," she smiled big and raced into Dwayne's arms, giving him a long drawn out kiss on the lips. "I'm going to change out of my fishing boots, and then I want to go to storage," Her eyes were wide when she laughed. "Gosh, I haven't seen that stuff in years. I can't remember what's in there."

"Well, it will be like Christmas. But first, we have to pick up the keys and sign the lease." Dwayne reminded her.

Tammy tugged on his hand. "Well, let's go! Screw changing my boots."

Dwayne laughed and followed her lead. He had no idea she would be so excited about getting the house. It made all the headaches and the times they had endured looking for a place well worth it.

"Wait, I have to grab my checkbook," Dwayne said as he pulled Tammy back.

"Okay, I'll meet you at the truck."

Dwayne nodded and headed back to the *Baywitch*.

Within an hour, Tammy held the keys to their new home tight in her hand. "I still can't believe the house is ours." She said as they headed over to their home.

Dwayne rubbed her thigh. "It's ours, babe. We'll be sleeping there tonight if you want to."

"Yes! I know we don't have beds right now, but we'll figure something out."

When they pulled up in front of the house, Tammy rested her head on Dwayne's shoulder and let out a big sigh. "Home sweet home."

Dwayne kissed the top of her head. "Come on. Let's go check it out. We need to break that key in."

Tammy couldn't stop smiling as she opened the small wooden gate and walked towards what was now her front door, and as she turned the key in the lock, she looked over her shoulder at Dwayne and beamed him a huge smile.

She stepped into their living room, which had brand new carpeting, and the entire house had a fresh coat of paint. Tammy looked over at the fireplace. "I want to make a fire tonight," she said as she hugged Dwayne.

Dwayne laughed. "What? It will be in the sixties tonight."

"I don't care. It's our first night in our new home." She had the entire day planned out. "I want to go to storage and bring all of our stuff here. I want to cook a big family meal and light a fire, and I want to do laundry."

"Laundry?" Dwayne said and cracked a laugh.

"Yes. I want to hear the washing machine while I'm cooking dinner. Just like a regular family home."

Dwayne raised his hands. "Okay. Whatever makes you happy."

"And I want to soak for hours in the bathtub," she laughed as she hugged herself and closed her eyes.

Dwayne and Tammy walked through the small house hand in hand, sharing decorating ideas and what they needed to buy. They had no furniture, so they would sit, eat, and sleep on the floor for a few days until they could check out some thrift stores. They had a tiny TV on the boat, which they could make do with for a while.

They stood in the backyard and decided on where to store the fishing gear. Dwayne told Tammy his plans for the garage, and none of them involved keeping the cars in it. Tammy didn't care. It warmed her heart to see Dwayne so happy when he talked about the workshop he would build.

"Okay, let's go to storage and load up the truck," Tammy said eagerly. "And afterward, we can go to the store and buy something for dinner and firewood. I want to make a big spaghetti dinner."

Dwayne laughed at her excitement. "Okay. Let's go." He echoed.

The storage unit was only ten minutes away, and no sooner had Dwayne opened the door, Tammy raced in and began grabbing boxes and hastily threw them in the bed of the truck.

"You want to take everything over today?" Dwayne asked as she continued to pile boxes on the truck's tailgate for Dwayne to slide in.

"Yes! That way, I can organize it. It's going to be so much fun going through all of this stuff."

Dwayne shook his head. "Okay, then we might as well bring all my stuff too, and I can organize the garage, and we can do away with storage altogether."

"That would be fantastic!" Tammy shrieked. "Now that we are paying rent, we need to save money where we can."

In record time, they made three trips to the storage unit and emptied it. Tammy spent the afternoon going through her forgotten treasures until it was time to pick up Matt from school.

"I wonder if Matt will be as excited as us about getting a house. He loves the boatyard and fishing so much he may hate the idea." Tammy questioned as they drove to the school in Dwayne's truck.

After she told him she saw her prediction was right.

"But I want to go fishing off the dock like I always do," Matt said from the back seat with his arms folded and a puckered lip.

Tammy's smile soon disappeared. "Sweetie, don't you want to see your room?"

Matt shook his head. "No! I want to go fishing."

Tammy looked over at Dwayne. "Well, shoot, I was afraid of this. He doesn't care about living in a house."

Dwayne chuckled. "Well, I think we saw this coming." He reached over and squeezed Tammy's knee. "Tell you what. Why don't I drop you off at the house, and I'll take Matt fishing for an hour?"

Tammy's smile returned. "That's a great idea. I still want to make us a fire and fix us a big dinner."

"You know what else I'm going to do tomorrow?" Dwayne said with a devious smile on their way back to the house.

"No, what?"

"Buy us a phone and get us a phone number."

Tammy shrieked. "Oh, that's right! We can finally get a phone, and I can call my mom without a bunch of quarters and tell her to book her ticket. Oh, she's going to be so excited." Tammy suddenly had a thought. "I wonder if Donna has told mom that she has moved to Colorado. I had promised mom I would take her to see Donna, but that was before Donna had moved. And I'll be

reminded again how mom wants to see all her daughters together."
Tammy shook her head. "Well, I won't worry about it right now.
There's too much good going on, and those thoughts will just spoil
my mood."

A few minutes later, Dwayne pulled up in front of their house.

She turned and looked at Matt sitting in the back seat. "Are you
sure you don't want to come in for a minute and check it out?"

Matt shook his head. "I'll see it when I get back, mom."

"Okay." She leaned in and kissed Dwayne. "You guys have fun."

Dwayne kissed her back. "We will. Love you."

While Dwayne and Matt spent the afternoon fishing, Tammy
was in her realm, doing what she could to the house without much
furniture. They planned to hit the thrift stores tomorrow and go
crab trapping the day after.

By the time the two most important men in her life returned
home, Tammy had a fire going and spaghetti cooking on the
stovetop. She had most of the dishes put away from the boxes and
made makeshift beds out of blankets and sheets, and was pleased
to find four pillows in a box.

Matt finally showed some excitement when Tammy showed
him his very own room with some early trophies of his sitting on
the windowsill and a few of his toys he hadn't outgrown.

That night they sat in a circle on the floor of the living room in
front of the fire and ate Tammy's homemade meal, and then she
surprised them with one of her finds from storage—Monopoly.

"Matt, you're old enough to play this game now. Wanna play?"

Matt nodded and helped his mom clear the plates to make
room for the game.

The night couldn't have gone any better for Tammy. Everything she had missed over the past three and a half years was
suddenly all available to her whenever she pleased. Even the

luxury of being able to stretch out on a floor while playing a board game was heaven.

Tammy decided she would give Matt the honors of taking the first bath and breaking it in. But only because she had plans to take a long bubble bath surrounded by some candles she had found in storage. Together she and Dwayne would break in the bathtub their way. She closed her eyes at her erotic thoughts and hurried Matt off to take a bath.

The next morning, after Tammy had taken Matt to school and discussed her career day with his teacher, she returned home, anxious for the phone company to arrive. Dwayne had called them first thing in the morning and then went to the store to buy a phone before heading to the boat to do some maintenance work.

It felt strange for Tammy not to go to the boat with him. It had been her home for the past three and a half years, and this was the first time she had spent over twenty-fours away from it. Tammy soon realized that living in a house again was going to take some getting used to.

By one o'clock, they finally had a working phone and a telephone number. Tammy had a long list of people she wanted to call and tell them the good news they could now call her.

She called her mom first and gave her the exciting news that she could book her ticket. Dwayne and Tammy already decided that they would buy bunk beds for Matt's room so she would have a place to sleep, and they would buy a foldaway couch for the living room for themselves.

It felt strange not having to feed the phone quarters to make a phone call, and after four rings, her mom finally answered.

"Hey, mom! It's Tammy."

"Hello Tammy, I was just thinking about you. Is everything okay?"

"It couldn't be better, mom. We got a house!" Tammy squealed into the phone.

Tammy heard her mother gasp. "You did. Oh, that's wonderful. I bet you will be glad to be off that boat."

"Actually, I kind of miss it, but I love the house too. It just feels weird having all the space and a backyard again."

"Oh, you've already moved in?" her mom asked.

"Yes. We moved in yesterday. It's only one bedroom. Dwayne and I sleep in the living room, but it's massive compared to the boat."

"Only one bedroom. Well, if I come over, where am I supposed to sleep?"

"We're going to get bunk beds for Matt's room; you can sleep in there."

"What a good idea. I would never have thought of that. I'm going to book my ticket next week." Her voice dropped a notch. "You know Donna moved to Colorado, don't you? She called me last week."

Tammy knew this was going to be part of the conversation and took a deep breath. "Yes, I do, mom."

"So, I guess I won't see her when I come over?"

"I'm afraid, not mom. Colorado is a sixteen-hour drive, and besides, we'll be fishing most of the time while you are here. You'll be in charge of Matt while we are gone." Tammy added, trying desperately to change the conversation and make her mother feel needed.

"Oh, my little Matt. How is he?"

"He's not little anymore, mom; he's almost eight. He's going to be thrilled when I tell him you're coming over."

"That's if he remembers me," her mom said with a hint of sarcasm.

"Oh, stop it, mom. Of course, he'll remember you. I have pictures of you on my wall."

"Well, I'm still not going to have all my daughters together, am I."

Tammy rolled her eyes. "Mom, You're going to see Matt and

me, and you'll meet Dwayne for the first time. Aren't you excited about that? Someday we will all be together. I promise."

"Of course, I'm excited about seeing you and meeting your fisherman friend."

Tammy chuckled at her mom's remark. "Mom, he's more than a friend; he's my boyfriend." Tammy checked her watch. She wanted to call Jenny in England before it got too late. "Listen, mom; I gotta go. I'm going to give Jenny a call. I've not talked to her in years. Now you can call me whenever you want."

"Jenny never answers her phone, you know. You'll have to leave a message." Her mom told her.

"Then I'll leave a message. I love you, mom. Call me when you have your ticket. I can't wait to see you in September."

After ending the call, Tammy immediately called Jenny's number and discovered her mom was right. Jenny either wasn't home or wasn't answering the phone. It was ten in the evening in England, so she assumed she was home. After five rings, the machine picked up, and after the ear-piercing beep, Tammy left a message. "Hey, Jenny! Guess who this is? It's your baby sister in America. I finally have a phone number. Call me," Tammy looked at the piece of paper in her hand and recited the new number that she had yet to memorize. "I can't wait to talk to you. Love you. Bye."

After leaving a message, Tammy made two more phone calls. One to Donna and one to her dad in Florida. The conversation with Donna was uplifting and pleasant. She and Jason loved Colorado, and they were thrilled and were settling nicely into their new home, but the call with her dad was disturbing.

After the initial hellos and I miss you, he told her his latest news. "We're moving to Ireland at the end of the month."

Tammy was stunned. First, Donna and now her dad. "What?" She shook her head. Trying to grasp what she had just heard. "Why and how long have you been planning this?" She asked with a slight edge.

"Joanne and I have been talking about it for some time, and we took a trip out there last month. I guess you were fishing. Anyway, we found a house, and we're going to make a go of it."

"But dad, why Ireland? I'll never see you."

John released a sarcastic laugh. "Tammy, you never see me now. You won't even know I'm gone. I'll be traveling back and forth to the States."

Tammy knew he was right. She hadn't seen her dad in almost five years. Like the rest of her family, they had become estranged, and she had a long-distance relationship on the phone with all of them. He had two more sons now, and Tammy had yet to meet them. He had done his usual fly-by visits while doing a book tour when Matt had just turned two, and then he saw Matt when he went to Florida the first year Tammy had fished. "Yeah, I guess you're right. Well, when you're in the States, you will have to visit your grandson. He's going to be eight soon, and he hardly knows you."

This time John had an edge to his voice. "And who's fault is that, Tammy? You are the one that chose not to have him come to Florida during the fishing season. Joanne offered to watch him every year."

"I know, dad, but I can't be away from him for three months again. That was horrible. I know he was okay with you, but being away from him that long was almost unbearable."

Tammy and her dad spoke for a few more minutes, but she had an urgency to get off the phone. Her father's news stunned her, and yet again, her family was becoming more spread across the globe. She believed her mother that her sisters would never be together again. She was determined to prove her mom wrong.

CHAPTER 10

For the remainder of the year, Tammy and Dwayne continued to fish for crabs off the Malibu coastline and did what they could to make their house a home.

Tammy had fun doing career day at Matt's school, and the children loved seeing her dressed in her slickers when she walked into the classroom with a lobster trap and some live lobsters in a bucket of ocean water. Many of the kids had never seen a lobster before, let alone touch one. The expressions on the kids' faces were priceless, and the look of pride that shined on Matt's face made it all worthwhile.

Even though they enjoyed the luxuries of the house, their lifestyles still revolved around the boats, and Dwayne and Tammy had a hard time adapting to living on land. Tammy noticed Matt was too. After school, he still wanted to fish off the docks at the boatyard, which resulted in them having a barbecue for dinner on the dock most nights and returning to the house after dark.

When they were not fishing, they spent their days in the boatyard either repairing or building traps and getting ready for the lobster season coming up in September, which would soon be upon them. But knowing Matt would be in his own home for the first time while she fished, bonding with his grandmother whom he had not seen in over five years comforted Tammy. Tammy had spent the previous months covering every detail for her mother's stay. She wanted it to go flawlessly and be as easy as possible for her mom. Tammy arranged with Louise to take Matt to and from school and leave her number by the phone in case of any emergency. The house had been cleaned from top to bottom, and there was no risk of them running out of food.

"So, are you excited about meeting my mom for the first time?" Tammy asked Dwayne as they waited patiently in the terminal of LAX airport for her arrival.

Dwayne turned to her and smiled. "Yes, I am. The only person I've met in your family is your sister, Donna. I went with you once when you visited her shortly after lobster season a few years ago."

Tammy squeezed his hand. "Yeah, I know. I hate that my family is so scattered. I'm so jealous of you when it comes to your family," Tammy confessed.

"You are?" Dwayne said, wearing a surprised look. "Why?"

"Because you are all so close, and you always have family gatherings on the holidays. I've met your entire family, and you've only met one of my sisters." Tammy released a heavy sigh. "I understand my mom when she tells me she wants to be with all her daughters. The last time she saw us all together was when I was twelve, and my sisters were fourteen. That was sixteen years ago. How sad is that?"

"Wow, that's a long time. No wonder she keeps bringing it up." Dwayne said as he glanced over at Matt. "Where does he think he's going?' Dwayne chuckled when he saw Matt was wandering off too far. He hollered loud above the chatter of people. "Matt!" He waved him back with his hand.

Tammy raised her arms above her head and stretched her stiff body. "Yeah. I'm just glad we're living in a house now, and mom can stay with us and be able to bond with Matt. I can't believe lobster season starts in two weeks. Where has the time gone.?" She gave Dwayne a cute smile. "This will be my fourth season fishing with you. Are you getting tired of me yet?" she laughed.

Dwayne took her in his arms and smiled. "I could never get tired of you."

"I can't wait to fish off the *Baywitch II* and see how she handles the season."

"Yeah, me too. I'll miss the old *Baywitch,* but she was just too expensive to run. This year we should have a better profit margin. Our new boat runs off diesel engines—much cheaper than gas, and we were able to build more traps over the summer. It should be a good year for us."

Tammy loved working with Dwayne. They had grown together as one when it came to fishing and knew what they expected from one another. It was a relationship that worked. They spent every hour of every day together, and sometimes that didn't seem enough for the two of them. In two days, they would leave to start the many trips to the island to drop off the gear before the season began.

"Nana's plane has landed," Tammy said with an edge of excitement to Matt, who was now sitting between her and Dwayne.

Matt's eyes grew wide before he jumped up from his seat and did a happy dance. Tammy stood too. "I wonder how long it will take her to get through customs? We've been here for over an hour already."

"Hopefully, not too long. Matt is getting restless. So am I, for that matter." Dwayne laughed.

It took another hour and a half before Tammy finally spotted her mother walking amongst a crowd of passengers. Tammy stood and raised her hand high before she squealed, "There she is!" She then grabbed Matt's hand and headed in her mom's direction with Dwayne close on her tail.

"Mom!" Tammy yelled over the loud noise of the terminal. It took Rose a few minutes to spot her daughter, but her beaming smile told Tammy when she did.

"Tammy!" Rose shouted.

Tammy embraced her mom with misty eyes and held her tight. "Oh, mom, I've missed you."

"I've missed you too, Tammy," Rose said with tears trickling down her cheeks.

Tammy stood back and looked at her mother. She was dressed in black slacks and a light purple sweater. Her hair, which hadn't changed, was still bleach blonde and her well-manicured nails looked perfect as always. "You look, great mom. And I love your hair."

Rose ran her fingers through her hair. "Thanks; I just had it done a few days ago." She scanned the area around them. "So, where is this grandson of mine?"

Tammy noticed Dwayne had held back while she reunited with her mom and motioned with her hand for them to join her. "Here, he is, mom." She said as Matt took her hand. "And this is my boyfriend, Dwayne," Tammy said with pride while squeezing his hand.

Rose pulled Matt in close to her and smothered him with kisses. Tammy laughed as she watched Matt winch his face from the wet kisses his nana was drowning him in. He had outgrown some of the smothering affections unbeknown to her mom.

Dwayne approached Rose and held out his hand. "Hi, it's finally good to meet you. Tammy talks about you all the time." He smiled. "She really misses you."

Rose held on to Matt's hand as she looked at Dwayne, taking him all in from head to toe. "Hi, Dwayne. Good to meet you too. So, you're the man that got my baby girl into fishing, eh?"

Dwayne gave Tammy a quick glance and wrapped his arm around her waist. "I sure am, and she's damn good at it."

That night Tammy and her mother cooked a chicken dinner together while Tammy told her some of her fishing adventures.

"You had a sea lion come on your boat?" her mom laughed while setting the table. "Why was it on your boat?"

"Go on, tell her." Dwayne laughed from the couch.

Tammy rolled her eyes and folded her arms. "Because I was throwing him fish from the boat even though Dwayne told me not to."

Her mom laughed louder and clapped her hands. "You still don't listen, do you, Tammy?"

"No, she doesn't," Dwayne butted in.

CHAPTER 11

The next day Dwayne and Tammy gave Rose a tour of the boatyard. Tammy was pleased to see the yard was busy, and her mum could experience it during the regular working hours. Another bonus was that Matt could join them because school was still on break.

As Tammy watched her mother walk precariously down the swaying docks, it reminded her of her first time with Dwayne, and she couldn't refrain from giggling quietly to herself. It was also the first time for her mom.

When Rose stepped onto the *Baywitch II,* she glanced around and looked down inside the tiny cabin; it was close to the size of the cabin of the old *Baywitch.* "You lived there?" Rose said in disbelief.

Tammy laughed. "It was the other boat we lived on, mom, but the cabin was about the same size."

"Good lord, Tammy. Where did you all sleep? And how did you even cook?"

"We managed. It was like we were camping every night."

Her mom shook her head. "I'll say." and continued to check out the boat. Every so often, she'd steady her feet by holding onto the rail. "I don't know how you did it, Tammy."

"I loved it, mom, but Matt is getting older and bigger, and now it is too small for the three of us. But Dwayne and I still live on it when we go to the island. It's kind of like a second home. We often come down here with Matt and spend the night on it because we miss it. Tammy threw Matt a proud smile. "But now that Matt is older, he sleeps in the cabin of the *Little Boat.*" Tammy pointed to the boat docked next to the Baywitch II. "That's ours too."

Rose turned her head and stared at the *Little Boat.* "That's a cute boat."

"It's the one I like to drive. Dwayne built it. There's nothing he doesn't know about the ocean and boats. He's taught me everything I know," Tammy said as she threw Dwayne a loving smile.

Her mom took a seat on one of the deck chairs and took in the view. "Gosh, it sure is pretty here. I can see why you love it."

Tammy glanced down the dock and saw Matt and Dwayne were walking to the end with fishing poles in their hands. Tammy's mind wandered-how did she ever get so lucky to meet such an amazing man? He was everything to her and then some. Lost in her thoughts, she shook her head and turned her attention back to her mom. "I love it here. I fell in love with this place the first time I came down. I knew that day I wanted to be a part of it." Taking a seat next to her mom, they sat for a few minutes in silence, mesmerized by the beauty of the water glistening in the sun and the sight of the occasional sailboat or powerboat cruising by.

The ocean breeze masked their faces and gently blew through their hair. Tammy leaned back and enjoyed the warmth from the rays of the sun reflecting off her face. She released a big satisfying sigh. Life couldn't get any better.

"I can see why you never want to leave," Rose said as she

became more at ease on the gently rocking boat and eased her head back into the deck chair and closed her eyes.

"Yeah, and Matt loves it too. I can't keep him away from the water. He's a fishing fool." Tammy laughed.

Rose sat up and reached for Tammy's hand. "You've come a long way, Tammy. I'm proud of you. Not too sure about the fishing thing, though. But I can tell you are happy."

Tammy squeezed her mom's hand, "I am a mom. I've never been happier."

"So, when are you leaving?" her mom asked.

"The day after tomorrow. So, Dwayne and I will work late tonight and tomorrow getting the boat ready and loading the traps. Which means you get to watch Matt at the house." She said with a large grin.

Rose matched her daughter's grin. "I'm looking forward to it."

Tammy stood up and glanced down to the end of the dock and saw Dwayne and Matt were still engaged in fishing. "Hey, mom, do you want to give fishing a go?" she asked with a devious smile.

Her mom cracked a sarcastic laugh. "Fishing! You're bloody joking, right?"

Tammy stood and held out her hand. "No, I'm not. It will be fun. Come on, let's join the boys. Matt would love it."

"I've never fished a day in my life, Tammy. Have you gone mad?"

Tammy laughed. "You've never been on a boat before, and look, here you are. Now come on. It will only be for a short while. Dwayne and I have to get to work if we want to leave on time."

Her mom shook her head in defeat and took Tammy's hand. "Okay, then. I'll give it a try."

"That's the spirit, mom," Tammy said in triumph.

Rose continued to mumble as they walked down the dock. "I can't believe you're making me fish. What if I get one? I won't know what to do."

"Ha! Mom, we will help you, don't you worry."

As they approached the boys, the rocking of the dock from their steps caused Dwayne and Matt to look over their shoulders.

"Nana!" Matt squealed. "I caught two Mackerel. Wanna see?" He said as he reached for a white bucket at his side with his free hand.

Rose peered into the bucket and curled her lip when she saw the two-shiny, slimy fish looking up at her with their large round glazed eyes. She took a step back. "Are they dead?"

"Yes, mom, they are dead," Tammy laughed. "We'll use them for bait in the lobster traps. It makes Matt feel like he's doing his part to help." Tammy said as she stroked the top of Matt's head. She leaned in and rested her hands on Matt's shoulders. "Hey, buddy. Do you want to show Nana how to fish? She's never done it before."

Matt looked up with bright shiny eyes. "Yes! Can I?"

"Sure. Why don't you give her your fishing pole?"

Matt stood up from where he had been sitting at the dock's edge and handed her the pole. "Here you go, nana. Now hold it tight, and when you feel a bite, yank it to set the hook."

"Yank it?" Rose asked with a puzzled look.

Matt jerked his pole up and down. "Yes, like this. See."

Rose nodded and took the pole in her hand. Dwayne stepped aside to give her some room and threw her a smile. "If it runs in the family, you're going to be hooked after your first fish like these two." He said as he gave Rose's shoulder a nudge.

"I can't see that happening," Rose said with a smirk. "Tammy takes after her dad. I can see she's not afraid of anything."

Rose stood at the edge of the dock next to Matt while Tammy stood back and took pictures with the disposal camera she had grabbed from the *Baywitch II*. She was sure this would be the only chance she could capture nana and grandson fishing together. It warmed her heart to witness such a moment that she would treasure for years to come, and she was sure Matt would too. Tammy clutched her hands close to her heart as she watched Matt show his nana how to pull the rod up and down in the water to attract the fish.

Dwayne, who still had a rod in the water, glanced over his shoulder in her direction and gave Tammy a loving smile. He knew this was a special moment for her.

After a few minutes, her mom suddenly squealed. "I think I got one!"

Tammy tucked the camera in her jacket's pocket she was wearing and raced over to her mom. She stood behind her and looked in the water from over her shoulder.

"What do I do?" her mom screamed as she held the rod with two hands and took a step back.

"Hold on to the rod tight," Dwayne yelled, wearing a huge grin. He patted Matt on the shoulder. "Show her what to do, buddy."

Tammy gave Matt some room as she watched with admiration her son give her nana instructions on how to reel in a fish. It was the cutest thing she'd ever seen.

"Go slow, nana. Pull the rod up, then wind some line in. Pull the rod up. Then wind some line in." Matt told her over and over, watching her every move.

After a couple of minutes, her mom screamed again. "I see it!"

Tammy looked in the water again and saw a silverfish splashing at the surface. "You got a Mackerel, mom." Tammy squealed as she patted her mom on the shoulder. "Show her how to take it off the hook, Matt." Tammy bellowed with excitement.

Rose quickly handed the rod to Matt. "No, no. Let him do it. I don't want to touch it."

Matt laughed at his nana's queasiness and happily took the rod from her and yanked the line out of the water where the fish landed on the dock in a frenzy. Rose squealed in disgust and dashed until she was a few feet away from the flapping fish.

"Oh, no! There is no way I'm touching that." Rose claimed from a distance.

In a few minutes, Matt laughed and had the fish free from the hook and in the bucket.

Tammy, who was still laughing at her mother's reaction, approached her mom and hugged her. "Well done, mom, you caught your first fish."

"And it will be my last," she said in defiance. "I'm not sure what you see in it, Tammy, but thank you for the experience."

"Well, before you go home, we will have to take you out on the boat. Maybe you will like that."

Rose shook her head. "I don't think so, Tammy. I get carsick. I can only imagine what I would be like on a boat."

"You do? I didn't know that."

"There are a lot of things you don't know about me, Tammy. How could you?"

Her mom's words stung her. Why did she have to continue to twist that knife? She knew what she was doing. Did she get enjoyment from making her daughter feel guilty? Tammy shook it off, just like she had done many times in the past. She wouldn't allow her mother to get to her. "Okay, mom. Dwayne and I have to get to work. I'm going to drop you and Matt off at the house, and we will see you tonight, okay."

"Ah, but mom, I want to stay here," Matt hollered from behind her in protest.

Tammy gave her son a stern look. "No, Matt. You're going home with nana. Now come on. Let's go."

Matt folded his arms and pouted as he walked behind his mom, dragging his feet.

Tammy turned and gave Dwayne a tender kiss on the lips as he stood at the end of the dock holding the two poles. "I'll be back soon. Love you."

"Love you too," he said as he gave her waist a gentle squeeze.

CHAPTER 12

To meet their deadline and leave for the island in just under two days, Dwayne and Tammy worked late into the nights at the boatyard. Traps needed to be repaired and loaded onto the *Baywitch II*. Tammy hasn't seen much of her mom or Matt. They were already asleep when they finally made it home to catch a few hours of rest themselves and left before they woke up.

Worried about how her mom was coping, Tammy called many times throughout the day to check-in. "Hey, mom, I'm just calling to see how everything is going and to see if you guys need anything."

It had been a long time since Tammy had heard her mom sound genuinely happy. She was almost singing when she spoke. "Tammy, this is the fifth time you've called me today, and as I said before, we are fine. I can't believe how grown-up Matt is. We are having a wonderful time together. This afternoon we are going to make Shepherds Pie. It's his favorite." Rose laughed. "He certainly has some British in him."

"Yes, he does, mom. He loves Scotch eggs too. Give him a big hug and kiss. I'm glad you guys are having a great time."

In a flash and with little sleep over the past few days, Dwayne and Tammy were ready to head out with their first load of traps. Tammy spent the early morning going over everything with her mom. Making sure she knew where Louise's number was. How to work the appliances and making sure they had everything they would need.

"I'll be fine, Tammy. Will you stop fussing and get out of here?" her mother said while practically pushing her daughter out the door.

Tammy laughed. "Okay. Okay, I'm going." She called Matt over and gave him a tight squeeze and a kiss on his cheek. "You be good for nana, okay?"

"I will," Matt said as he wiped the moist spot on his cheek.

The sound of a horn came from the street. Tammy knew it was Dwayne who was waiting in the truck. "Okay, I gotta go. I love you guys. We should be back in late tomorrow night for the second load of gear and then probably head back out again the next morning," she said as she gave them both one last hug before heading out the door.

"When do you sleep?" her mom asked.

"On the boat, or we may come home for a quick shower and a nap. It depends on how it goes. You are in charge now, mom."

Tammy waved to her mom and Matt from inside the truck, who stood outside the door, yelling goodbye and waving. She leaned over and gave Dwayne a peck on the cheek. "Okay, let's go before I start crying."

Dwayne rubbed her shoulder. "They'll be fine. It's not like your mom has never taken care of a child before. She raised three girls, remember."

"Yeah, I know," Tammy said, giving her mom and Matt one last wave as Dwayne pulled away from the curb.

Their hard work had paid off, and they were right on schedule. Within an hour, they were heading down the main channel on the *Baywitch II*. Tammy was at the helm driving the boat while Dwayne checked the traps were all securely tied down.

For the middle of September, the weather was glorious, with bright blue skies and no clouds. The wind was light, and the spray of salt-water felt refreshing against Tammy's face. She loved the beginning of the season and what would be their first trip out to the island in six months. She still enjoyed the solitude of it and the freedom they inherited being away from the mainland.

"How's it looking back there?" Tammy yelled over the sound of the roaring engine.

Dwayne steadied himself as he headed to the helm to join her. "Everything looks good. I checked the weather, and it looks like it's going to be sunny and calm all day. We should have a nice crossing."

Ten hours later, they were pulling into Northwest harbor at San Clemente Island. They saw Mitch on the *Sea-Life* was anchored with a load of traps. He waved from his deck and then a few minutes later called Dwayne on the radio to say a howdy. They chatted for a few minutes.

"Happy to hear you had a good crossing. Some new boats are showing up this year. One just left the harbor an hour ago to dump gear." Mitch told Dwayne. His tone told Dwayne he wasn't too pleased with more boats fishing the island.

"I guess word travels fast about the good season we had last year," Dwayne said.

"It sure did. I don't think these guys realize, though, that it's a short season out here. As we all know, the weather gets too rough to fish pretty quickly."

Dwayne chuckled. "Well, they'll soon find out."

It took Dwayne and Tammy twelve days and four trips to drop all two hundred plus traps at the island. Over that time, they made it home twice to take hot showers and check on Matt and her mom. But it seemed Tammy had nothing to worry about. Their smiles told her everything was fine.

On their last trip and with all the traps now at the island, they loaded the *Baywitch II* with all their supplies and had the *Little Boat* in tow.

Tammy sat at the helm and drove while Dwayne checked the towline. It all looked good.

"You know I've been thinking," Dwayne said with a devious grin that Tammy has gotten to know so well.

"What?" she asked with her eyes narrowed. What was he up to now? she wondered. Tammy sped up the boat as they left the main channel and hit the open waters.

Dwayne raised his voice over the elevated noise. "Well, we have fifty extra traps this year, and you've been doing this for a few years now and even have your own permit."

Tammy had a feeling he was setting her up for something. "And?" she said with a piercing stare.

Dwayne threw her a large grin, showing off his pearl white teeth. "How about you run the little boat by yourself this year, and I'll pull the deeper traps from the *Baywitch II*?"

"What!" Tammy shrieked. She checked the compass to make sure they were on course and then quickly set the autopilot so she could reply to Dwayne's ridiculous idea. "Why do you always do this to me?"

Dwayne laughed. "Do what?" he said while shrugging his shoulders.

Tammy rolled her eyes. He knew what he was doing. "You always put me on the spot like this with no warning. It's how you got me to drive the *Little Boat* for the first time years ago."

"And it worked, didn't it?" Dwayne laughed. "I think this will work too. We have more traps to pull this year, and if you start at one end and me at the other, we'll get them pulled faster."

Tammy made a frustrated grunt. "I don't know, Dwayne. I've

never driven the *Little Boat* by myself at the island before, let alone pull traps. I'd have to do everything. Drive the boat, pull the traps, and measure the lobsters. Oh, and let's not forget, we need to re-bait the traps." She shook her head. "That's a lot for one person."

"Yes, it is, and I'll have to do the same." He gave her one of his sexy smiles that always weakened Tammy. "Think of it as precautionary measures."

Tammy creased her brow. "What do you mean?"

"What if I get injured? You need to pull traps by yourself if I can't. Remember my arm. When it went numb, something like that could happen, but far worse. This is our only source of income. We need to be prepared, and I'm surprised at myself for not having thought of it sooner." He said while giving her shoulders another tender rub.

Tammy released a heavy sigh and pulled away from his hands that were still resting on her shoulders. "You always know what to say. Don't you?" Tammy said while rolling her eyes. "Okay, I'll give it a go. But we won't meet in the middle; I can guarantee you that. You'll have two-thirds pulled by the time I've only pulled a third."

"Don't underestimate yourself. You're damn good on the boat. It might surprise you just how well you do."

Tammy gave him a loving smile. He always believed in her. "Thanks for the vote of confidence, but I don't know about this."

"I think you'll be fine."

CHAPTER 13

ammy was pleased to see all the regular boats from the previous years had returned, along with the two new boats Mitch had mentioned.

They were the last to arrive in the harbor, and after setting the mooring and tying off the *Little Boat* alongside the *Baywitch II*, Dwayne got on the radio to say hi to a few of the captains.

Tammy waved at those close by who she now considered friends. "Hi, Tom!" she yelled across the water.

Sound carries well across the water. Tom heard her and yelled back. "Hey, Tammy. Good to see you back for another season."

"I wouldn't miss it for the world." Tammy hollered. Dwayne covered his ears and struggled to hear himself on the radio.

"Tammy! Hush, I'm on the radio."

Tammy rolled her eyes. "That's why I'm hollering at the guys because you are hogging the radio."

Dwayne gave her a sarcastic grin. "Smartass."

The sun was setting rapidly on the horizon, so Tammy fixed them some soup and rolls for dinner after Dwayne had finished talking on the radio.

"That was good soup. Thanks." Dwayne said. "Let's get the *Little Boat* set up for you. We must make sure you have everything you will need. We can load the bait on there too," he added.

"I'm not so sure about this, Dwayne. What if I mess up or if the *Little Boat* breaks down?" Tammy said as she handed him a box of mackerel.

"You're going to be fine, and I also told a few other captains that you would fish on your own tomorrow and to keep an eye out." He nudged her elbow and gave her a wink. "They are pretty impressed by you. If you can't get a hold of me on the radio, they can help. Especially if I'm on the backside of the island where I don't get a signal. You can always call one of them if you need help. Okay?"

Tammy nodded. "Okay."

They worked hard for the next few hours, so in the morning, both boats would be turnkey ready, and by midnight Tammy was prepared to call it a night.

The next morning Tammy woke before Dwayne because of a restless night worrying about fishing on her own. It was a huge step for her to be in charge and make all the decisions. She had always relied on Dwayne to fix things if something went wrong. Tammy realized how much she took him for granted and understood why he insisted on her learning to fish independently. It was a huge responsibility, but she was ready.

Being careful not to wake Dwayne, Tammy tried her best to crawl over him to get out of their confined sleeping quarters but was unsuccessful. As she rolled her body over his, he stirred and pulled her back. "Where do you think you're going?" he said in a sleepy state with his hair in a tangled mess.

"I can't sleep. I'm going to make some coffee. Do you want some?"

He smiled and locked his hand around the back of her neck. "Not before you give me a kiss."

Tammy returned the smile and leaned in until their lips

touched and gave him a long, drawn-out kiss. "Man. You're better than a cup of coffee," she said before kissing him again.

Dwayne lowered his hand and gave her naked butt a playful squeeze. "And sleeping next to you naked every night out here sure brightens my fishing trips."

Tammy laughed and smacked his naked chest. "Okay, before we start anything here, I'm getting up. The sun is coming up, and we need to get a move on."

Dwayne Saluted her. "Aye aye, captain. I can call you that now, you know. You're captain of the *Little Boat*."

Tammy pulled herself off the bed and thought about what he had said. "Yeah, I guess I am." She smirked.

Dwayne swung his legs over the side of the bed and sat on the edge as he watched Tammy pull on a pair of jeans and top. "It feels good, doesn't it?" He said, looking proud.

"Yeah, it does." She giggled. "Captain Tammy. I like that."

Once Tammy was dressed, she left the cabin, so Dwayne had room to stand and do the same. It was still dark outside, but the sun peeked over the horizon. Tammy breathed in the fresh ocean air. She couldn't think of a better way to wake up. A steaming hot cup of coffee while they bobbed around in the middle of the ocean at a remote island. It was something she would never get tired of.

She scanned the harbor and saw floodlights illuminated on the decks of the other boats. Tammy knew how they were feeling. The day before the opening of the season, everyone was eager to get their traps baited in time for the opener. She watched from the deck chair as the other boats' crews did their last-minute chores while she drank her early morning beverage. A few minutes later, Dwayne appeared and grabbed the coffee off the helm that Tammy had made for him.

"So, are you ready to go?" he asked as he leaned back against the rail of the helm and took a sip of his drink.

Tammy took her last sip and stood up. "As ready as I'll ever be."

"That's my girl," Dwayne said as he approached her and gave

her a peck on the lips. "You'll be fine. I have all the faith in the world. I'm going to make sure you get off okay, and then I'll fire up this beast and head for the far side of the island."

Tammy freed her slickers from the hook at the helm and slid into them. She then grabbed her boots from inside the cabin and put them on. "Okay, I'm ready," she said with an edge of nervousness.

"Damn, you're the cutest fisherman out here. I'm so lucky." Dwayne said before giving her one last hug and a passionate kiss on the lips. "I'm so proud of you."

"Tell me that after today. Let's see how I do first."

Dwayne smacked her butt as she stepped onto the *Little Boat* and fired it up. "Okay, untie me." She yelled.

"Oh, I love it when you talk dirty to me," he chuckled. "Now, you know where you are going, right?"

Tammy nodded. "Yes, we discussed it last night. I'll go over to the east side where the swell is low in the mornings and then head around castle rock and meet you somewhere down the line over there."

"You got it. Okay, I'm going to push you off," Dwayne said as he untied the last line at the stern of the boat. "I love you," he hollered as Tammy drove away from the *Baywitch II*.

Tammy smiled and yelled over the motor. "I love you too."

When she was a distance away, it suddenly hit her that she was in charge of the *Little Boat's* entire fishing operation. "Wow!" she said out loud before the sound of a horn startled her. She looked to her right where the other boats were anchored and saw Mitch was standing tall, waving at her. Tammy smiled and waved back vigorously. It felt good to have these guys finally on her side and rooting for her.

With both hands firmly on the wheel, she steered the boat and headed out the harbor. "You can do this, Tammy," she said out loud, feeling confident.

CHAPTER 14

*T*ammy was pleased that the weather was on her side for her first day of being solo. The ocean was flat with hardly any swell, and the sun reflected off the surface of the clear water. Today would be a good test for her to handle the boat by herself and retrieve the traps to bait them. Her task was to pull as many traps as she could, fill them with bait, and toss them back in the water. Tomorrow would be the big day, where she would pull the traps for lobsters and do all the tasks independently.

It took her roughly ten minutes to spot the first trap, and she immediately slowed down the boat so she could ease up on it. She took a deep breath, "Okay, here we go. Trap number one."

Tammy had watched Dwayne pull up to the trap hundreds of times and was thankful that she had been paying attention. With her gaff in one hand, she steered the boat with her other and hooked the line perfectly before putting the boat in neutral and wrapping the line on the pulley. "Yes!" She screamed in triumph as she saw the trap break through the surface of the water and land on the trap table. "I knew I could do this!" she squealed as she skipped across the deck to grab some bait.

Still beaming like a Cheshire cat and feeling mighty proud of herself, Tammy plugged the trap with bait and secured the door. Before pushing it over the side, she grabbed the radio microphone. "Dwayne. Dwayne, you got me?"

A few seconds later, she heard his masculine voice over the radio. "Yeah, I got you. Is everything okay? Over"

"I did it! I pulled my first trap. Over."

Tammy heard him laugh before he spoke. "See, I knew you could do it. You should be proud of yourself. Over."

Tammy had forgotten they were on an open channel and suddenly heard the cheers of Mitch coming through the speakers. "Yeah, Tammy! Well done. Holler if you need anything. I'm out."

"Will do. Thanks, Mitch. Over," Tammy replied before getting Dwayne back on the radio.

"Dwayne, are you still there? Over."

"Yeah, I'm here. I'll be out of radio contact in about twenty minutes. Give yourself a big pat on the back from me. I'm so proud of you. I'll see you on the other side. Over," he laughed.

"Okay. Be safe. I'm out."

Tammy returned the mic to its holder and was flattered that Mitch had come on the radio to congratulate her. It was comforting to know that the rest of the fleet knew she was on the boat alone and would assist her if need be. Suddenly she didn't feel so isolated.

After pushing the baited trap into the water, Tammy put the boat in gear and worked the rest of the line without incident and felt like she was ready to fish the traps on her own tomorrow. It took her a good two hours to bait the rest of the line before she headed around castle rock, where she would meet up with Dwayne somewhere down the line up ahead.

She was eager to hear his voice. She hadn't spoken to him in hours. She needed to know if he was okay. She didn't like that he was out of radio contact for the first part of the day but felt a little at ease when Dwayne told her a couple of other boats would fish the backside of the island at the same time as him. When she finally heard his voice over the radio, three hours later, she immediately slowed down the boat and put it in neutral.

"Tammy! Tammy! You got me? Over."

"Yes, Dwayne, I got you! I'm so happy to hear your voice. Over."

"So, how did you do? Over."

"Good! There are no problems, and the boat is running fine; I've baited about ten traps on the other side of Castle Rock. Where are you? Over."

"I'm coming down the same line. We should meet up in a few hours. Well done. I'm out."

Tammy couldn't wait to see Dwayne. They had fished side by side for the past four years, and she preferred it to fishing solo. As much as she felt proud of herself for her accomplishments today, she didn't like her loneliness. She missed the laughs she and Dwayne had shared while fishing together and the adventures they had while exploring new parts of the island. And when she had stopped to take a lunch break before heading around Castle Rock, she found it to be a lonely experience and cut her break short.

Tammy baited another thirty traps before she spotted Dwayne off in the distance and immediately called him on the radio.

"Dwayne! I see you! Do you see me? Over."

"Hey Tammy, I see you! How are you doing out there? Over."

"Missing you. It's lonely out here. Over."

Dwayne laughed. "Tell me about it. Over."

Suddenly Mitch's voice came over the radio. "Get a room, guys," he laughed.

Tammy laughed and hollered into the radio. "The *Baywitch II* will rock tonight. I can tell you that."

"Ha! I gotta love your style of fishing, guys. You have it made. I'm out."

"See Ya, Mitch," Tammy hollered.

Tammy couldn't help but feel excited as she and Dwayne's boats were getting closer. She felt like she had been at sea for days.

It was the loneliest day of fishing she had ever experienced. When she was in close range to the *Baywitch II*, she screamed and waved her arms high above her head. "Dwayne! Dwayne!"

Dwayne waved back, wearing a huge smile that melted Tammy's heart as always. He turned off the boat, leaned against the helm, and waited for her to get closer. "Tammy, I've missed you. How was it?"

When she was near enough that she didn't have to yell, Tammy turned off the motor and beamed Dwayne a big smile. "I've missed you too. I did okay, but damn, it was lonely out there by myself. I'm not sure if I like this." Tammy confessed.

"Yeah, I hear ya. It's a whole different ball game when you're out on your own." He threw her another smile. "Listen, we are all done. We've baited all the traps between us. Meet me back at the harbor, and we'll discuss it some more."

"Sounds good," Tammy said before firing up the boat again.

Back at the harbor and with both boats tied securely, Tammy couldn't wait to feel Dwayne's muscular arms around her. She had missed him so much.

"I'm so proud of you, Tammy. I knew you could do it." Dwayne said to her after a long, drawn-out smooch. He held her tight as they conversed about their day apart.

"Thanks, it was nerve-wracking at first, but I kept picturing you driving the boat and how you did it, and it helped me a lot."

They were the first to return to the harbor, but Dwayne wasn't surprised since they were using two boats to bait the gear.

Tammy slid out of her slickers and then grabbed two Pepsis from the ice-chest. She scanned the empty harbor and smiled. She loved where she worked. She noticed Dwayne had also pulled off his slickers and was sitting in one of the deck chairs smoking a cigarette. She took a seat next to him.

Dwayne held out the pack of Marlboros. "Want one?"

"Yes, I've only had about four all day. It's hard to have a smoke when you have to do everything yourself." She took a long drag, enjoying every satisfying moment the rush of nicotine was bringing her.

"So, did you have fun?" Dwayne asked.

"Yes and no. I like the sense of pride I felt all day, and knowing I could handle the boat and traps on my own was comforting, but God, the isolation part sucks. I hated it when you were on the backside of the island. I did nothing but worry about you. I was relieved when I spoke to you on the radio and knew you were okay."

"Yeah, I didn't like it either," Dwayne admitted.

"I hated not being able to check in on you, and I miss the fun we had fishing together. We laugh all the time. I didn't laugh once today, and that was a drag too."

"Are you saying you don't want to fish alone anymore?"

Tammy leaned back and rolled her eyes in despair. "I don't know, Dwayne. I don't want to disappoint you, but what if something happens to you on the backside? I would never know. That's a scary feeling."

Dwayne reached over and took her hand. "Tammy, you could never disappoint me. What you did today took a lot of guts. Don't ever say that. Believe it or not, I agree with you."

His confession surprised Tammy. "You do?"

"Yes, I do, and I have an idea."

"Okay, I'm listening," Tammy said as she sat up and anxiously waited for him to tell her more.

"I think you should continue to fish alone for practice." He immediately saw the disappointment on her face. "But it doesn't have to be all day. How about you go and fish the quiet side where it is always flat in the mornings by yourself, and I'll fish up to castle rock? We meet back in the harbor, unload the lobsters and fish the rest of the day around castle rock and beyond together on the *Little Boat* and leave the *Baywitch II* in the harbor?"

Tammy jumped up from her chair and threw herself in his lap

as she hooked her arms around his neck. "I love that idea. Yes, it's brilliant."

Dwayne leaned in and gave her a tender kiss. "Great, then that's how we will do it from now on. No more lonely days of fishing."

Tammy smiled and kissed him again. "I sure do love you."

"I love you too, babe."

CHAPTER 15

For the next three years, Tammy was pleased that things ran smoothly for her and Dwayne. Her mom had so much fun watching Matt for the nine weeks they fished San Clemente Island that she came back every year after that. Tammy left worried free. She watched the relationship grow over the years between her mom and son. The love seeped from their eyes when they reunited. What they had was special. But the constant reminder that her mother still yearned to have all her daughters together was something her mom would never let go of.

"I know, mom, but I don't know how that is possible right now," Tammy said during her mom's last visit.

"That's what you always tell me. I've not seen Donna since she moved to Colorado, and I've only met her husband once. It's just awful, Tammy. Families shouldn't be this far apart from one another," her mother ranted. "And when are you coming to England? You've not been back since you left. That was fourteen years ago."

Tammy rolled her eyes. She's had this conversation too many times. "Mom, I can't afford to go to England. It wouldn't be just me. What about Dwayne and Matt? Do you know how much three tickets would cost? And let's not forget, we wouldn't be making any money. Fishing doesn't have vacation pay. We just can't do it, mom. I'm sorry," Tammy told her.

She expected her mom to come out this year again and take care of Matt. It would be her fourth year and Tammy's seventh year of fishing. Tammy was so proud of her son, who was almost eleven. Since he was old enough to understand, he had been eager to learn as much as he could about lobster fishing, just like his mother many years ago. He couldn't wait to return home from school and finish his homework so he could help get the traps ready for the season. But what Matt enjoyed the most was when he didn't have school, he would join them on the *Baywitch II* and help pull the traps at Malibu.

Today was one of those days. It was the first week of March, and they were getting ready to wrap up the lobster season and took the *Baywitch II* so they could bring some gear home. Tammy and Matt stacked the traps while Dwayne drove the boat. In between traps, Tammy stood and watched with pride when Dwayne would let Matt have a go at steering the boat.

When they returned to the dock, with the boat loaded with traps, Tammy fell into Dwayne's arms. "I'm exhausted. I wish we were done."

Dwayne glanced at the sun that was setting. "It shouldn't take more than an hour to stack these traps in the yard."

Tammy watched Matt jump off the boat and chase a duck off the dock. "Where does he get his energy? He is not the least bit tired." She placed her hands on her hips. "Okay, let's do this. I want to be home before dark. It's pizza and a movie night."

After taking turns to shower, Tammy ordered the pizza and settled on the couch with her two favorite guys to watch a movie when the phone rang. Dwayne turned to reach for the cordless phone but saw it wasn't in the cradle. "Where's the phone?" he asked. "You're always misplacing the phone, Tammy," he laughed.

Tammy looked at the empty cradle. "Oh, shoot. I think I had it in the kitchen last. I always forget to put it back. I'm sorry."

Dwayne tapped her knee as he stood up. "It's fine. I'll get it." He said as the phone continued to ring.

He answered it before the answering machine kicked in. "Hello. Dwayne here."

Dwayne heard the chirpy voice of his dad. "Hello, son. It's your dad."

"Hey, Dad, how's it going?"

"It's going good, son, but your mother and I have been having a conversation, and I wanted to give you a call."

Dwayne couldn't hide the worry in his voice. "Is everything okay, dad?"

"Oh yes, everything is fine, but we were just trying to figure out how long you and Tammy have been together."

"Hold on a sec, dad." Dwayne pulled the phone away from his mouth and hollered to Tammy, who was still in the living room watching the movie. "Hey Tammy, how long have we been together?"

Tammy hollered back, "About seven years."

He repeated her answer to his dad. "Seven years."

"Are you two ever going to get married?" his dad asked.

Dwayne laughed and hollered to Tammy again, humorously. "Hey Tammy, are we ever going to get married? Dad wants to know."

"I'm sure we will someday," Tammy replied—distracted by the movie.

"When?" his dad asked.

Dwayne shrugged his shoulders—amused by his dad's questions and threw out a random date. "I dunno. August second."

"Is that okay with Tammy?" his dad asked.

"Is August second, okay?" Dwayne hollered to Tammy.

"Sounds good," Tammy said, still distracted by the movie.

But Charlie wasn't done. "Where?"

"Where what?" Dwayne asked.

"Where will you get married?"

Dwayne thought quickly. "Your house."

"Great!" Charlie shouted away from the phone to Dwayne's mother. "Hey, Cathy, Dwayne, and Tammy are getting married in five months at our house. We have a wedding to plan."

Dwayne heard his mother cheer in the background and chuckled.

"I gotta go, son. Your mother wants to talk about the wedding. She is so excited. I'm sure she will call you later. Love you, son. Bye."

Dwayne sat stunned, looking at the now silent phone in his hand. "What the hell just happened?" He chuckled to himself and was still wearing a huge grin when he returned to the couch.

"What are you smiling about?" Tammy asked as she placed a hand on his knee and made room for him on the couch between her and Matt.

Dwayne's smile got bigger. "I guess we're getting married."

Tammy's jaw dropped. "What? I thought you were joking."

Dwayne shook his head. "Nope. That was my dad. When I told him we'd been together seven years, he asked when we were getting married. You said August second was okay, so that's the date, and it will be at my dad's house."

Tammy gasped. "Holy shit! You're kidding me. We're getting married."

Matt screeched. "you're getting married? Dwayne will be my dad?"

Tammy couldn't contain herself and jumped off the couch and began skipping around the room. "We're getting married. Oh my god! I can't believe it." She raced back over to Dwayne's side and gave him a hard kiss. "Pretty sneaky of your dad, I must say."

Dwayne laughed. "Yeah, it was. He had me propose to you without even knowing it."

Tammy laughed. "You're not regretting it, are you?"

Dwayne cupped her face in his palms and kissed her tenderly. "Oh, hell no. You're the best thing that ever happened to me."

Tammy leaned back against the cushions of the couch. "Wow! I can't believe I'm getting married." She narrowed her eyes at Dwayne. "I only plan on getting married once, you know. You realize you're stuck with me for the rest of your life?"

Dwayne took her hand and gave her a smile. "That's just fine with me."

Tammy let out a loud, cocky laugh. "So not only do we have to get ready for lobster season this summer, but we also have a wedding to plan."

CHAPTER 16

$\mathcal{T}$ammy didn't know how they pulled it off, but with the help from Dwayne's family and some close friends, her wedding day had quickly arrived. Tammy stood outside on the lush green grass of Dwayne's parent's house, where everything looked perfect for the big day. She admired the beautifully decorated tables with white and pink roses for their one hundred guests. The white arbor where she would become Dwayne's wife stood tall and decorated with ivy, roses, and carnations.

Tammy looked off to the edge of the lawn and saw that the caterer and band were busy setting up their equipment and buffet tables. It was early August, and the heat of the sun showed its strength. "Oh, the guys are going to die in their tuxedos," Tammy whispered under her breath as she wiped a bead of sweat from her brow. Tammy glanced at the shimmering water in the pool and thought how inviting it looked.

She went inside and admired the three-tier cake that stood elegantly on the large dining room table, safe from the expected 102-degree scorching temperatures.

Tammy was pleased when she got the news that her dad was

flying in from Ireland for the wedding to give her away, and Donna was also going to make it from Colorado. It was peak season for Jason's tree trimming business, and they buried him in work and wouldn't be able to come out with Donna, but he had called that morning to congratulate them.

Tammy's mother Rose flew out a month earlier than her normal time when she normally watched Matt in September to help Tammy with any last-minute plans. Tammy loved having her at the house for an extra month.

Donna also stayed at the house and slept on the living room floor, and their dad, John, got a room at a hotel right across the street.

On the eve of the wedding, over dinner with Tammy and Dwayne's families, Tammy wondered if this was as close as it would get to have her mom's three girls together. It saddened Tammy when Jenny had told her they wouldn't make it to the wedding. With the short notice of a wedding, they didn't have enough time to apply for a visa for the family, and then there was the expense and time away from work was also a factor. Tammy understood but couldn't help but feel the void at the table.

Tammy hadn't seen her parents together since their divorce almost twenty years ago. She admired them from across the room and saw the sparkle in their eyes as they chattered to one another. Tammy was happy to see they had risen above their differences and were now good friends and knew from their body language and the caring smiles they shared that they carried a special place in their hearts for one another.

Now on the morning of the wedding, with tears in her eyes, Tammy held hands with her mom and Donna, "I can't believe I'm getting married in just a few hours." she cried.

Donna cracked a laugh. "It's about time, sis. I wouldn't miss this for the world. Does Dwayne know what he is getting into?" she joked.

Suddenly Tammy heard the familiar sound of Dwayne's truck

pull into the driveway. Tammy had driven her car to Dwayne's parent's house with her mom and sister. Her dad had stayed behind and rode with Dwayne. "Shit!" Tammy shrieked. "Dwayne's here. I don't want him to see me until the wedding. It's bad luck."

Donna laughed again. "Didn't you see him this morning when you woke up? And haven't you shared his bed for the past seven years?"

Tammy rolled her eyes. "Yes, but that doesn't count. Come on; we gotta disappear," she said, grabbing her mom's hand and hurried them to the east side of the house where the ladies would get ready.

A few hours later, Tammy stood in front of a full-length mirror with her mom and sister on either side. Her long white dress, which flared at the bottom, hugged her body perfectly. If she had brought the dress instead of renting it, it would have cost her eight thousand dollars instead of the five hundred weekends rental rate. She only planned on getting married once and couldn't fathom spending an obscene amount of money for a dress that would not see the light of day after her wedding.

Tammy's tears flowed when she saw herself in the mirror. She couldn't believe she was a bride.

"Don't cry." Her mother whispered as she tried to hold back her own tears. "You'll ruin your make-up."

"How do you want to wear your hair?" Donna asked.

"Definitely down. I hate my ears and forehead," Tammy laughed.

Donna nodded. "Good choice. You have beautiful hair. Why don't you have a seat, and I'll curl it at the ends?"

Tammy's eyes sparkled, "Ooh, I love that idea." Tammy watched as her sister did her magic. "Wow, that looks great. Where did you learn to do hair?" Tammy asked.

"From other strippers at the club when I lived with you. We all did each other's hair."

"Donna!" Rose gasped.

"What, mom? I'm not ashamed of it. I did what I had to do."

Tammy raised her hands. "Okay, enough, guys." She took another look at herself in the mirror. "Okay, I'm ready. Where's dad?"

"He's waiting outside," Donna said, who was Tammy's matron of honor and led the way. "Let's go, sis. The music is playing."

Rose leaned in and gave Tammy a light kiss on the cheek before leaving the room. "I'm so proud of you. You look beautiful."

Tammy gave her a caring smile, "Thanks, mom."

Tammy listened to the music and then heard the familiar wedding tune of *Here comes the bride.*

Donna shook her hair and raked her fingers through it. "That's your cue, sis. It's your last chance to run," she laughed.

Tammy slapped her sister's arm. "You're terrible. I have no intention of running. Dwayne is the best thing that has happened to me."

"He sure is. We have both found our perfect men. I don't know what I'd do without Jason. He saved me." Donna played with Tammy's hair one last time. "We've come a long way, sis."

Tammy smiled. "We sure have."

"Okay, everyone is waiting to see the beautiful bride, including Dwayne, who is out there waiting for you. Now go get him." Donna said with a huge smile.

Tammy nodded, took a deep breath, and followed her sister out of the room. She smiled and struggled to hold back her tears when she saw her dad, looking sharp in a grey suit. His arm was bent at the elbow, ready for Tammy to take it.

"Hi, Dad," she whispered.

"You look beautiful," her dad said with a smile.

Tammy hooked arms with her dad, and together they walked to the arbor where Dwayne was waiting. She nodded and smiled at all the familiar faces of friends and family that were there to share this special day. She couldn't help but feel like the luckiest woman in the world. Before Tammy stood, the man she had met and fallen in love with over seven years ago, and today he was to become her husband.

She admired how he stood tall and assertive with glassy eyes, dressed in a black tuxedo, a white shirt, and a black bow tie. It was the first time she had ever seen him in a suit of any kind, and he looked dashing and delicious. His long blonde hair cascaded over his shoulders and blew gently in the breeze. He turned to face her as she walked toward him. He winked and gave her one of his heart-warming smiles that melted her heart many years ago. Tammy smiled back and couldn't believe she was about to marry the gorgeous man that stood before her.

Standing next to Dwayne were their two sons, Matt and Justin, both also dressed in tuxedos. She smiled at the boys, looked down at Matt's hands, and saw he had the ring box.

By the time Tammy and her dad reached Dwayne, the music had stopped, and silence fell upon the crowd. Her dad looked so proud as he let go of Tammy's hand and gave her a light kiss on the cheek before taking his place next to Dwayne's brothers. Tammy took a deep breath, faced Dwayne, and took his extended hand.

Dwayne smiled and whispered. "Hi."

Tammy laughed. "Hi."

Their guests heard them, and soft laughter erupted amongst them.

The sun was high in the sky and radiated its intense heat as Dwayne and Tammy said their vows.

A few minutes later, the minister smiled. "I now pronounce you man and wife."

Dwayne and Tammy kissed passionately to the sounds of the loud cheers and whistles coming from their guest. And when the music played, they danced.

By the end of the ceremony, the temperatures were now soaring in the late nineties, and Tammy laughed when she saw Matt rip off his bow tie and undo some buttons. "Why don't you and the other kids go in the pool? I told everyone to bring swimming trunks. Yours are in the house."

Matt's face lit up. "Can I?" he screamed as he ran off to tell the other kids.

Dwayne and Tammy celebrated with their family and friends into the early evening. They still had to drive to San Diego for what would be their short two-day honeymoon, which was all the time they could take because fishing wouldn't wait.

Tammy said goodbye to her dad, who would leave the next day. "Thank you for coming, dad. It meant a lot." Tammy said from her dad's arms. "I'll call you soon."

"You've found yourself a fine young man there, Tammy. I may not say it often, but I'm proud of you."

Tammy closed her eyes and squeezed her father's waist. "Thanks, dad."

Tammy turned to her sister. "No fighting with mom while I'm gone," she joked. "I know how you guys can be. Dad is taking my car home, so you, mom, and Matt can ride with him."

"Donna took Tammy's hand. Thanks, sis. I'll be heading back home in a couple of days. It's going to be fun hanging with mom and Matt until then. We will be fine. I promise there will be no fighting. I'm older now," she laughed.

Once in the truck, Tammy rolled down her window and waved at her family and friends standing in the driveway. "I love you guys!" she yelled. She turned to Dwayne and smiled. "I love you too."

Dwayne pulled her in close and kissed her hard on the lips. The crowd screamed, "Get out of here and go get a room." Dwayne laughed as he put the truck in reverse and backed out of the driveway.

CHAPTER 17

*T*ammy leaned against the tall stack of traps in their backyard and wiped her brow. She was tired, but her spirits were high. Another lobster season was behind them, and after catching up with all their bills, she was pleased to see they still had money left in the bank.

"God, It's a warm one, and it's only March," Tammy said while trying to catch her breath after stacking the last trap. She pulled her aching body away from the traps and arched her back. "I need an ice-cold Pepsi and a cigarette."

"Sounds good." Dwayne hollered from the other side of the yard where he was coiling rope into a barrel.

Tammy returned a few minutes later with two sodas and took a seat at the patio table, anxious to light a cigarette. "Here you go."

"I'll be right there," Dwayne said, dropping the rope.

Tammy lifted her sore legs onto the nearby chair and released a heavy sigh. "God, I'm so tired." She took a hit from her cigarette and closed her eyes. A few minutes later she heard the phone ring from inside the house. "Damn it. Why does it always ring the minute I sit down?" She groaned in agony as she slowly returned her feet to the ground and pulled herself up from her comfy chair. "I'll be right back," she said as she entered the house.

After the fourth ring, she picked up the phone. "Hello." There was silence. Tammy repeated herself, "Hello?" Tammy thought she heard the faint sound of crying. Worried, she spoke with an edge and louder. "Hello! Who is this?"

"Tammy, It's Donna," she said between heavy sobs.

Tammy held the phone tight with both hands. "Donna, are you okay? Why are you crying?" Tammy waited anxiously for her to speak, but all she could hear were the increasing sounds of sobbing. Tammy felt the panic rise to her chest. "Donna, what's going on? Talk to me," she said, raising her voice and feeling scared.

"It's Jason." Donna cried into the phone.

Tammy's heart hammered beneath her chest. "What about Jason? Is he okay?"

Donna sucked back her tears. "I'm at the hospital. He had a seizure."

Tammy felt her knees turn weak and stumbled over to the couch. "What? Oh my god, is he going to be okay?"

"I don't know yet. They have to run all kinds of tests."

"When did this happen?" Tammy asked as she clenched her still racing heart.

"About two hours ago. We were coming back from the movies, and he suddenly lost control of the truck. His eyes rolled to the back of his head, and his body jolted uncontrollably. It was horrible. I grabbed the wheel and steered the truck to the side of the road, where we ended up in a ditch. The car behind us stopped and made sure we were okay and then went to go find a phone to call 911." Donna took in a sharp breath. "Jason was unconscious by then. He had hit his head on the steering wheel. I thought he was dead."

"Oh my god, Donna. Do you want me to come out there?"

Donna's voice seemed a little calmer when she spoke again.

"No. No, you have Matt to take care of. You can't bring him here. I don't want him to see his uncle like this. His sister Terry moved out here last month; she is here with me."

Tammy released a sigh of relief. She was thankful Donna was not alone. "Oh, that's good to know. Is there anything I can do? I feel so helpless."

"No. I'm just sitting here with Terry waiting for the test results to come back, which might be hours."

Suddenly the familiar annoying phone booth recording came on. "Please deposit fifty more cents to continue with this call."

"Damn it! I ran out of change," Donna snapped down the phone.

Tammy spoke quickly. "I love you, sis. Hang in there. I'm sure he's going to be okay. He's young and healthy. Call me collect as soon as you have any news. I don't care what time it is."

"Okay, Tammy, I will. I love you too. Bye."

"Bye," Tammy replied in a somber tone.

Still shaken by the news, Tammy remained on the couch for a few minutes trying to process what her sister must be going through and how terrified she must be feeling. Tammy couldn't even imagine and wished she were at the hospital with her.

Dwayne immediately saw the sadness in her eyes and the look of worry she wore on her face when she returned outside. He stopped what he was doing and rushed over to her. "Hey, are you okay?" he said while placing his hand on her shoulder.

Tammy looked at him with her glassy eyes, fell into his arms, and cradled her head against his chest.

Dwayne felt a rush of fear and wrapped his arms tight around her trembling body. "Hey, sweetheart. You're scaring me. Who was that on the phone?"

Tammy sniffed back her tears. "It was Donna."

Dwayne rubbed her back and kissed the top of her head. "Is she okay? What's going on?"

"It's Jason. He had a seizure, and he is in the hospital."

Dwayne pulled back, his jaw dropped, and he gasped. "Oh, no! Is he going to be alright?"

Tammy shook her head. "She doesn't know yet. She's at the hospital with him. They are running a bunch of tests. I told her to call me as soon as she knows anything."

Dwayne fell into one of the patio chairs, like Tammy; the news stunned him. "But he's so healthy. He works outside all day, climbing and trimming trees. The last time we saw him, which I know was a while ago, he looked great. Are they sure it was a seizure?"

Tammy took a seat next to him. "That's what Donna told me. I guess we'll know more after they've run the tests," Tammy shook her head in despair. "God, poor Donna. She told me Jason's sister moved out there last month and is at the hospital with her. That makes me feel a little better; otherwise, I would have found a way to get out there. But she doesn't want Matt to see Jason the way he is."

Dwayne nodded. "That makes sense. Let's wait to hear from her, and then we'll decide what we're going to do."

Tammy gave him a loving smile. He always knew how to put things in perspective. It was one thing she loved about him. "You're right. I don't want to over-react. I must stay calm for Donna's sake, and I won't say anything to Matt until I know what's going on."

Worried about Jason, Tammy had a restless night and was concerned when she still hadn't heard from Donna by morning. She desperately wanted some answers and called Donna's house, but as she predicted, she got the answering machine. After the recorded message had played, Tammy spoke. "Donna, it's Tammy. I'm so worried about you guys. I couldn't sleep last night. Call me as soon as you can. Love you."

With her back to the kitchen doorway, she was startled when she heard Dwayne's voice behind her. She turned and saw him leaning against the doorjamb with a sadness lingering in his eyes and his arms folded.

"No news?" he asked.

Tammy shook her head and ran her hand through her hair. "No."

Dwayne took her in his arms, and Tammy wrapped her arms tightly around his waist and rested her head on his chest. For the next few minutes, they stood in silence and just held each other close.

"God, I hope Jason is going to be okay," Tammy said, feeling safe in Dwayne's firm grip.

"Me too. Why don't I make you some coffee while you wake Matt for school? I'm sure we'll know more later today."

For the rest of the morning, after Tammy returned from taking Matt to school, the mood in the house was somber. Every time the phone rang, Tammy's heart skipped a beat, hoping it was Donna with some news, but sadly it wasn't.

"I need to keep busy," Tammy said after spending the last hour cradled in Dwayne's arms on the couch.

"Do you want to go work on the crab gear? We need to get some traps in the water this weekend, and I promised Matt he could help us."

Tammy stood up from the couch. "Sure. That's a good idea. I'll bring the phone outside in case Donna calls."

Tammy struggled for the next hour, trying to stay focused on attaching the doors to some new traps, but she lost it when she poked her finger on a piece of wire. "God, I can't stand this! Why doesn't she call?" Tammy yelled as she threw her pliers across the yard and licked on the blood trickling down her finger.

Her outburst startled Dwayne, who stood close by putting new zincs in the traps. He reached over and took her hand. "Hey, calm down. She will call us when she can. She's got a lot to deal with right now. Don't be upset with her. Put yourself in her shoes."

Tammy suddenly felt embarrassed by her selfish act. "You're right. God, I'm sorry. I'm just scared, that's all."

"I know you are. I am too, but Donna will call when she has news."

Suddenly the phone rang from the patio table where Tammy had set it. Tammy gasped and covered her heart with her hand. She looked at Dwayne with wide eyes and raced over to the table. Dwayne quickly followed and rested his hand on her shoulder as she picked up the phone.

"Hello," Tammy said, unable to hide the anxiety she was feeling.

"Tammy, it's Donna." Her voice was flat.

Tammy turned and took Dwayne's hand. "Hi, Donna. How is Jason?"

Donna's next words scared her. "Not good. He's in surgery."

Tammy squeezed Dwayne's hand and looked at him when she spoke into the phone. "Surgery? For what?"

Donna took in a deep breath. "They did a brain scan and found a tumor. It's pretty big, but they won't know if it's benign or cancer until after surgery."

Tammy held her hand up to her mouth and choked back her tears. "Oh my god, Donna. I'm so sorry. When will you know?"

"Sometime later today or tomorrow."

"Is Terry there with you?" Tammy asked.

"Yes. I've not slept in two days. We're going to stay here until he's out of surgery, and then I'm going home to take a shower and try to sleep for a few hours. I want to come back tonight. I need to be here." Donna cried.

Tammy squeezed Dwayne's hand hard, not believing what she was hearing. "Do you want me to come out there?"

"No, Terry is here. Let's see what the results are. I'm hoping it's just a fatty tumor, and he will be fine. I'll let you know as soon as the doctors tell me. I have to go. I love you, sis."

"I love you too, Donna."

"What's going on?" Dwayne asked after she had hung up the phone.

"They found a tumor on his brain. Donna says it's big, and he's in surgery right now."

"Oh my god. Is he going to be okay?"

"They won't know until after surgery. They need to find out if it's benign or not. God, this is horrible. What if it's cancer?"

"Let's not go there, okay. We have to think positive and hope for the best." Dwayne took her hand. "Come on. Let's forget about working on traps today. Let's go for a drive up the coast to Malibu for a little while and try to clear our heads. I'll buy you lunch. Donna won't be calling for a while. It will do us both good."

Tammy gave him a warm smile. Yet again, he knew how to make her feel better. "You're right. Let me change out of these dirty clothes. A drive to Malibu sounds good."

CHAPTER 18

*D*onna called the following morning when Dwayne and Tammy were in the backyard loading crab traps into the truck to take to the boat.

Tammy threw off her gloves and raced to the phone that lay on the patio table. She took a seat with bated breath, answered the phone. "Donna, is that you?"

Donna's voice sounded flat, and from her sniffs, Tammy knew she had been crying. Tammy sensed the news wouldn't be good.

"Yes, it's me," Donna said in a somber tone.

"So, what's going on? How's Jason?" Tammy asked, trying desperately to hide the fear in her voice.

Donna broke into heart-wrenching sobs the minute she spoke. "He has cancer, Tammy!" she cried.

Tammy's jaw dropped, and she put the phone on speaker so Dwayne could hear, who had joined her at the table and was holding her hand. Dwayne shook his head and raised his hand to his brow in disbelief.

"Oh my god. No!" Tammy shrieked.

Donna continued to cry, sucking in the air between her words. "They found a tumor the size of a goddamn lemon. How could that be? He's never felt a thing."

"Did he ever complain of headaches?" Tammy asked.

"Jason is hard-headed and had never complained about anything. He hates the doctors. If Jason had headaches, he never told me about them because he knew damn well I would have dragged his ass to the doctors."

"And they said for sure it's cancer?" Tammy asked in a soft voice.

"Yes. they told me it was a Global blastoma grade-four tumor."

Tammy glanced over at Dwayne and creased her brow. "What does it mean?"

Donna's crying intensified. "It means he only has about six months to live."

Tammy gasped, and Dwayne squeezed her hand tight. "What! Are they sure?"

"Yes, they are sure. They removed ninety-nine percent of the tumor, but they couldn't do a complete removal because of where it is on the brain, and that little piece will grow back and kill him."

Tammy was numb. She didn't know what to say. "But how can that be? He's so young. He's supposed to turn forty this year."

"I know." Donna cried. "I don't know if he will make it. Oh, Tammy, what am I going to do?"

Donna's tears tore at Tammy's heart, and she wished more than anything that she was close by and could hold her sister tight and give her the support she needed. Tammy didn't need to think about her next words or discuss them with Dwayne. "Donna, we're coming to see you," Tammy said as she gave Dwayne a hard stare.

Dwayne nodded, and Tammy threw him a grateful smile.

Donna sounded not only surprised but also relieved. "You are?"

"Yes, we are. We'll drive there. Matt is out of school next week. I want him to come too. Jason is his uncle. Is that okay?"

"Of course. Yes, That's fine." She paused and whispered in a calmer tone. "Thank you."

"Hush. There is no need to thank me. You are family, and so is Jason. I just wished we weren't so far away and saw more of each other." Tammy released a heavy sigh and wiped away her tears. "Oh, Donna, I can't believe this is happening. Why, Jason?"

"I swear I can't get a break in life," Donna said with a sharp tone. "I'm finally happy, and now I'm going to lose the guy that made it all happen."

Tammy had no words. There was nothing she could say that would ease the horrific pain her sister felt. And then it hit her. Donna would become a widow at the young age of thirty-six. How could life be so unfair? Tammy wondered. Donna had already had her share of trying times, and now this. Tammy tried to comfort her sister as best she could for the next few minutes until Donna told her; the doctors were there to talk to her.

"Okay, Donna, I'll let you go. We'll be there next week but call me when you can, okay."

"I will. I love you, Tammy."

Tammy's voice was flat. "Love you too, sis."

After hanging up the phone, Tammy let her tears fall. It was the first time in her life that she had to deal with someone dying who she knew and cared about. She couldn't wrap her head around the thought that Jason would not be with them next year. How could such a healthy, young man be facing death in just six months? "What are the odds the doctors are wrong?" Tammy asked Dwayne, who was now standing behind her with his chin resting on her head as he embraced her from behind.

"I hate to say it, but pretty slim, I would imagine," he said as he buried his head in her hair as he tried to hold back his own tears.

"I'm sorry I told Donna we would go see them before talking to you first. I just need to support her somehow," Tammy confessed, still cradled in Dwayne's arms.

"It's fine. I would have suggested it, anyway."

Tammy freed herself from Dwayne's hold and twisted her body until she met his eyes. "There's another reason I want to go."

"What's that?" Dwayne asked.

"If what the doctors are saying is true, then this trip will probably be the last time we will see Jason alive. It's kind of our last goodbyes."

CHAPTER 19

A week later, after driving for sixteen hours, they pulled into Jason and Donna's driveway. It was their first visit to Colorado, and Tammy wished it were under better circumstances.

Before their trip, Tammy and Dwayne sat Matt down and had a heart-to-heart talk with him about Jason and told him that soon he would fly with the angels and that they wanted to see him before he left. Tammy wasn't sure if Matt quite understood what they were trying to tell him, but the sadness she saw in his eyes told Tammy that he probably did, but she remained strong for her son and refrained from breaking down and sobbing in front of him.

Donna must have heard them pull into the driveway. Within minutes she stood at the side of the car before they stepped out. Immediately Tammy cried and quickly exited the car. "Donna." She sobbed as she ran into her sister's arms.

Tammy couldn't help noticing how fatigued her sister looked. Her skin was pale, and the sparkle had disappeared from her eyes. Her hair was uncombed and a tangled mess. The bathrobe looked too big for her frail skinny frame.

"Oh, Donna, I'm so sorry. I don't know what to say. I still can't believe it."

"I know me neither. Jason is inside. I try not to cry in front of him. So, let's pull ourselves together before we go into the house." Donna said, showing more strength than Tammy had at that moment.

Tammy nodded and broke away from their embrace. "Okay. I didn't think he'd be home from the hospital yet."

"He just got home yesterday."

"How is he doing?" Dwayne asked who was standing next to a confused Matt as he had just watched his mom and auntie cry heavily in each other's arms.

Donna wiped her eyes with her hand. "As well as can be expected. He's frail, of course, and has constant headaches. He stutters, which is an aftereffect of the seizure, and he also has a hard time remembering anything. He has also lost a lot of weight, so don't be alarmed."

Feeling more composed, Tammy took Donna's hand. "Come on, let's go inside. Show me where the kettle is, and I'll make us some tea." Tammy said with a subtle smile.

Donna followed suit and broke a small smile. "Sounds good. Thank you so much for coming out. Terry is staying here too. You'll get to meet her soon. She just ran to the store."

"Stop thanking us. We want to be here." Tammy told her as she led them into the house.

Once they were inside, the first thing Tammy noticed was that all the curtains were drawn.

"Sorry it's so dark in here, but Jason can't stand the sunlight with his constant headaches," Donna told her.

Donna led them through the living room and into the kitchen where, to Tammy's surprise, Jason sat at the table drinking coffee. Tammy noticed straight away that Donna wasn't kidding about his weight loss. She hardly recognized him. She couldn't believe that the man before her used to be the meaty rugged guy that had the strength of a bull and was now skin and bones with sunken shallow eyes, and half his head was shaved and partially covered with a bandage. He looked over at them, and through all his pain, he smiled. Tammy struggled to hold back the tears that were ready to burst and smiled back.

"Hi, Jason," she said as she approached the table. She saw Jason was about to stand.

"Oh, please don't get up." She turned to Matt, who hadn't said a word since they arrived.

Jason saw the boy's uneasiness and raised his hand. "Give me five there, buddy," Jason said with a forced smile and a strained, cracked voice.

Matt smiled at his uncle, giving him a high five, and then took a seat next to him.

Dwayne was the last to reach the table and shook Jason's hand before taking a seat. The vibe was tense and uncomfortable. Tammy and Dwayne didn't know what to say to Jason. They were numb and still in shock by his appearance.

Jason was the first to speak. "Thanks for coming out, guys. I appreciate it." Jason said and then shook his head. "Can you believe this shit?"

Tammy continued to fight back her tears. "No, and it's not fair." Tammy hesitated before continuing but needed to know. "Is there nothing they can do, Jason?"

Jason took Donna's hand, who stood beside him with her hand resting on his shoulder, and gave her a loving smile. "Oh, sure, they can feed my brain with radiation and my veins with Chemo to slow down the inevitable."

"Well, isn't that a good thing?" Tammy asked.

"Not really. It may give me an extra three months, but I'll be so sick from the treatment. What's the damn point?"

Tammy creased her brow. "So, what are you saying?" fearing she already knew the answer.

"I'm not doing any of the treatments." Jason raised his hand.

"Before you say anything or try to talk me out of it, Donna and I have discussed it. I don't want to prolong this any more than I have to and put Donna through any more suffering. I want to go out with some bit of dignity."

Tammy looked over at her sister, who gave her a slight nod. "I understand, Jason. In fact, I admire you." Tammy said in a soft voice.

Donna left Jason's side and went to the corner of the room, where she grabbed a cane. "Jason has to take a nap soon, but he likes to walk around the yard first." She looked over at Dwayne. "Why don't you and Matt go with him? Tammy and I will make some tea and sandwiches for everyone."

"Sound good," Dwayne said as he took the cane from Donna.

Tammy watched with a torn heart as Jason stood slowly with the aid of Dwayne.

"God, Donna, I don't know how you are coping with this?" Tammy said as she looked out the kitchen window at the three guys.

Donna stood next to her. "I have no choice. I have to be strong for Jason."

"I don't need to get too personal. But are you going to be okay once... well, you know?"

Donna gave Tammy a half-smile. "You can say it—once he dies."

Tammy shied away. "Yeah. Will you be okay, financially?"

"Yes, I will be for a while. This house is paid for thanks to some money Jason's dad left him. Jason has saved some too. I should be okay."

Tammy was relieved and rolled her eyes. "Oh, good. That makes me feel a little better."

A few minutes later, they heard the front door open and close. "Oh, that must be Terry back from the store. Thank god she is staying here too. She said she would stay as long as she needs to."

Terry entered the kitchen to carry a bag of groceries and set it down on the counter before introducing herself. "Hi, you must be Tammy; I'm Terry," she said with an extended hand.

Tammy ignored her hand and opened her arms and embraced her. "Hi, Terry. I'm so sorry about what is going on with your brother."

"Thanks. I still can't believe it. He's my only and baby brother. He's always been there for me and our sister, Carol."

"Oh, that's right, I forgot Jason had two sisters. Is she here?"

Terry shook her head. "No, she lives in California and has kids. She's going to be coming out next month sometime."

Tammy saw the resemblance between her and Jason. They both had the same high cheekbones and silvery grey eyes. Terry's hair was long and blonde, just like Donna's, and for a moment, Tammy thought they looked like sisters. She knew how close they had become since Donna had married Jason, and it showed. Tammy knew that when she and Dwayne returned home, Donna would be in excellent hands. Terry had promised to be there and guide her through the heartbreaking journey they were about to endure. For Tammy, it was a comforting thought.

ammy and Dwayne stayed in Colorado for as long as possible, which ended up being almost two weeks. School break would soon be over, and if they didn't start fishing for crabs soon, they would have to dig into their small savings account to pay for the upcoming bills.

During their stay, they tried to help Donna in any way they could by cooking meals, going to the stores, or cleaning the house. Whatever Donna needed, they tried to be there for her along with Jason's sister, Terry.

Jason, Dwayne, and Matt bonded in a bittersweet way. Dwayne and Matt spent many hours with him out in the yard where Dwayne would fire up the barbecue some afternoons, and he would talk to Jason about guy stuff, fishing, hunting, cars, and motorcycles. All of which were hobbies they both shared.

In Dwayne's earlier years before he met Tammy, he had spent most of his late teen years and early twenties on motorcycles. There were days when he and Jason would sit in the garage and admire Jason's polished shiny Harley Davidson Knucklehead, and

Dwayne listened intently as Jason talked with pride about the motorcycle he restored from the ground up.

Tammy and Donna had many tearful moments cradled in each other's arms in disbelief over what was happening. Tammy couldn't believe that Jason was dying a slow death, and there was nothing no one could do to save him. How could life be so cruel? Tammy kept asking herself and why Jason? The man that took her broken sister in, loved her unconditionally and finally gave her the life she deserved. How was Donna ever going to recover from this? Tammy couldn't even imagine.

On the day they were leaving to return to California, the emotions were high for everyone. How do you say goodbye to someone when you know it would be for the last time and that you would never see him again? Tammy remembered her sister's words. *I have to be strong for Jason,* and Tammy knew she would have to be too.

Jason laid on the couch with two pillows supporting his head, and a light blanket covered his frail body. Tammy sat gently on the edge of the couch, being careful not to squish him while everyone else stood behind her. She took his hand and gave it a gentle kiss. Jason, whose eyes were half-closed, giving her a weak smile. It took all her willpower to hold back her tears as she spoke. "I'm so sorry we can't stay any longer. I really wish we could. I'll be calling Donna every day to see how you are doing okay."

Jason nodded. "Thank you for everything. You take care of each other. You have a beautiful family, Tammy."

Tammy sniffed back her tears that were trying to escape. "I will. I love you, Jason."

Jason gave her hand a gentle squeeze. "I love you too, Tammy."

With ease, being careful not to disturb him, Tammy lifted herself off the couch and turned to Matt. "Why don't you give your uncle a kiss goodbye on the cheek, and after we will wait outside for Dwayne with Auntie Donna."

Matt, who now understood that Jason was dying, sauntered

over to his uncle and laid his head gently on his chest. Tammy turned away and wiped her now moist eyes with her hand.

"I love you, Uncle Jason."

"I love you too, buddy," Jason said as he slowly lifted his arm and cradled his nephew.

"Okay, sweetheart, let's go wait outside Tammy said once Matt stood away from the couch. "I'll see you outside," Tammy whispered to Dwayne. She gave Jason one last caring smile, left the room, and found Donna sitting on the front step smoking a cigarette.

"I didn't see you come outside," Tammy said before lighting a cigarette of her own.

"I snuck out while you were saying goodbye to Jason."

Tammy sat next to her sister, and once again, they cried in each other's arms. "Are you sure you're going to be okay?" Tammy asked. "I'm so worried about you."

Donna sniffed hard. "Yeah. Terry will be here. I don't know how but I'll get through this."

They remained on the steps embraced until Dwayne came out, and after one last emotional goodbye, they got in the truck. Donna stood on the steps and waved with tears gushing down her cheeks. Tammy was doing no better. She waved her hand high out of the window and screamed, "I love you, Donna!" as Dwayne backed the truck out of the driveway.

Tammy kept her promise and called Donna every day. On the days she was fishing Malibu, she'd call the minute she was home. Sometimes she had to leave a message because after eight, Donna turned off the phone so it wouldn't wake Jason.

By late July, Tammy and Dwayne had begun the grueling task of getting ready for lobster season. Rose, Tammy's mother, would arrive in September like the previous years to take care of Matt while they fished the remote island. But this year, she was going to go to Colorado first before coming to California. Like Tammy, their mom and Donna had spoken often on the phone. Jason was now bedridden and on morphine for the pain. They all knew his time was near, and Rose insisted on being there for Donna when Jason was finally at peace.

Rose arrived in Colorado in the first week of August. Four days later, while Dwayne and Tammy worked on the gear in the backyard, Donna called with the devastating news that they knew was inevitable.

"He's gone, Tammy. Jason is finally out of pain." Donna cried down the phone.

Tears flooded Tammy's eyes. "Oh my god, Donna, I'm so sorry. Where's mom?"

"She's right here next to me."

Tammy could hear her mom's sobs in the background. "Tell her; I love her. She's too upset to talk, and so am I."

Donna told Tammy of Jason's passing—that he passed peacefully in his sleep after weeks of living in excruciating pain. After Tammy reluctantly hung up the phone, Dwayne pulled her into her arms, where she immediately buried her head in his chest and cried hard for the death of Jason and her sister, who was now a widow.

Matt must have heard his mom's loud cries and came out of the house, strolling with his head hung low.

Dwayne suspected he knew and held out his arm. "Come here, buddy."

"Uncle Jason is dead, isn't he?" Matt said with tears pooling in his eyes.

Tammy raised her head and wiped her eyes before extending her arms. "Yes, he's gone, sweetheart. Come here."

Matt's lips quivered, and tears flowed down his cheeks as he ran into Dwayne and Tammy's arms for comfort and remained there for some time. It was the first time Tammy and her son had experienced the death of someone they loved. Tammy was numb, and it broke her heart. Jason's passing devastated her and seeing her son experience such raw emotions at such a young age. It was something she couldn't make better for her son, and that too tore at her heart.

Honoring Jason's wishes, Donna had Jason's body flown out to California seven days later, where he was laid to rest next to his father, not too far from the house where Donna had lived with him before they left the state.

After the emotional services, Donna returned to Colorado with their mom and Terry. Rose insisted she'd stay with Donna until Tammy and Dwayne left for the island, which was only a few weeks away.

CHAPTER 21

*H*aunted by images of Jason's slow death in the house they had lived in, Donna sold it within a year and bought a new one twelve-miles away. Terry kept her promise to her brother to take care of Donna and has been by her side ever since Jason's passing by moving into a house nearby. Slowly, with Terry's help, Donna tried to ease back into her life without Jason, but her wounds were raw—her heart shattered. As heart-wrenching as it was, Tammy called her often and listened as her sister poured her heart out. "I'm so lost, Tammy. I don't know if I can go on without him. He was my everything. He took care of me and loved me for who I am. He didn't care about my history. I'll never find another Jason."

Her sobs tore at Tammy's heart. She had no words to comfort her. Instead, she cried with her and let her speak about her pain.

"This hurts so much. Why does life have to be so cruel? Haven't I gone through enough? This isn't fair. I don't deserve this, and Jason didn't deserve to die. He was such a good man." Donna cried to Tammy.

For the first time, Jason's death made Tammy realize just how precious life is and how short it is. Now more than ever, she wanted to fulfill her mother's only wish of being reunited with her three daughters. Her mother wasn't getting any younger, and as much as Tammy hated to admit that her mom was showing small signs of aging such as forgetfulness and confusion.

But three years after Jason's death, Tammy still had not accomplished it, and it taunted her daily. Matt was now fourteen, and like Tammy, he had caught on quickly to all the grueling chores that came with fishing lobsters. Alongside his parents, Matt worked every season getting the gear ready and was often Dwayne's deckhand when they fished crabs in Malibu.

Tammy's mom continued to come out every year and watch Matt while they fished the island, and this year was no exception. She arrived just under a week ago, and Dwayne and Tammy were ready to embark on their tenth year of fishing together.

The first week of the season was always full of high expectations and hope. It was the week Dwayne and Tammy expected to make the most money during the entire season. The lobsters had not been fished in six months, so the season's first catch was usually the best.

Like every year, Dwayne and Tammy left the dock in debt, but amazingly they always got caught up after their first trip. Tammy didn't mind that they weren't getting rich from fishing and weren't saving a lot of money. It's what they loved to do. Tammy got used to living on the edge with elevated nerves until they paid the bills. She conditioned herself over the years. It was all part of the fishing, and it will always work itself out. And every year, it had. Fishing carried them through the year, provided a home for them, and allowed them to work together as a team and spend their days on the ocean. Tammy couldn't think of a better place to work.

They made the crossing in good time and pulled into the harbor just before the sun went down and connected with the other boats via radio. They had seen a few of the captains over the previous weeks when they had dropped off their gear, but there were a few they had not seen or spoken to since the last season. For Tammy, it was always good to return to the fleet that felt like family over the years of fishing together.

The eve before baiting the traps always had an essence of excitement in the air. Every year was going to be the year that they would all have a record catch and fill their bank accounts.

Many of the crew members and captains did not sleep that night, including Dwayne and Tammy. There was always too much to do, and everyone was anxious for the sun to rise so they could begin baiting the traps because the sooner they baited, the sooner the traps would start to fish—tonight was no exception. Dwayne and Tammy worked hard into the morning hours and only got two hours of sleep before leaving the harbor in the *Little Boat* to bait their traps.

They baited all two-hundred-fifty traps by nightfall on little sleep and with aching bodies from prepping the night before. They pushed themselves through their pain and only stopped a few times for short five-minute breaks.

When they returned to the harbor, they spent the rest of the evening getting both boats ready for pulling the gear the next day. For the past few years, it has worked well with Tammy pulling traps on her own on the *Little boat* in the morning and then meeting Dwayne in the harbor at noon so they could pull the rest of the gear together.

After another night of very little sleep, Dwayne and Tammy were eager to pull the first trap of the season and said their good-byes with a quick kiss before driving out of the harbor in separate boats.

Tired but excited about what the season may have in store, Tammy hummed a cheerful tune as she made her way over to the first set of traps.

Ten minutes later, she had the rope to the first trap of the season in the pulley and anxiously waited for it to spring out of the water and land on the trap table, and when it did, she was shocked by what she saw.

The trap was empty—not even a short lobster. In all the years they had fished the island, this had always been a good spot.

Tammy's jaw dropped. "What the hell?" she gasped. "Well, that's not a bloody good start." Being the first trap, Tammy tried her best not to feel discouraged, and after refreshing the bait, she quickly dropped it back into the water, eager to go on to the next one.

She wasted no time and sped off to the second trap and quickly pulled it out of the water. It was no better than the first one. "Frigging empty!" Tammy cussed. "God, we'd better have something in the third one. This is eerie," she said out loud, feeling somewhat worried.

After pulling five traps and only getting three short lobsters, she should have at least twenty keepers by now; Tammy was beyond worried. It scared her. "Where the hell are all the lobsters?" She said with her lips quivering. "I have to call Dwayne and see if it's any better at his end. God, I hope so."

Tammy put the boat in idle and pulled the microphone off its cradle. "Dwayne, you got me? Over."

It took Dwayne a few minutes to come back. "Yeah, I got you. Over."

Tammy noticed his flat tone and could tell he wasn't happy. "Are you catching anything? Over."

"I have two keepers out of ten traps. I hope it gets better than this. Not a good way to start the season. How about you? Over." Dwayne said, sounding somewhat discouraged.

"Well, you've done better than me. I've pulled five traps and gotten only three shorts." She raised her voice a notch. "What the hell is going on? Over."

"You're kidding! Well, shit, this isn't good. I'm going to give Mitch a shout and see if he's doing any better. If he is, he probably won't tell me, though. Fishermen never tell." Dwayne said, followed by a forced laugh. "I'll call you back in a few minutes. I'm out."

Tammy hung up the microphone and thought about all the money they had invested in getting to the island and how much they were in debt. "Shit. This isn't good," she whispered under her breath.

While she waited for Dwayne to get back to her, she pulled three more traps out of which she got one legal lobster and three more shorts, which had to be thrown back into the water. "Hurry and grow up, so I keep you," she yelled at the small lobsters as she tossed them overboard.

The sound of Dwayne's voice over the radio startled her. "Hey Tammy, you got me? Over"

Tammy quickly reached up and grabbed the microphone. "Yes, I'm here. So, did he tell you?" she asked with bated breath.

"Yep. He's not catching any either. He said he has six lobsters out of twelve traps, and the other boats aren't doing that great either."

A rush of panic swept through Tammy. "Dwayne, this is not good. What are we going to do? Over."

"Maybe the lobsters don't know it's opening day. Over." he joked, trying to make light-heart of the situation that had him concerned, but he didn't want to worry Tammy. "We'll talk more back at the harbor. How many more traps do you have left to pull? Over," Dwayne asked.

"About twenty. Over."

"Okay, I'll see you back at the harbor when you are done. Call me when you are heading back in. I'm out."

After pulling the rest of the line, Tammy was even more discouraged. Before heading back to the harbor, she called Dwayne to let him know she was done. She returned with eight lobsters when normally she should have at least fifty to a hundred from the line she had just pulled.

CHAPTER 22

The *Little Boat* was much faster than the *Baywitch II,* and Tammy reached the harbor before Dwayne. While she waited for him, she put her measly catch of lobsters into a receiver and restocked the bait. Fifteen minutes later, she heard the familiar sound of the *Baywitch II* and saw Dwayne heading her way.

When he was close enough, he waved, wearing a solemn look. "This doesn't look good," Tammy muttered under her breath.

For the first time, after a day's catch, Dwayne tossed her line without smiling. Tammy didn't smile either as she tied off the boat.

Once the boats were secured and the motors shut off, they could talk. "So, how did it go?" Tammy asked as she stepped on to the *Baywitch II.*

"Lousy," Dwayne replied, still wearing a frown. "I got fifteen lobsters."

"Well, that's better than my eight," Tammy said. "What the hell are we going to do?"

Dwayne put his lobsters in the receiver with the ones Tammy caught and rinsed his hands off in the ocean water. He turned to face Tammy, looking concerned. "I don't know . The day isn't over yet. Maybe the rest of the gear will be better."

"And if it's not?" Tammy said with her hands on her hips. "We are screwed. We owe so much money back home. And how are we supposed to come back out here if we don't have the money to buy more bait and fuel?" Tammy said with an edge to her voice.

Dwayne shook his head and brushed by her. "I don't know yet, Tammy. I don't have all the answers. You know as well as I do this is the worst opener we've ever had. Let's pull the rest of the gear and see what it's like before we fret over what we don't have."

"Easy for you to say. I'm scared, Dwayne."

Dwayne rubbed her shoulders and cracked a small smile. "It will be okay. Maybe the moon has something to do with it. I don't know, but I won't get discouraged so quickly. Now come on, the clock is ticking." He said as he jumped on the *Little boat* and fired it up.

The rest of the day wasn't any better. Trap after trap, they pulled up empties or ones with shorts and very few keepers. As the day dragged on, the words between them became fewer and fewer. They were both on autopilot, doing the tasks together that they had done for years. But this year, there were no cheers or claps or joyful laughter—just frowns and many cuss words when another trap came up empty.

On their way back into the harbor, Tammy shouted above the loud noise of the motor. "Now, do you feel discouraged?" Tammy said with sarcasm. "And I'm also a little worried, I might add."

Dwayne ignores her question. "This is so frigging weird. I don't get it. And it's not just us. No one is catching any lobsters. Where the hell did the lobsters all go?" He slowed down the boat and headed to their mooring. A few of the other boats were back, including Mitch on the *Sea Life*.

"I'm going to swing by Mitch's boat and see what he thinks."

Tammy nodded and glanced over at the *Sea Life*. "He's on the deck waving at us. Maybe he has some good news."

A few minutes later, they pulled alongside Mitch's boat. Tammy threw him a line, and once they were tied off, Dwayne turned off the boat.

"Hey, guys. I hope you did better than I did today. It is the worst I've ever seen it out here." Mitch said with his arms folded.

Dwayne shook his head. "I doubt it. We're going to be lucky if we have fifty lobsters. That won't even pay for fuel." Dwayne moaned.

Mitch nodded. "I hear ya. There's nothing out here. Kinda freaky, don't you think?"

"I'd say if this doesn't change in the next day or so, I don't know what we're going to do," Dwayne said. He turned and looked at Tammy, who was sitting on the edge of the boat. "Tammy is pretty worried. I can't say I blame her."

"You're damn right, I'm worried," Tammy snapped.

Dwayne forced Tammy a smile before speaking to Mitch again.

"Yeah, we need that kick start here, and it just ain't happening this year. You know how it is. You leave town owing everyone money and can't return until we can pay them," Dwayne laughed.

Mitch cracked a laugh. "Yeah, you got that right."

"I think we will stick it out another day and see what tomorrow is like before we make any hasty decisions," Dwayne said, seeking approval from Tammy.

Tammy nodded.

"Okay, man. Well, we're going to head back and get ready for tomorrow. Good luck out there."

"You too, man," Mitch said as he untied their line and tossed it over to Tammy.

Tammy couldn't think it could get any worse, but the next day proved her wrong. By the end of the day, exhausted and emotionally drained from worry, Dwayne and Tammy were at a loss on what to do.

After returning to the harbor with their nerves on edge, they hosed and cleaned the *Little Boat* in silence. Once she finished, Tammy grabbed the straps to her slickers and spoke with a sharp tone. "So, what are we going to do? Am I cutting bait for tomorrow, or can I take these damn things off?"

"I don't know, Tammy. What do you want to do?" Dwayne said, matching her tone.

Tammy rolled her eyes. "You're the captain, you tell me."

"Don't pull that with me, Tammy. We are in this together." He snapped and shook his head before softening his voice. "Tell you what. Before we get into a fight, let's drop everything and have some hot chocolate. We'll calm down and discuss our options."

Tammy mellowed her tone, "Sounds like a good idea." she agreed as she peeled off her slickers and hung them on a hook behind her. "I'll have the drinks ready in a jiffy."

Ten minutes later, Tammy smacked her lips from the sweet taste of the chocolate sliding down her throat "Damn, that tastes good." She leaned back in the deck chair and closed her eyes. She loved these rare moments where she felt like she was being rocked gently to sleep by the swift motion of the boat swaying in the harbor.

Dwayne had taken a seat next to her, and he, too, had his eyes closed as he thought deeply about what they were going to do.

"You know we don't have any choice but to stick it out here. We are committed to all the traps we have in the water, and all the bait will go bad if we don't use it," he said.

Tammy sighed, "I was afraid you were going to say that?" She sat up and took another sip of her drink. "But what if the rest of the week is just as bad? How are we going to pay all the bills we owe and have enough money to come back out?"

"I don't know yet, Tammy. We are going to have to wait and see where we stand by the end of the week."

"Well, from what I can see, it doesn't look very promising." She shook her head and sighed again. "Where the hell are all the bloody lobsters?"

"A few of the guys are saying it's because of El Nino."

Tammy creased her brow. "The what? What the hell is that?"

"It's when the surface waters are warmer than usual. When we have an El Nino, the lobsters don't crawl as much. Whether it's a myth, I don't know. But this is the year of the El Nino, and we don't have many lobsters. So, what does that tell you?"

Tammy shook her head and gulped down the rest of her drink before pulling herself up out of her chair. "All I know is if we don't start catching some lobsters pretty soon, we're going to be in deep shit. I guess I'll go cut some bait if we are going to stay here."

Tammy and Dwayne worked hard for the rest of the week, from sunrise to sunset. They spent hours moving gear in the hopes the new spots would bring them a good catch. They baited with extra bait and measured the smaller lobsters twice in case they were right on the brink of being legal. They couldn't afford to make any mistakes and throw away a keeper. Each day they became more discouraged as the catches became fewer and fewer. They were tired and sore. Their muscles ached, and their tempers grew short.

"Fuck! I'm sick of this!" Tammy screamed after they had pulled another empty trap.

The tension on the boat was strong. Spirits were low, and Tammy was at her wit's end. Most days, they pulled the traps in silence, and each time another empty trap came up, Tammy held back her tears and yelled a few choice words to vent her frustrations.

Each night back in the harbor, Tammy yearned to go for a long walk to gather her thoughts. But there was nowhere to go. She was stuck bobbing around on a thirty-foot boat. For the first time in all her years fishing, she didn't want to be there. She had known from day one that every year was a gamble. They forked out thousands of dollars, hoping they would make ten times or more back. Their gambles had paid off until now, but this trip had Tammy afraid for their future. How would they ever climb out of the hole they had dug themselves into?

On their last day, any hopes they had of getting a good catch were gone. They just went through the motions of pulling their gear as quickly as they could. They wanted to pack up and head back to the mainland as fast as possible to sell what lobsters they had. Afterward, they would then try to figure out what the hell they were going to do.

CHAPTER 23

*W*ithin twelve hours of returning to the mainland, feeling exhausted and with little enthusiasm for the rest of the season, Dwayne and Tammy sold their smallest catch ever from an opening season. They made just enough to catch up on their rent and pay a few of the other outstanding bills. The rest would have to wait until next month. Tammy just hoped their next catch would be better. "Hey, let's not say anything to my mom about how terrible fishing has been. I don't want her to worry," Tammy said on their way back from the store.

Dwayne nodded. "Sure."

Tammy was beyond distraught. For the first time since she had fished, she was scared and feared what the rest of the season might be like. She couldn't believe how drastically the catch had dropped, and it wasn't just them; all the boats at the island had one of their worst openings ever. She and Dwayne had worked so hard, and like every year, they were expecting a good payoff with extra money left in the bank. But so far, their goals were nowhere near being reached.

"What are we going to do?" Tammy said, "My mom will leave in three weeks. Fishing Malibu won't cut it."

Dwayne reached over and rubbed her thigh. "I know. There was a message from Stan, an old fishing buddy of mine I'm still in contact with. He is fishing off Dana Point. He wants me to call him. Maybe he has some ideas. I'm sure everyone has heard how bad it is out at the island by now. I'll call him as soon as we get home."

Tammy folded her arms and leaned back. "Isn't that north of San Diego?"

"Yes, it is," Dwayne replied.

"Okay, and remember, don't say anything to my mom."

When they arrived home, Tammy joined her mom and Matt in the backyard while Dwayne made his phone call. Matt was always super excited when they returned. He was always so eager to share with her his adventures with his nan, which is what he now called her. The worry that consumed her derailed her return home. Tammy forced her smiles as she tried to listen to Matt's recap of his week with nana. But she heard none of it. Her mind was distracted. Anxious to hear about Dwayne's phone call with Stan.

Dwayne told her he had set aside enough cash to buy more bait and fuel, but they would have nothing after that. They desperately needed a good catch on their next trip, but he feared it might be a repeat of the last one.

Tammy couldn't wait any longer. She was dying to know what Stan and Dwayne discussed and told Matt she'd be right back.

She walked into the living room just as Dwayne was hanging up the phone. Tammy stood in the doorway, leaning against the doorjamb with her arms folded. "So, what was all that about?" She said with a sense of urgency.

Dwayne, who was sitting on the couch, showed a slight smirk when he spoke. "Stan says they are slaying them down in Dana Point. Every day his traps have been plugged."

Tammy's jaw dropped. "What? How can that be?"

Dwayne shrugged his shoulders. I have no idea. I guess the El Nino is good for the coastal waters."

Tammy rolled her eyes. "Just our luck to be fishing in the wrong spot during an El Nino."

"Stan says we should move all our gear down there. He said we'd make a killing."

Tammy gasped, and her eyes grew wide too. "You're kidding, right?"

Dwayne's smirk reappeared. "I'm not sure if I am. I would like to see for myself before committing."

"And how do you plan on doing that?" Tammy asked.

"Stan has offered to take me out on his boat early tomorrow morning, and I can see his traps as he pulls them."

Tammy nodded. "That's not a bad idea. What time would you be leaving?"

"Well, it is a two to three-hour drive from here, and he leaves the dock at five, so I need to leave no later than two in the morning." Dwayne hesitated. "But I also want to take some of our gear down there in the truck."

Tammy shook her head and scrunched her brow. "What. But we have no gear here except for the sixty bare ones in the backyard, and they have no rope and aren't ready to fish yet."

"Those are the ones I'm talking about. Look, what if they are slaying them down there? Wouldn't it be a good idea to have some gear with me to dump in the water? Instead of racing back here."

Tammy ran his idea through her head. "Yeah, I guess," she mumbled, feeling defeated. She checked her watch. It's already three o'clock. "So, what are you saying? We need to hustle and get the gear in the yard ready?"

"Not necessarily all of them right now. I can probably fit only fifteen in my truck. Let's rig those up and load them in the truck. It will take a few hours, and then we can work on rigging up the rest. Whatever we don't get done, you can finish up while I'm with Stan."

Tammy walked across the room and took a seat next to Dwayne. "So I guess we are not heading out to the island tomorrow?"

"I'm not too excited about that place after last week. I'd like to go check out Dana Point and decide what we are going to do when I get back."

Tammy patted his thigh. "Okay, Captain. You're the boss. Now I just gotta figure out what I'm going to tell my mom."

"Just tell her the truth. We're trying a new spot. No big deal."

"Yeah, you're right. I don't know why I'm afraid to tell her. It's not like she pays any attention or knows where we fish in the first place." Tammy laughed. She smacked Dwayne's leg before pulling herself off the couch. "Well, those traps aren't going to rig themselves. Let's go do this," she said as she motioned with her hand for Dwayne to get up. "I'll put Matt to work too. He's a good helper."

For the rest of the afternoon and well into the night with the floodlights lit, they worked hard getting most of the traps rigged, and with Matt's help, they stacked fifteen of them in the bed of the truck.

When ten o'clock rolled around, Tammy insisted Dwayne stop working, take a shower and try to get at least a few hours of sleep.

"You can't go all night and then be out on a boat all day with no sleep," Tammy barked when Dwayne protested.

Dwayne knew better than to argue. He had lost this battle. "Fine. Are you going to be able to finish the last dozen traps?" Dwayne asked.

"Yeah, I got this." She turned and gave her son a loving smile. "You are done too, Matt. Why don't you go inside, wash up before Dwayne jumps in the shower, and watch some TV with nan? It's almost your bedtime."

Matt scrunched his face, "but mom."

"No, buts Matt. You've been a tremendous help, but it's getting late."

Matt folded his arms and let out a heavy sigh before heading into the house. "Fine."

Tammy shook her head and chuckled at his mannerism before heading back to work by herself with the floodlights illuminating the yard and the radio playing in the background. By midnight she had all the traps rigged and stacked by the back gate, ready to go if needed. She was filthy, her body was sore, and it exhausted her. She was too tired to take a bath and made a pot of coffee for Dwayne before crawling into bed next to him, and before she fell asleep, she woke him with a smooch and a cuddle.

Dwayne stirred and smiled when he felt Tammy's arms embrace his chest.

"Time to get up, sweetie," Tammy whispered in his ear, kissing him on the cheek before she closed her eyes.

"Hey, babe. How did it go?" Dwayne whispered in a sleepy voice. She didn't reply, and then he heard her faint breathing through her nose. He soon realized she was already asleep. He smiled at the thought and, with care, gently slid out of her arms and left the room.

CHAPTER 24

*T*ammy slept undisturbed for a good solid seven hours. She couldn't remember the last time she had gotten such a good night's rest. She was thankful for her mom being there to take care of Matt. Tammy had watched over the years, the close bond that had formed between Matt and her mom. They had something special that couldn't go unnoticed.

Tammy didn't like that she couldn't communicate with Dwayne while he was out on the boat with Stan. Her mind wouldn't rest. The anticipation of how they did was driving her crazy. If the catch was good, what will Dwayne's next move be? She didn't even want to think about what they would do if it were bad.

Her questions would soon be answered when she heard Dwayne's truck pull up in the alley and park in front of their garage. She was outside coiling rope with Matt while her mom sat at the patio table, reading a book, and drinking hot tea.

Eager to hear his report of the day, Tammy dropped the half-coiled rope on the ground. "I'll be right back," she told Matt as she raced through the back gate to join Dwayne.

When he exited the truck, Tammy was just walking around to

the driver's side. She paused; his beaming smile told her he had a good day.

"Tell me; you have good news," Tammy said as she wrapped her arms around him and pulled him in close. "I've missed you."

He looked ragged and tired. His clothes smelt of bait, and his skin felt dry from the sun. He beamed her another smile, squeezed her tight, and gave her a long hard kiss. "It was better than good. It was unbelievable! I've never seen so many lobsters in one trap."

Tammy's eyes grew wide. "Really!" She wiped a fish scale off his cheek. She was worried about him. As much as she wanted to talk about what he wanted to do next, he needed to rest. "You look so tired. Why don't you take a shower and a nap? We can talk later about what you want to do."

Dwayne took both her hands and gave her a hard stare. He shook his head. "No, I want to take more traps down there while the fishing is good. No one knows how long it will last. If it sticks around, we can make up for the awful catch we had last week."

Tammy gasped and rolled her eyes. She placed her hands on her hips and gave him an icy stare. "Dwayne, you can't drive back down there. You need to get some rest."

Dwayne shook his head. "I'll be fine. We need to get the rest of the traps to the harbor and in the water. It's going to take three trips. Stan said he would take them out on his boat first thing in the morning if we have them stacked on his dock and ready to go."

Tammy used a sharper tone. She didn't like his plan, and she hated it when he acted so hard-headed. "I won't let you drive all that way with no sleep."

Dwayne cracked a sarcastic laugh. "You have no choice, Tammy. I'm not missing out on this opportunity. I'll be fine."

Tammy folded her arms. "Yes, I do have a choice, Dwayne. We both do. Especially for our safety, and it's not safe for you to drive. You've hardly slept in the last twenty-hours." She pondered for a minute and then smiled at him. "Tell you what. Help me stack the next load onto the truck, and I'll take them down."

Dwayne questioned her. His face was masked with surprise and uncertainty. "What? are you sure?"

"Yes, I'm sure, and I won't let you talk me out of it. Write the address and the boat slip number. We can relay. While I'm gone, you rest, and I'll do the same when you take the second load down."

Dwayne raised his hands in defeat and laughed. "Okay, you win. I know when I'm defeated. Matt can help too."

Tammy smiled. "Good Idea. Hey Matt!" Tammy hollered.

It took them an hour to load the truck, and by four, Tammy was on the freeway driving to Dana Point. She hoped to be there in two hours, but an hour into her drive, the traffic was crawling at fifteen miles an hour. She spat out her words. "Shit, I forgot about rush hour." The traffic was going to cost her another hour.

By the time she reached the unfamiliar marina, the fishing boats were quiet, tied up to the docks with no one on board. She was the only one there. Tammy walked down the ramp onto the dock lined with lobster boats searching for Stan's vessel called *Fishing Fool*. She released a smile when she came upon it almost immediately. "Well, that's good it's close to the ramp," Tammy whispered and scanned the area around the boat in search of a good place to put the traps. She found the perfect spot on the other side of the boat and wasted no time to grab the first load.

Her first task was to climb on top of the stack of traps and untie the hand truck Dwayne had remembered to grab at the last minute. After struggling with the tight knots Dwayne had made, she used all her strength to lift the heavy metal hand truck over the top of the traps while keeping her balance as she lowered it to the ground. Her chest heaved, and she sucked in air as she slowly eased herself down the traps and off the truck. "Well, that was a chore," she gasped.

After she rested for a few minutes, she climbed the stack again to untie the top traps and then wondered how she would get them down by herself. She didn't want to overthink it and put on her gloves she had stuck in her back pocket and pulled a trap forward.

Tammy took in a deep breath, and with both hands, she grabbed the heavy trap and pulled it to the edge, where she balanced it as she climbed down and planted her feet firmly on the ground. She stood on her toes and stretched her body to the max and smiled when she discovered she could reach the trap. Slowly she inched the heavy trap more to the edge, praying it wouldn't come crashing down on top of her. When it was finally at a pivoting point, she pulled hard and took the full weight of the trap, guiding it to the ground as she let out a loud painful grunt. "Fuck, that's heavy!" She hollered. "Why do they always seem much heavier when they are out of the water?" Tammy repeated the maneuver two more times until she had three traps stacked on the hand truck. "God, this is going to take forever, and we have two more trips to do. This is bloody insane." Tammy complained as she pushed the heavy load toward the ramp. When she reached the top of the ramp and out of breath, she stopped and peered down the steep ramp. "Now, how the hell am I going to wheel this down there?" She feared it would gain speed and get away from her.

Again, Tammy took a deep breath and slowly pushed the hand truck to the crest of the ramp. "Well, here goes nothing." She planted her feet firmly on the wooden ramp as she inched the hand truck down the incline by taking baby steps. It took all her strength to hold it back from getting away from her, and as she neared the bottom, she felt she was losing it and ran the last four feet. "Fuck!" She yelled as she finally touched the dock where she stood the hand truck upright and leaned forward, gasping for air. Tammy keeled over and rested her hands on her knees as she sucked in oxygen. "Shit, I have to do that five more times. I'm going to bloody kill myself."

After catching her breath, she found the strength to push the heavy load of traps to the dock next to the boat. She rested again before stacking them. "This is bullshit. We better get some friggin lobsters after all this." Tammy cursed as she wheeled the empty hand-truck up the ramp to grab another load.

It took her just over an hour to take all the traps down to the dock. By the time she was finished, beads of sweat had poured from her brow. Her hair was drenched, and her soaked t-shirt stuck to her moist back. Tammy could hardly lift the hand truck into the bed of the truck and released a loud moan as she slid it up onto the tailgate and pushed it with a hard shove.

By eight-fifteen, she was back on the freeway heading north. She was pleased to see rush hour was over and made it back to the house within two hours, even after stopping to get gas.

It surprised her to find Dwayne already awake and dressed, packing some last-minute items.

"Oh man, you look beat," Dwayne said when she staggered into the house, holding her back. He walked across the kitchen and held out his arms.

Tammy welcomed his embrace and rested her head on his chest. "That was a lot of frigging work for one person. My back is killing me." She looked around the room. "Where's Matt and mom?"

"They are in Matt's room doing a jig-saw puzzle. Tell you what. I'll have Matt help me load the next stack. Why don't you go soak in the tub and get some rest?"

Tammy smiled and pulled herself out of his embrace while squeezing her side. "You don't have to ask me twice. There's gas in the truck. Wake me up when you get back; I'm going with you on the boat. I want to see the catch for myself."

Dwayne kissed her forehead. "You are such a trooper. It's one reason I love you. I'll see you in a few hours."

CHAPTER 25

wayne returned at two o'clock in the morning feeling and looking as tired as Tammy did when she had made her trip. He knew they would have to leave no later than three-thirty to make it to Stan's boat by six, and even that was cutting it close. But he had to get at least an hour of sleep before making the trip one more time. He set the alarm for three and let his clothes fall off his body onto the floor before quietly crawling into bed next to Tammy, who was sound asleep.

When the alarm went off, Dwayne turned, mumbled, and pulled the sheets over his head. Tammy stirred and was surprised to see Dwayne lying next to her. She gave his shoulder a gentle nudge. "Dwayne, wake up."

"Five more minutes," he whined from beneath the covers.

"What time did you get home?"

"About an hour ago," he groaned.

Tammy nudged him again. "I'm sorry, I know you're tired, but we have to get up. We can't be late. Stan may leave without us." She pulled the covers away from her body and stood to her feet. "I'm going to go make us some coffee. Come on, babe, wakey, wakey," she said before giving him another nudge.

Dwayne rolled onto his back and pulled his head up out of the comfort of the covers. He rubbed his eyes and yawned. "Okay, I'm up."

Before leaving, Tammy snuck into Matt's room, where he was sleeping on the top bunk. She tip-toed across the room and kissed his hand softly that was hanging over the edge. "I'll see you tonight, buddy."

She left a note for her mom, thanking her for being there, and then quietly tip-toed out of the house.

With it being so early, there was no traffic, and they reached Stan's boat in record time with even thirty-minutes to spare, which gave them enough time to load the traps onto the boat.

"You made it," Stan said before taking a hit off his cigar and a swig of coffee, which he held in his other hand.

Dwayne shook his hand. "Yeah, neither one of us got much sleep last night. We took turns bringing the gear down while the other one slept."

Stan cracked a laugh. "The things we do to catch a lobster."

Dwayne nodded. "No, kidding."

Stan turned to Tammy and smiled. "So, you are the Mrs."

Tammy gave him a friendly smile and held out her hand. "I sure am. I've heard a lot about you."

Stan gave Dwayne a devious smile. "What have you been telling her?" he chuckled.

Even if Dwayne hadn't told her that Stan had been fishing for over twenty years, Tammy saw the signs. He was older than Dwayne. Probably in his late 50s. Like most fishermen that had spent their days being baked by the sun while on the ocean. His skin was dry and rough looking. His dark brown hair was mid length and had no style. He wore a black t-shirt that showed off his buff, tanned arms. It was something Tammy had noticed on all the fishermen she had met—no matter how old they were; their arms were always muscular from hauling gear all day.

Tammy soon discovered that Stan ran a tight ship. Five minutes before the top of the hour, Stan fired up the boat while she and Dwayne finished loading the last five traps onto the deck. Stan checked his watch. "We'll be heading out in approximately five minutes. If there's anything you need from your truck, you'd better grab it now."

Dwayne glanced over at Tammy. "Need anything?" he asked.

Tammy shook her head. "No, I'm good. I already put the ice chest on the boat."

"Okay, then we're out of here," Stan yelled above the loud sound of the engine. "Dwayne, I'll let you untie the boat," he said from the helm.

Tammy jumped on the boat and stood out of the way so the two men could prepare to leave the dock.

It didn't take them long to reach their destination, and within a half-hour, Tammy was baiting the first of their traps to prepare for them being dropped in the spots Stan recommended.

"You could give these traps a few days' soaking if you wanted to. Nothing is going to eat the lobsters like at San Clemente." Stan told Dwayne as he pushed the first trap over the side and into the water.

"That's good to know," Dwayne hollered as he grabbed another baited trap.

It took them a couple of hours to get all the traps in the water, and then they headed over to Stan's gear and anxiously waited for him to pull up his first trap.

Tammy stood close to Dwayne and the trap table and peered into the water to watch the trap immerse.

When it landed on the table, Tammy gasped. The trap was plugged with lobsters. Most of them looked legal too. "Holy shit!" Tammy squealed. "It's loaded. And the lobsters are huge."

Dwayne beamed her a smile. "I told you."

Stan handed her a gauge. "Here, why don't you measure them, and I'll drive to the next trap."

"A lot of them don't need to be measured," Tammy laughed. "I can tell just by looking at them they are twice the legal size."

The number of lobsters that were in the trap stunned Tammy. By the time they had finished measuring the lobsters, Stan had thirty legal lobsters in the barrel. "Wow! That's incredible," Tammy said. She quickly baited the trap and tossed it over the side before they grabbed the next one close by.

They continued down the line, and each trap was just as good as the first one. Stan did not have one empty trap and very few shorts. By the end of the day, Tammy felt excited about the few traps she and Dwayne had in the water. Stan's catch that day was as good as a normal opener at the island.

"Is it always this good out here," Tammy asked as she jumped off the boat onto the dock and tied the line around a cleat.

"No. I've never seen it this good before. It's normally like Malibu, but this El Nino we have this year makes the lobsters crawl for some reason."

"Not at the island," Dwayne chuckled.

Stan shook his hand. "Well, I hope this turns it around for you. Let me know how it goes. Do you have any more gear you can put in the water?" he asked.

"Nah, it's all on the island."

"Well, you might want to think about bringing some down here."

"That's not a bad idea. I'll think about it." Dwayne shook his hand. "Thanks for everything. You've been a great help."

"My pleasure. Now I gotta tend to these lobsters. We'll talk soon, guys."

They left Stan to tend to his business, and once they were in the truck, Dwayne turned to Tammy and draped his arm over her shoulder. "What do you think about heading out to San Clemente and grabbing some more gear to fish here?"

Tammy creased her brow and gave Dwayne a sharp stare. "You're kidding, right?"

"No, I'm not. I'm serious. It's where the lobsters are, and we need more gear in the water if we are going to make any kind of real money."

Tammy leaned her head back and closed her eyes for a moment. She didn't like Dwayne's idea. "But it will take us a day to get there and then another day to get back here, and that doesn't count pulling the gear out of the water and stacking it on the boat." She shook her head. "And then we still have to bait and put them in the water here. When the hell would we sleep? I'm still exhausted from last night."

Dwayne rubbed her shoulder, "I know. I'm tired too. We could do it in shifts and drive through the night to the island. We could be on the *Baywitch II* by this evening. It has fuel, and we have bait in the freezer. What do you say? If we push ourselves, we could be at Dana Point with a boat full of traps by late tomorrow night. We could spend the night on the boat at a guest dock and dump them the next morning."

Tammy buried her head in her hands. "Oh, I don't know, Dwayne. I am so damn tired as it is."

"You can sleep in the truck on the way home. I'll drop you off at the house so you can rest some more while I get the boat ready and load up the bait."

Tammy shook her head. "No, that's not fair. I won't have you do all the work."

Dwayne gave her a loving smile. "Does that mean you'll do this with me?"

"Yes, I guess. We are in this together, after all."

Dwayne planted a big kiss on her lips. "Yes! Okay then, Let's get going. I'm excited. Aren't you?"

Tammy laughed at his enthusiasm. "I'll start getting excited after I've gotten some rest—no need to drop me off at the house. I'll come down to the boat and help you load up the bait. We can go to the house together and pack some food and clean clothes. I hope Matt will still be awake. I miss him, and I want to say goodbye to him and see how mom is doing."

Tammy fell asleep as soon as they were on the road heading north. She slept soundly for the next two hours. It was only when the truck came to a full stop and woke her up. She looked out the window and saw they were in front of their house.

"Hey, we're here, sleepyhead," Dwayne said as he gently nudged her shoulder.

Tammy rubbed her eyes. It was still light out. "What time is it?" she asked.

"Almost seven. I want to be on the boat within the hour."

"Sure. I just need to clean up and grab a few things and pack our food."

Matt came out to greet them and asked with wide eyes about the fishing. Tammy couldn't hold the excitement in her voice and told him about the amazing catch Stan had and that they were heading out to the island to grab more traps to take to Dana Point.

"Can I go?" Matt asked.

"No, you can't go. You have school."

Matt let out a loud moan of disapproval. "God, I hate school." He moped into the house.

Dwayne and Tammy made it to the boat in record time, and by eight-thirty, they had everything loaded, and we're heading down the main channel for a long ten-hour crossing to the island.

Dwayne was at the wheel, but Tammy could see how tired he was. He kept rubbing his eyes, and she watched as they periodically closed for a few seconds. He was exhausted. Tammy approached him and took his hand. "Hey, why don't you go lie down for a bit and get some rest. You've not slept in almost thirty-six hours. I can drive for a while."

Dwayne smiled at her. "Are you sure? It's a clear night, and the stars are out. You shouldn't have any problems."

"Yes, I'm sure. Let me grab my jacket, and then I'll take the wheel."

He leaned in and gave her a soft kiss on the lips. "Thanks. A nap would be good."

Tammy drove for the next four hours while Dwayne slept with no interruptions. She wanted him to sleep as much as he could because she knew once they reached the island around six in the morning, there would be no time for rest. He emerged from the cabin with his hair uncombed and his clothes wrinkled, but what caught Tammy's attention was his large grin.

Hey handsome. "Feeling better?"

Dwayne steadied himself as he climbed the last two steps onto the deck, looked out at the vast ocean, and saw Catalina behind them.

"Oh, wow, we're on the backside of Catalina Island."

"Yes, you slept for a good four hours." Tammy stood up from the Captain's chair. "Now it's my turn. Wake me up when we are almost there."

Before she left, Dwayne took her in his arms and gave her a long sensual kiss. "You're amazing."

Tammy tilted back her head and laughed and patted his chest." You're not so bad yourself. I love you."

He squeezed her waist." I love you too. Now go on, get some sleep." He said as he patted her behind.

As much as Tammy needed sleep, she never had slept well on a boat, especially moving at eight knots across the ocean. She had slept little over the past twenty-four hours, and as exhausted as she was, she couldn't fall asleep. For the next few hours, she laid wide awake, feeling frustrated, and finally gave up on sleep.

"What are you doing up?" Dwayne asked, looking surprised to see her.

"I can't sleep. And I got bored." She laughed and walked over to Dwayne's side, where he cradled her in his arm. Dwayne shook his head. "You're going to be sorry."

By the time they reached the harbor a little after six in the morning, Tammy felt the fatigue immensely and would have given anything to be curled up in her bed right about now instead of being on a cold, damp boat on a remote island. They were not surprised to see the harbor empty. It was light out, and the boats were probably out pulling their gear already. Dwayne didn't want to lose time calling them on the radio and wasted no time driving over to the first trap while Tammy balanced herself to put on her slickers, which was always a challenge on a moving boat.

For the next five hours, Dwayne and Tammy pulled fifty traps and stacked them on the boat. Tammy struggled with the last ten. Her back burned from the constant heavy lifting, and every time she grabbed a trap, she winced her body in pain and could barely coil her fingers around the wire to get a good grip on the trap. Each one seemed to weigh heavier than the previous one. Every time she dragged one off the trap table to stack it, she released a loud moan of agony.

"We better get some goddamn lobsters after this," Tammy hollered as she steadied herself against a stack of traps while a large swell passed under the boat. When it had passed, and the intense rocking subsided, Tammy took her place with the gaff while Dwayne drove to the last trap.

It was almost eleven o'clock by the time they had fifty traps tied down on the *Baywitch II.*

"How are you holding up?" Dwayne asked, looking concerned. "I want you to go down below and get some rest. You've been going for over thirty hours and only slept for a few hours in the truck."

Tammy was about to protest, but Dwayne raised his hand.

"And before you try to start an argument, I'm ordering you. I'm not asking you." He gave her a wink. "I'm using my captain's rank, okay."

Tammy arched her back to pull out a few of the knots she was feeling. It didn't work. Her back was on fire. Her entire body ached as though she had never experienced it before, and she was on the verge of tears. It hurt to walk or raise her arms. Her legs felt like lead weights, and she dragged her feet as she made her way to the cabin. "No argument from me. I'm in so much pain right now." Tammy looked at the steps that descended into the cabin. She feared her legs would not carry her and inched her body lower to the ground until she was sitting on her behind.

Dwayne looked down from the helm, wearing a puzzled look. "What are you doing?"

"My legs are killing me. I'm afraid I'll fall if I try to walk down the steps, so I'm going to scooch down them on my butt."

Dwayne snickered. "Okay, and you can't come back until you have gotten some sleep. Captain's orders."

"Aye, Aye, Captain," Tammy said sarcastically.

I t surprised Tammy that she dozed off, but it didn't last long. The seas were growing, and the swells rocked the *Baywitch II* vigorously, and from inside the cabin, it was much more intense. Fearing she might be thrown from the bed by an angry wave, Tammy pulled herself to her feet and held onto the table for balance. Tammy peeked out of the cabin window and saw it was still light and suddenly jolted her head back when the ocean smacked the plexiglass of the cabin window. "What bloody time is it?" she whispered out loud and scanned the cabin. "Ten bloody years, and we still don't have a damn clock on this boat." Tammy pulled up her sleeve and squinted at her watch. It was two o'clock in the afternoon. She slept for roughly two hours.

"How are you doing up there?" Tammy hollered up to Dwayne. But he couldn't hear her over the loud engine. Tammy braced herself as another wave crashed against the hull before attempting to climb the steps up to the deck. She stopped midway and held on as the boat rocked heavily for a moment before climbing the last few steps.

When Tammy stepped out onto the deck, the sudden chill stung her face. Dwayne sat at the helm, bundled in a sweatshirt with the hood up. He hadn't seen her, and when Tammy rested her hand on his shoulder, he jumped.

"Damn, you scared me," he said as he turned his upper body to face her.

"Sorry, I didn't mean to." Tammy was disturbed by how tired he looked. His eyes were dark and heavy, and his skin was pale. "Are you okay?"

"Yeah, hanging in there. You didn't sleep much."

"Nah. You know I have a hard time sleeping on the boat. I got a couple of hours in, though. I'm good."

Tammy watched Dwayne closely as he continued to drive and saw his eyes close for a few seconds before he'd shake his head and rub his eyes. She counted him doing it four times in five minutes and nudged his arm. "Why don't you let me drive. You're falling asleep."

"No, I'm not," Dwayne said defensively as he held the rail for support.

Another wave hit the boat, and Tammy quickly took hold of the back of the captain's chair. "What's with this bloody ocean? I didn't hear of any weather coming."

"It just picked up a short while ago. I'm sure it will pass. Just some winds are making the swell increase," Dwayne said before giving his eyes another rub.

Tammy had seen enough. "Okay, that's it. Get up. I'm driving; lie down. You've been going since last night," Tammy said, using a stern voice.

Dwayne didn't argue and stood up from the captain's chair. "Okay, stay on that course." He said, pointing to the compass. "The autopilot is on, but we both know it goes off course a bit, so keep an eye on it. It's a new course. We're going to Dana Point, not the Marina."

"I know," Tammy said as she took a seat, pushing Dwayne

towards the steps of the cabin. "Now go on, get out of here. I'm going to wake you when we are an hour out of port if you are still sleeping. I don't know the harbor. You will have to take us in."

Dwayne nodded and disappeared down into the cabin.

Tammy yanked her sweatshirt off the hook where it hung by the wheel, and while bracing herself with one hand, she slid it over her upper torso and welcomed the warmth before making herself comfortable in the Captain's chair. "Man, it's rough out here." She scowled while holding the wheel tight.

The waves continued to roar for the next hour, slamming the boat hard with bodies of water. The swells were not huge but big enough where Tammy had to be constantly holding onto something for balance. "How the hell does Dwayne sleep in this shit?" Tammy called out as the boat rocked hard from side to side. "I hope it's not going to be like this the whole way," she added while looking out at the white-crested waves. "I don't know if my body can take eight more hours of abuse from the ocean," Tammy complained as another wave threw her off balance and into the wall of the helm. The side of her body hit the wall hard. "Ouch! That bloody hurt."

Finally, after two more hours of increased swells and wind, the weather calmed down, and Tammy eased her hold on the wheel and gave her cramped hands a rest. She checked her watch. They still had another four hours to go before they would be an hour out of Dana Point. Amazingly, Dwayne had slept through the rough seas and was still sound asleep when Tammy peeked her head through the doorway of the cabin. Tammy checked the skies and noticed clouds were rolling in and off to the distance and saw where the clouds meet the ocean. "Oh, wow! That looks like a fog bank." Very rarely had they hit fog, and when they did, Dwayne had always taken the wheel because it was so easy to get off course. Tammy had considered waking up Dwayne but waited until they were closer. "I'll let him rest some more. I've got this."

Tammy kept her eyes peeled to the open waters ahead of her as the boat neared the thick fog bank that spanned for miles across the surface of the ocean. She wondered how thick it was and what her visibility would be like. But she wouldn't know until they were in the thick of it. Doubting herself and her inexperience, thoughts of waking Dwayne crossed her mind again, but this was an opportunity to gain the experience she lacked, and she chose to let him sleep. Her stomach churned with nerves as she grabbed the wheel and looked ahead at the eerie fog bank.

The clouds were getting denser and closer to the boat. Tammy checked her compass and saw the boat was still on course. She stuck her head out the side of the helm and felt the dewy mist in the air. In about an hour, the sun would go down. Tammy wondered if there would be enough time to pass through the fog before the skies turned dark?.

The tunnel of fog showed no mercy and engulfed the *Baywitch II* within minutes, leaving Tammy with a sense of isolation from the rest of the world. Tammy tightened her grip on the wheel. The thickness of the fog hindered her ability to see twenty feet in front of her. Regret and panic consumed her. "Fuck. I can't see a damn thing." Tammy expressed her fears out loud to herself. "I'm so friggin scared right now. What if there is another boat up head? I might hit it." Tammy's brow dripped with sweat, and her hands trembled around the cold metal wheel at the helm. Tammy released a huge sigh of relief after checking the radar and saw no flashing green dots, which meant there were no other boats in the area. "That's good there aren't any other boats near us." The compass told her they were still on course as she crawled along at a slow six knots.

Tammy scanned the entire perimeter of the boat and saw nothing but thick fog for what seemed miles. "Man, this is creepy" The fear of a drifting log or debris in their path prompted Tammy to slow down the boat even more. The last thing they needed was a hole in the boat. Still clutching the wheel, frozen with fear, Tammy's hands trembled. "God, what was I thinking? This is too bloody scary." Afraid to leave her station for even a second, she cried for help. "Dwayne!" But the loud noise of the engine blanketed her voice.

The minutes turned into what seemed hours. Her arms were tired from constantly steering, trying to stay on course. The aching she felt in her heavy, misty eyes caused the radar and compass to be a blur. Tammy gave her head a vigorous shake. When she did, the wet strands of her hair whipped her face. "Damn it! When is this going to end?"

When the skies darkened to the color of coal, Tammy searched hard for stars and saw none. They had been her savior many times in the past and guided her home. Dwayne had told her one time when her eyes were tired from looking at the compass to pick a star and follow it. They never move, and it will lead you home. Since then, it had worked, and Tammy had preferred the navigation of a star over a compass. They were her angels in the sky and provided a sense of security. "I can't see one star. Where are you? My angels. I need you," Tammy cried.

From lack of sleep, Tammy strained to keep her eyes open or stay focused. The blanket of fog confused her bearings. There was no glimpse of a coastline. They were completely shielded from the rest of the world. Tammy tried to erase the horrific images that haunted her head of them crashing on the shore or, even worse, slamming into another boat and possibly killing themselves or someone else. "God, I wish Dwayne would wake up. I have no idea if I am still on course." Angry with her stupidity, Tammy stomped her feet and screamed. "I don't want to do this anymore."

Tammy had lost all track of time and remained glued to the helm, desperately seeking for any signs that the fog may be lifting. After what seemed like an eternity, she believed it finally was. Suddenly she could see a few feet beyond the bow and then fifty feet more. She screamed with joy when she was able to see a hundred feet, "Oh my god, we are coming out of the fog bank." Tammy jumped up and down and cried happy tears. "We are going to make it. I did it." Tammy smiled and looked up to the skies. "Hello, stars. I've missed you." and then suddenly jumped back when she felt something touch her shoulder.

"Hey, it's only me," Dwayne said, who stood behind her.

Tammy spun around and threw herself into his arms, "God, you scared me. I'm so happy you are awake. What a bloody ordeal I had."

Concerned, Dwayne broke free of their embrace. "What do you mean? What happened?"

"We hit a fog bank. It was bloody awful, and it lasted for hours."

Dwayne's jaw dropped, "You're kidding? Why didn't you wake me?"

"I was afraid to leave the wheel. I couldn't see shit. What if we hit a log of something for that few minutes I had left? I was so frigging scared. I never want to drive in the fog again."

Dwayne gave her a huge grin.

Tammy wasn't amused. "What are you smiling about? It wasn't funny, Dwayne."

"Don't you see what you did? And you did it all by yourself. I've always been afraid to let you drive in the fog because you can become so disorientated and get lost fast." He pulled her in his arms and kissed her hard on the lips. "But you didn't panic and drove through it and kept your wits about you. Give yourself a big pat on the back, girl. I'm so proud of you."

Tammy rested her head on his chest. "I'm so tired. I think I will be able to sleep on the boat for once."

"Go on. Go down below and sleep the rest of the way. I've got this. I love you. Well done!"

She gave him a long, drawn-out kiss. "I love you too." And went down below.

The silence of the motors and the stillness of the boat woke Tammy from her well-needed sleep. She yawned and stretched, stopping mid-way when pain shot up her back. She winced. "Ouch!" Her back was on fire.

Dwayne must have heard her and peeked his head through the cabin doorway. "Are you okay?"

Tammy moved slowly, holding her side as she slid her aching body out of bed. "Yeah, my damn back is on fire. Are we here?"

"Yes, we are. Do you want to lie down some more?"

"No. I need to walk around." Tammy looked through the cabin window and saw it was dark outside. "What time is it?

"Almost midnight."

Tammy used her hands and crawled out of the cabin to the deck, where Dwayne helped her to her feet. "Wow, it took us a long time to get here."

"Yea, the fog slowed us down. That was smart of you to slow down the boat."

"Yes. I slowed way down. I could have walked faster. It took forever."

Dwayne rubbed her shoulders, and Tammy hunched her back to reap the full benefits of his massaging hands. "God, that feels good. I'm so bloody tired." She pulled herself to a standing position and scanned their surroundings. There were six other boats tied in slips where they were docked. A few were sailboats and the rest commercial boats. "So, where are we?" Tammy asked.

"We're in Dana Point harbor."

"And what is the plan, Captain?" Tammy said with a hint of sarcasm.

"Well, I figured we could leave around five and bait these traps as we dump them, and then after, we can pull the traps that have been soaking for a few days. What do you think?"

"Okay, then. Let's go down below and grab some sleep. We only have a few hours."

Tammy had a restless night and got little sleep. She woke in a foul mood and to the sound of her stomach growling. Acid came roaring through her stomach with hunger pains. Living off granola bars and cans of tuna fish were not cutting it.

She didn't know what time it was and again wished they had a clock in the cabin. It was pitch black inside the boat, which told her it was still the wee hours of the morning, but she was too irritated and hungry to go back to sleep. Her hands searched for the flashlight stashed under the pillow in the dark. Once it was in her hands, Tammy held her breath and realized the boat was too quiet. The gentle snores from Dwayne couldn't be heard. She patted his pillow and discovered he was not lying next to her.

Puzzled, Tammy pulled herself out of bed and threw on a pair of jeans and sweatshirt before heading up to the deck. She looked around the boat and up and down the docks. Dwayne was nowhere to be found. "Where the hell is he?" Tammy whispered, checking her watch. It was nearing four, and they needed to leave in an hour. She scanned the docks for a guest bathroom, spotted it at the end, and then noticed Dwayne's exiting one and stepped off the boat to meet him half-way.

"Hey, good morning, beautiful. Did you get some good sleep?" Dwayne asked, looking all perky and wide-eyed. Tammy didn't know how he did it.

Tammy frowned. "No. I didn't get hardly any, and I'm so bloody hungry."

"We'll grab a can of tuna and orange juice before we head out, okay."

"I'm sick of bloody tuna. I want a damn meal," Tammy snapped.

Dwayne gave her a smirk. "Well, look who got out of bed on the wrong side." He chuckled. "Tell you what, after we finish for the day, we'll dock the boat at the guest dock and go look for a restaurant, and I'll buy you a nice meal."

"I can't wait. I'll probably eat two meals. I'll meet you back at the boat. I'm going to use the restroom."

They left the dock at five and were eager to pull the few traps that had been soaking for the last few days, but they needed to unload the traps they had on the boat first.

Tammy struggled through the morning, getting each trap ready to dump while Dwayne drove the boat to the various spots. Over the past few days, her body had not recovered from the intense labor she was continually putting it through. She didn't know if she could make it to the end of the day. She was so tired that she was on the verge of tears. Any kind of body movement was followed by excruciating pain. Her back was on fire, her hands were swollen, and she could hardly move her fingers. Her legs were stiff, and she could barely feel her feet. Tammy was sure of it because of the way her boots felt extra tight around her ankles. She struggled to keep her balance on the moving boat and many times stumbled back into the stack of traps, thankful Dwayne was facing the other way. She didn't want to do anything to prevent today's achievements from happening and hid how much her body hurt from him. This season was already off to a terrible start, and if Dwayne knew the intense pain she was experiencing, he would insist they'd not work today. Tammy just wanted this to be over with. She wanted to go home and sleep in her warm bed after sitting down to a home-cooked meal and taking a hot bath with plenty of bubbles. Taking a day of rest would mean putting all those luxuries off for another day.

Tammy envied Dwayne's stamina, but it's what kept her going. He was definitely the backbone of their fishing business and kept their spirits high even through the low times. She loved how he always looked out for her and made no plans for their fishing adventures without talking them over with her first. He treated her as an equal partner, and she admired that about him.

After they dumped the last trap, Tammy wiped her brow and looked at the empty deck. It was a glorious sight.

Wearing a huge grin, Dwayne rubbed his hands together. His eyes were wide. "Are you ready to go pull some traps now and see how many lobsters we have?"

Tammy knew she should be excited, but for the first time, she wasn't feeling it. She just wanted to go home. "How do you do it? You just keep going."

Dwayne laughed. "Money, baby. It's all about the money. How are you holding up? Are you okay?"

Tammy lied. "Yeah, I'm fine. Just a little tired. I'll feel better once I see that first trap plugged with lobsters."

"That's my girl. Come here and kiss me."

It took them twenty minutes to get to the first trap that had been soaking since they left for the island over three days ago. Tammy finally felt the adrenaline rush she was used to each time they approached a trap. She was in position, holding the gaff ready to hook the line as Dwayne drove up to it.

"Got it!" she yelled in triumph.

Dwayne gave her a huge smile as he watched her wrap the line around the pulley. "Okay, here we go—trap number one. Bring me the money, baby!" he yelled.

Tammy laughed and peered beneath the surface of the water as she anxiously waited for the trap to make an appearance through the murky water.

When it broke through the water and landed on the trap table, their hearts sank. The trap was empty.

"What the fuck?" Dwayne said in disbelief.

"Oh, come on! You're kidding me! Not again," Tammy snapped. "This is bullshit!" she yelled. "Now what?"

Dwayne tried to calm her down. "Maybe it's just this trap. Let's stack this one and move it to another spot and go to the next one."

"I'm sick of stacking and moving traps," Tammy screamed as she yanked the trap from the table and slid it to the back of the deck with force.

Dwayne waited until she was safely holding the rail before putting the boat in gear and heading to the next trap. The second trap wasn't any better. It had one legal lobster and two shorts.

"I don't understand. Where the hell did the lobsters go? Three days ago, Stan's traps were plugged," Dwayne said in despair.

"Are we fishing in the right spot?" Tammy asked.

"Yes, look out there. The guys are all fishing here. There are buoys everywhere. I don't get it."

"Just our fucking luck," Tammy said as she stacked another trap. "And where are we supposed to dump these traps? We've never fished here before. We have no idea what the hell we are doing, Dwayne."

For the first time, Dwayne came unleashed. "I don't freaking know, Tammy. Your guess is as good as mine. You're right! I don't know what the hell I'm doing. We both saw the lobsters in Stan's traps and took this chance. Well, it looks like it was a bad decision. I just hope it gets better."

Tammy softened her tone. Dwayne was right. It was both their choice to make a move; it was wrong of her to blame Dwayne. "Me too. Let's go."

After pulling ten more traps and only getting a few legal lobsters, Tammy broke down into tears. "I'm so sick of this, and I'm so bloody tired. Where the hell are the lobsters?" she cried.

Dwayne turned off the boat. He was just as upset and tired as Tammy, but he refused to give up hope. "Hey now. I'm sure it's going to get better. Hang in there, okay. Why don't you take some time out and chill for a bit?"

Tammy shook her head and snapped. "No! I've worked too damn hard. I want to be there when we finally catch some lobsters. I'll be fine. Come on, let's keep going."

Dwayne nodded. "Okay." He fired up the boat to head to the next trap.

By the end of their line, Tammy was mortified. They caught twelve lobsters. "What are we going to do, Dwayne? These lobsters won't even buy us groceries for a week. We are so screwed." Tammy stood next to Dwayne at the helm as he drove back to the guest dock. Neither one smiled. Dwayne turned to Tammy, his face long and his eyes distant. "I don't know. I'm going to call Stan over the VHF radio when we get back to the dock and see how he did. I hope he is still on the boat."

Tammy looked away and wiped a tear that had escaped. "I don't know how we are going to pay our bills. We owe two months' rent, slip fees, and two truck payments. And god knows what else."

Dwayne reached across and rested his hand on her shoulder. "Let me talk to Stan first before we fret about bills. He may have an answer. He's fished here for years."

"I hope so. How much longer do we have before we reach the dock."

"About fifteen minutes," Dwayne replied.

"I'm going to go lie down. I'm so sore. My body is so damn battered. And for what? I'm so pissed off right now," Tammy snapped as she headed down into the cabin.

As soon as he tied the boat up to the dock, Dwayne wasted no time trying to reach Stan on the radio.

"Hey, Stan. You got me? *Baywitch* here. Over."

There was silence.

Dwayne tried again. "Stan. It's Dwayne on the *Baywitch*. Have you got me?"

A few seconds later, Stan's voice came over the radio loud and clear. "Hey, Dwayne. I got you. Over."

Tammy had heard the conversation and crawled out of bed. She moaned with every move and crawled up to the deck, and remained quiet while the two men spoke.

"Hey, Stan. We just got in from pulling the traps we had soaking for a few days. Not many lobsters. Nothing like the pull you had the other day. I was wondering how you did today. Over."

"I hear ya on that, Dwayne. I had a lousy catch today, and from what I hear, none of the boats had a good catch. Over."

Dwayne's face turned pale, and the little smile he had soon disappeared.

Tammy's jaw dropped, and her eyes turned wide.

"Oh, wow, that's not good. So where do you think all the lobsters went? It's like they just disappeared. Over."

"I have no idea. Strangest thing I've ever seen. I'm going to give it another go tomorrow. If the traps are empty again, I hate to say it, but the mad crawl might be over. Which will really suck for you guys after all the traps you moved over here? But that's fishing; you just never know. Over."

Dwayne gave Tammy a worried look as he spoke over the radio. "Well, I hope that's not the case. Let me know when you get in tomorrow. Over."

"I sure will. Have a good night. I'm out."

Dwayne replaced the mic in its cradle. His eyes looked dazed.

"Are you okay?" Tammy asked.

"I'm just worried. It sounds like the lobsters are gone. No one had a good catch today."

"We're really screwed if that's true. We've invested so much bloody time and money. How the hell are we ever going to recover from this?"

"I don't know, Tammy. I'm not going to think about it until tomorrow. Let's hope the lobsters are back."

Tammy tugged at the straps of her slickers and yanked them down her arms. When her arms were free, she pulled the slickers down her legs as fast as she could and over her boots. Tears streamed down her face like a leaky faucet. The brokenness finally unleashed something inside of her. She picked up the slimy slickers and threw them hard at the stack of fifty traps on the deck of the Baywitch. "I am so frigging done with this shit," she yelled at the top of her lungs. She wanted to be heard above the roaring noise of the engine. She steadied herself as a wave passed under the boat. "I'm sick and tired of chasing god damn lobsters all over this fucking ocean. Look at me. I'm a bloody mess!"

Dwayne stood at the helm. "Look, I'm sorry, okay. But we both knew we were taking a chance by coming here. We'll take these traps we have on the boat to Malibu and just fish Malibu for the rest of the year."

Tammy raised her hands. "No, I'm done, Dwayne! I've had it. We won't make enough money to live and pay what we owe if we fish Malibu so early. I can't do this anymore. I'm sick and tired of being broke all the time and being away from Matt. These last few days have almost killed me, and for what? We're still no better off."

Dwayne's jaw dropped. "Are you saying you're done for the day? Do you want to take a break? What are you trying to tell me, Tammy?"

Tammy collapsed onto the deck of the boat and leaned against the traps. She brought her knees to her chin and buried her head in her hands. Her tears were heavy.

Dwayne took the boat out of gear and left it idle. They were in open waters on their way back to Marina Del Rey with fifty traps, which they planned to drop off in Malibu the next day. He checked his surroundings; the boat was safe and approached Tammy. He knelt at her side and rested his hand on her shoulder. "Tammy, talk to me. What's going on?"

Tammy lifted her head. Her face was drenched with tears. "I can't do this anymore, Dwayne. I'm so tired. My hands are wrecked." Tammy held them up. " Look at them. The cracks are so deep they are bleeding. I can barely move my fingers. And look, my fingers are so swollen that my wedding band is cutting into my flesh. My body is so sore that I can hardly move. I have never worked so goddamn hard in my life and have nothing to show for it."

Dwayne cradled her in his arms. "Come here. It's okay. We'll get through this."

Tammy pushed herself away and shook her head vigorously. "No, Dwayne! You don't understand I can't do this shit anymore. I'm packing it all in. I'm done. Every year is a gamble on whether or not we make money. Some years we barely make it, and this year did it for me. I can't live with the stress anymore. I want to get a regular job where I get a damn paycheck every week and not wonder where the next dollar is coming from."

Dwayne's face turned pale. His eyes were shallow. "You're serious, aren't you? This is it?"

Tammy nodded. "I'm afraid so. I'll still fish for fun with you. I love the ocean. I just can't work my ass off like this. I miss Matt. He is growing up so fast, and I'm missing out on so much. I want to be a mom to him before he gets too old to need me. I miss my friends." She released a slight chuckle. "Shit, I don't have any close friends. I'm gone too much to make any." She took Dwayne's hand and looked at him with sad eyes. "I just want to be homebound for a while."

"Wow. Well, if that's what you want. I'm not going to force you to fish. I'm behind you one hundred percent. I want you to be happy. But what will you do?"

Tammy leaned her head back against the traps. "I don't know. Maybe I'll start a boat wash-down and detailing business. I'll help you get these traps to Malibu and the ones left in Dana Point, but after that, I need to find something else to do."

Dwayne squeezed her hand. "Okay, but I'll miss you on the boat. I'll have to hire a deckhand."

"Matt can help you, and I can help you get the gear ready. I just don't want to travel miles across the ocean anymore."

"It's okay. You've been a trooper. Do what you have to do. I love you."

Tammy's body collapsed into his lap. "I love you too. Thank you. I'm so tired. I'm going to go lay down."

CHAPTER 26

Tammy took both of Dwayne's hands and held them tight. "Are you sure this is what you want to do? Don't make any hasty decisions."

Dwayne shifted on the bench where they sat in the backyard of their home. "Yeah, I'm sure. Fishing is not like it used to be. I'm struggling just to pay the expenses. Fishing for spider crabs and you doing boat wash-downs keeps us afloat. You quit three years ago, and it's not been the same since," he confessed. "I hate going to the island by myself and being away from you and Matt." He gave Tammy a serious stare. "I'm done. I want to do something else with my life."

"Well, what would you do? Work on boats all year? You'd hate that."

Their two dogs joined them, Sprity, a feisty Jack Russell, and Harley, a mix between an Australian Shepherd and a Hikitia Husky. When Tammy began spending more time at home, she had convinced Dwayne to get a couple of dogs. It made her feel safer when Dwayne was gone fishing for weeks at a time. Tammy smiled at her canine companions and gave them both a playful back rub. "Hey, guys." She said as she leaned down and allowed them to lick her face.

Dwayne shrugged his shoulders. "I don't know yet. Tell you what, let's go camping. We will be away from the boats and the marina and give it some more thought. We'll spend some time with Matt and see what our options are."

Tammy gave him a large grin and patted him on the thigh." Yeah, Matt is seventeen now. I'm not sure how many more camping trips we have left with him before deciding it's not cool anymore to go camping with his parents. When do you want to leave?"

"How about in the morning?"

"Sounds good. I'll go tell Matt and start packing." Before she left, she nuzzled nose to nose with the dogs. "These guys would love to go camping, too, I bet."

~

"So, we've spent three days camping and still haven't decided on whether or not you want to quit fishing," Tammy said as she threw two rolled-up sleeping bags into the back of the truck. She turned her head and saw Matt was busy taking down his tent, and the dogs were chasing ground squirrels down into their holes.

Dwayne used the tailgate of the truck for a table to pack up a lantern. "I don't know what to do. I'm burned out. I'm not getting any younger."

Tammy lifted a tote and slid it in the bed of the truck. "Well, whatever you decide, I'm behind you one hundred percent. We'll manage."

"Do you miss it?"

Tammy turned to face him. "Miss what?"

"Fishing."

Tammy propped herself up on the tailgated and used it for a seat. "Yeah, I miss it. I miss working with you and being on the ocean, but I don't miss not being home or being away from Matt and being dog ass tired all the time. Fishing for me now is a hobby and not a job, and I'm okay with that." She held up her hands. "And look, I have fingernails too now." She laughed.

Dwayne nodded. "Yeah, I've been around the ocean my entire life. I'll never be able to give it up completely."

Tammy rubbed his arm and gave him a loving smile. "And there's no reason you should. You'd still have the *Little Boat* if you quit, right? You wouldn't sell that, would you?"

"Oh, heck no. I have to have at least one boat."

"Well, then. The ocean would be at your disposal whenever we all need a fishing fix. That's what I do now. I jump on the *Little boat* with you and Matt for a fun fishing day on the ocean."

Dwayne paced around the truck and raked his fingers through his hair. "God, I don't know what to do."

"Hey, honey. No one is asking you to make a choice. When the time is right, you will know, and until then, don't stress over it, okay."

"Yeah, you're right. Come on, let's finish packing up and get on the road." He looked over at Matt, who was playing with the dogs. "Almost ready, Matt?" he hollered.

"Yeah, I'm coming. Just gotta grab these two chairs," Matt yelled.

"Hey, I have an idea," Dwayne said from inside the cab where he sat behind the wheel, waiting for Matt and the dogs to climb in the back seat.

"What's that?" Tammy asked.

"Instead of taking the regular route home, let's go the back way over to the five freeway. It's pretty country back there, and it would be nice to do some exploring on our way home."

Tammy beamed him a smile. "Good idea."

Dwayne fired up the truck and turned his head to look at Matt. "What do you think, Matt? Do you want to do some exploring? It will extend our camping trip for a few more hours."

"Sounds great!" Matt said with enthusiasm.

Tammy opened the glove compartment and pulled out a map. She opened it and studied it for a few minutes. "It looks like we take Maricopa highway, which is the thirty-three."

Dwayne nodded. "Yep, that's right. I used to ride my motor-cycle through there. It's pretty. You'll love it."

Tammy's eyes sparkled. "Oh, I'm excited." She looked at the map again. "I guess we will have to turn onto Lockwood Valley road, and that will take us to the five freeway."

Dwayne backed out of their campsite. "Let's go." He said and gave Tammy a loving smile.

Tammy settled back in her seat and glanced out of the window as the truck drove to the exit. Soon they were the only vehicle driving on an endless two-lane highway with spectacular views of mountain ranges and pine trees that went on for miles.

Tammy sat up to take it all in. "God, it's just gorgeous out here. I've not seen another car since we left the campground." She reached over and placed her hand on Dwayne's thigh and gave it a gentle squeeze. "It's so peaceful, and it's only two hours away from home."

Dwayne scanned the views. "It sure is."

"We need to do this more often. I'm so relaxed right now," Tammy said as she leaned back in her seat.

"It would be nice to move to the country and retire, don't you think?" Dwayne stated.

Tammy looked at Dwayne with a creased brow. "Retire? I'm only in my late thirties, and you are in your forties. Retirement won't be happening for a while, I'm afraid." She took in a deep breath. "But yeah, to retire to a place like this would be awesome. I grew up in the country in England, and I miss it. I miss the small, close-knit community. I get so tired of the city and the rat race sometimes. We're always on the go." She released a heavy sigh. "Ah, if only," she chuckled.

Dwayne squeezed her hand that was still resting on his thigh. 'Well, it's nice to dream."

"Look, I see houses," Tammy said as they drove along Lockwood Valley road. "What town is this?"

"I have no idea. I never made it out here."

"Wow, to live out here would be something. They have no neighbors. I wonder what people do for a living?"

"Who knows? Maybe they are retired or have a long commute."

Tammy sat up straight and took everything in. The little town mesmerized her and kept her eyes glued for more houses peeking through the pine trees. "Look, there is a sign up ahead. It says Frazier Park three miles.

"It must be another small town," Dwayne said.

"Oh, fun!" Tammy squealed.

Soon they were surrounded by more houses nestled amongst the pine tree. Tammy looked to her right. "Look, a pond and people are fishing in it. How cute is that, and look, there is a playground for the kids too?" Tammy said, her voice exploding with excitement.

"There's a baseball field too," Matt said from the backseat."

"You like this town, Matt?" Tammy asked.

"Yeah, it's pretty cool. It's so quiet. Not many cars and only a few stores."

Dwayne pulled up to a flashing red stop signal and looked to his left. "I wonder where that road goes?"

Tammy followed his stare. "Let's go take a look."

Dwayne made the left turn. They pulled up to another stop sign. "This must be the main road that goes through the town. Look, they have a few stores and some restaurants," Dwayne said as he made a right.

Tammy looked across the valley and up at the tall mountain covered with pine trees. "And look at that view. This town is based at the bottom of that mountain."

"That must be Frazier Mountain. They have everything they need here, and I've not seen one traffic light."

Tammy beamed Dwayne a smile. "Let's come back next weekend and explore this place. I want to see more of it."

"I'm spending the night over at my buddy's house next weekend. We're going fishing, remember?" Matt butted in.

Tammy turned her head to look at him. "That's fine, me and Dwayne can come up. She rubbed Dwayne's leg and gave him a flirtatious smile. "What do you say?"

"Sounds like a plan to me."

CHAPTER 27

"I've been thinking about this place all week," Tammy said as Dwayne took the Frazier Park exit off the freeway.

"Me too." He turned to Tammy and grinned. "We should see if there are any real estate offices and go check out some houses. What do you think?"

Tammy creased her brow. "You want to buy a house up here? What will you do for a living? I don't see an ocean nearby, or boats for that matter. You haven't officially quit fishing. And I do boat wash-downs for a living, don't forget."

"I know. I just want to look around. We're up here. We might as well."

Tammy shrugged her shoulders. "Okay. It won't hurt, I guess. Then we can try out that pizza place I saw last week."

Tammy and Dwayne scanned the signs over the buildings in search of a real estate office. A few minutes later, Tammy hollered. "There's one! Pull into that driveway."

Dwayne saw where she was pointing and parked in front of the building. "I wonder if they are open on Saturdays," Dwayne said.

"Well, the only way to find out is to try the door," Tammy said, wearing a sarcastic grin as she stepped out of the truck.

Dwayne reached the front door of the office before Tammy and pulled the handle. The door swung open in his direction. "They are open." He smiled.

A pretty, middle-aged woman sat behind a desk studying some papers. She looked up over glasses. "Hi. Can I help you?"

Dwayne approached her desk and extended his hand. She smiled and gave him a firm handshake. "Yeah. We're just checking out the town and we're wondering if there were any properties we could check out. This is my wife, Tammy, and I'm Dwayne."

She gave them a friendly smile. "I'm Kate. We have some listings," she said, turning to a file cabinet against the wall behind her.

"This is a charming town. We passed through it on our way back from camping last week and came and checked it out." Tammy said.

Kate spoke as she fumbled through the file cabinet. "I love it here. I've been here for over twenty years. The people are great, and we all know and watch out for each other." She pulled out a file. "Here you go. This is a list of all the houses for sale in Frazier Park and the surrounding towns. I'll give you a map and my business card. If you see anything and want to go inside, call me. I'd be happy to show you around."

Dwayne took the papers and browsed through them. "Wow! This is great thank you so much." He looked at the papers again and then at the map. "This one doesn't look like it's too far. It says it's on Lillie Lane."

"Yep. About five minutes away."

Tammy took the papers from Dwayne's hand and studied them. "Is that the right price?" Tammy asked.

"Yep. It's an old house. No one has lived there for over fifteen years. It's going to need a lot of work. You'll find the prices of the property up here pretty cheap."

"I'd say," Dwayne replied. "That's a fifth of what houses cost in the city." He turned to Tammy and took her hand. "So, do you want to go check it out?"

Tammy smiled. "I do."

Dwayne shook Kate's hand. "Thank you so much, Kate. We'll be in touch."

Kate smiled. "My pleasure. If you decide to move up here, you will love it."

Tammy studied the map while Dwayne put the truck in gear and headed into town. "Keep going straight up that hill," Tammy said and pointed up ahead.

A few minutes later, Dwayne spotted Lillie Lane. "There it is."

Dwayne turned the truck onto a dirt road and started checking the addresses. Halfway up the street, he spots it. "There it is on the left."

Tammy crouched her neck and looked through the window on Dwayne's side. "Oh, wow! She's not kidding. It needs a lot of work. It looks like something out of an old John Wayne movie." Tammy chuckled.

"Come on, let's go take a closer look," Dwayne said eagerly and turned off the truck.

Tammy looked at the old wooden rickety fence surrounding the property. It had a good lean to it. "I wonder how old this fence is," she said as she walked through the gate.

"Probably as old as the house," Dwayne chuckled.

Tammy took in a deep breath and filled her lungs with the fresh air. "God, the air up here is as good as the ocean, and look at that view. We can see the entire mountain from here."

"Yeah, we're pretty high up. The map says five thousand feet."

"They must get snow here. God, it's been ages since I've seen the snow." She grabbed Dwayne's hand. "Come on, let's look around."

"This is a big lot. Much bigger than we have at home, and look, there is an old garage, another building, and then some kind of covered area over to the left," Dwayne said excitedly.

Tammy pulled Dwayne toward the old cabin. "It's a cute place, but man, will it need some work. Not trusting the old wooden steps that led up to the house, she lightly placed her feet on each step, in fear they may cave beneath her."

"Careful," Dwayne said, who was close behind her. "This whole place may collapse."

Tammy laughed and peeked through the dusty front window on the porch. "It looks pretty big inside."

Dwayne stood next to her and admired the heavy wooden door. "I think this whole place needs to be torn down. There's no way we could bring it up to code. But man, the size of the property is great, and I love that view."

"Who would have thought such a place existed just a few hours out of The Marina. I could see us living here. The dogs would love it."

"You do?" Dwayne said. "What are you saying? You want to move here?"

Tammy skipped down the steps and spun around in a circle with her arms spread like an eagle. "Well, look at this place, Dwayne. We could make this a home. I could grow the garden I've always wanted. We'd have all this space. It's perfect. And look, since we've been here, not one car has gone by."

"I hear you. But what would we do for a living?"

"I have no idea," Tammy laughed. "Who says we have to move up here right away. We could come up on weekends and fix it up, and besides, Matt is still in school. He only has two years left. I wouldn't pull him out of school."

Dwayne gave Tammy a sweet smile and took her in his arms. He kissed her passionately on the lips and gazed into her eyes. "I like your way of thinking. I wouldn't mind changing our lives over a period of time. I guess you could call it a slow transition. I could still fish while we figure out what we want to do."

Tammy gave him a big grin. "Really! You like the idea of living up here too?"

"I do. Shall I call Kate, or do you want to look at some other places?"

"No. This is the one. It's screaming home to me, and I don't need to look anywhere else. Call Kate."

"Well, instead of trying to find a phone-booth, let's just go back to her office. I'm sure she's still there."

Tammy wrapped herself in Dwayne's arms and smiled. "Are we really going to buy this place?"

"I don't know, Tammy," Dwayne Laughed. "We've never bought a house before, but the price sure is affordable. Just don't get your hopes up, okay."

"I won't. Come on, let's go. I don't want to miss Kate."

Tammy and Dwayne couldn't stop smiling when they left Kate's office over two hours later. Tammy leaped down the steps and did a sexy twirl at the bottom. "I can't believe we may be homeowners soon."

"Me neither. I didn't have any plans to put an offer on the house today, and not only that, it's the first and only house we've seen."

"I know me neither. I can't wait to tell Matt."

CHAPTER 28

*T*ammy sat outside at the patio table with her morning coffee and admired the beautiful view of the mountain. She had done so for the past ten years since she and Dwayne had taken the plunge and brought their diamond in the rough piece of property. She inhaled deeply, her arms extended into a full stretch, and filled her lungs with the refreshing air. "God, I'll never get tired of this." Tammy enjoyed her morning ritual of having at least two cups of coffee while reading a couple of chapters from a good book. Afterward, she would be ready to feed their seventeen chickens and what she believed to be now over one hundred pigeons.

The chickens were among the first things they had bought when they finally moved full time to the mountains—two years after they had purchased the property.

Matt had graduated high school just shy of nine years ago and still lives in the city where he has been an electrician ever since. Dwayne's son Jason moved out of state and has his own family now. He keeps in touch and tries to visit a few times a year.

The marina's two-hour commute soon grew old, and they cut

ties with the marina completely. Dwayne quit fishing, sold both boats, and was able to fix up the guest house, which is where they have been living for the last eight years.

It had been a struggle in the beginning. While they worked on making the guest house livable, they lived in a tiny trailer left on the property when they bought it. Dwayne worked in construction for the first few years, and Tammy dove into the new internet technology and began an online sales business. She also helped Dwayne on some of his jobs and spent a lot of time working on their property. She especially loved the weekends because that was the time they spent working together building the guest house. She missed working with him.

Tammy had no regrets. She loved the slower pace of life, the sparsely populated town, and the friendly people that had welcomed them with home-baked apple pie and new friendships. Tammy planned on checking her vegetable garden after the birds had been fed and giving it a good soak before the scorching sun rose high in the sky. Tammy wasted no time starting the garden and looked forward every year to picking her fresh vegetables and bringing them to the table. It was a dream of hers to have a garden someday, but it had been impossible while fishing and gone for weeks at a time.

Tammy looked over at the main house and chuckled. It still looked exactly like it did when they first bought the place, except the master bedroom was now her office. Complete with a computer and everything she needed to run her online business. They hadn't planned to live in the guest house for over eight years, but their only free time was on weekends when they didn't have to work. The guest house, or as they liked to call it the Tiny house, was cozy and easy to maintain, but the downside was they had no room for guests, which both their parents had pointed out when they saw the place for the first time.

Even though Tammy no longer fished, her mom missed America and continued to visit every year. When they moved to the mountains, she would stay in the hotel just out-of-town by the freeway.

They had long talks over tea at the patio table outside the tiny house. "I can't wait to see the new house built, Tammy." her mom had said on many of her visits.

"Me neither." Tammy would laugh. "One day, it will be done, and you can stay in the tiny house. Our problem is, we only have weekends to work on it."

Tammy was pleased that her dad had made a quick visit when he was in the states on a book tour a few years ago, and since then, his first question had always been when he called, "How is the house coming?"

Tammy would try to talk to her dad at least once a week. Now that she had a computer, she helped him with book orders from his website. Stored at her house was an inventory of his books, and when orders were placed, Tammy shipped them out. A shipment was expected any day now with his latest book. Her dad had been calling every morning to see if they had arrived. Tammy hoped to see a UPS truck pull up in front of her gate this afternoon so she would have good news for her dad tomorrow.

Tammy looked up and smiled. Dwayne suddenly appeared at the doorway of the tiny house. He yawned and raked his hands through his uncombed hair. The sunlight glistened on his bare chest as he felt for his cigarettes in the shorts he wore and joined Tammy at the table.

"Morning, beautiful," he said as he took a seat and lit a smoke. "Want one?" he asked, holding out the pack.

Tammy reached over and took a cigarette. "Sure." She leaned back and took a deep drag. "Man, I love these mornings. What time do you have to leave?"

"As soon as I'm dressed and loaded up the birds." He glanced at his cell phone he had just set down on the table. "In about half an hour, I guess."

Tammy took a sip of her coffee. "Did you ever think you'd get back into falconry?" Dwayne shook his head. "Nope. If it weren't for that falcon I heard a few years back; I'd still be doing construction."

Tammy chuckled at the memory. "Yep. That ignited the fire again, and within a few months, you had a falcon. Now, look at you. You quit construction, have six falcons, and do bird abatement for a living. You went from the ocean to the sky," Tammy laughed.

"Yeah. It was back in my teens when I started it. Way before I met you." he chuckled.

"I know. I remember you telling me. I would have loved to know you back then." Tammy said with a loving smile.

"So, what are your plans for today?"

Tammy released a heavy sigh. "Well, I'm hoping my dad's books arrive today so dad will get out of my hair and quit calling me all the time. I also have a ton of work to do in the office." She petted Harley, who rubbed his back against her legs. "And I'll take these two for a good hike." She said as she gave Harley a mean back rub.

Dwayne leaned in and gave Tammy a peck on the cheek before standing to his feet. Okay, I have to get out of here. I love you. I'll see you tonight."

Tammy smiled. "Okay."

Tammy checked her cellphone. It was almost three o'clock. "Where the hell is the UPS guy? God, I hope those books come today." Tammy mumbled as she walked across the yard to the tiny house with Harley and Sprity following closely behind. She turned around and looked at them. "Yes, I know you want to go for a walk, but I can't leave yet. I'm afraid I'll miss the USP truck." Tammy suddenly froze. "Shh, do you hear that?" Tammy asked her dogs as she raced to the front fence. "It sounds like a truck." She leaned over and looked down the street. "Yes! It's UPS."

She grinned. "Oh, please stop here," she begged out loud. A few minutes later, her wish came true.

Tammy beamed at Tom, the UPS driver, with a huge smile when he stepped out of the truck.

"Afternoon Tammy. I have a heavy package for you."

"Yes, they are my dad's books. He's been calling me all week about them. Can you set them on the front porch for me, please?" Tammy asked as she opened the gate.

"Sure, no problem."

After Tom had left, Tammy wasted no time calling her dad in Ireland. She hoped her Dad would answer the phone and not his new wife of three years, who she had never met or knew. She still considered Joanne her other mom, even though she and John had divorced many years ago. Tammy still kept in touch with Joanne as often as she could. She might not be her father's wife anymore, but she will always be family to Tammy.

Tammy released a sigh of relief when she heard her dad's voice on the phone. "Hey, Dad, it's Tammy. Your books came."

"Well, about bloody time. I'm glad to hear it. I'm going to email you some addresses of readers that have ordered the book. Can you ship them out tomorrow? And Andrew will put the book up on the website, so you'll be in charge of the orders."

"Got it, dad."

"So, how's the house coming?" John asked.

Tammy rolled her eyes. He never failed to ask. She gave him her usual answer. "Fine, dad. Maybe it will be done by the time you visit again."

"That would be nice. Listen, I have to go. Thanks for letting me know the books have arrived."

"Sure, no problem. Love you, dad."

"Love you too."

Tammy ended the call and gave her two dogs, who sat at her feet, a huge smile. "Guess what, guys! We can go for a walk now. Come on, let's go."

Tammy spent the next morning loading up her car with books she had packed for shipping last night. Dwayne had left for work a few hours ago, and she wanted to get to the post office early so she would have the rest of the day to do other projects that she had planned. She stood back and looked at the pile of manila envelopes on her back seat from readers anxious to read her father's book. She was so proud of him and what he had accomplished. "What an amazing feeling it must be to have people order a book you wrote," Tammy mumbled to herself as she put the last few envelopes in her car. "I'm going to write a book someday." She confessed out loud. "And I know exactly what it's going to be about." She added with an attitude before pushing the car door closed. "Now, where the hell did I put my keys?"

Tammy headed into the office to begin the dreaded search for her keys when the phone rang. She looked at the number on the caller ID and didn't recognize it. "Hello?" she asked with some uncertainty.

An unfamiliar male voice came on the line. "Hello, is this Tammy?"

"Yes, it is. Who is this?"

"I'm a friend of your dad. My name is Jeffery. I'm afraid I have some sad news."

Tammy heard him take a deep breath. It scared her. "What is it? Is my dad okay?"

"I'm so sorry, but your dad passed away early this morning."

CHAPTER 29

*T*ammy screamed at the top of her voice. "Oh my god! No!" Her knees buckled, and she fell to the floor. Her sobs were fierce. "How can that be? I just spoke to him last night. He sounded fine. He was happy after I had told him the books had finally arrived."

"It was very sudden. He had a heart attack."

Tammy shook her head in disbelief and rocked herself. Tears pooled from her eyes. "I can't believe this—not dad. He was only sixty-nine. He was supposed to be around for another twenty years." Tammy's heart ached from the pain, knowing she would never see her father again or hear his voice. She couldn't hold back her tears long enough to talk. Her body trembled, and her hands shook. "I'm sorry I have to go," she said as she hung up the phone.

It was then that she let herself go and screamed, "No, dad! No! Oh my god, dad! Why you?" She brought her hand up to her mouth to muffle her pained cries and continued to rock back and forth with her knees tight up under her chin. "This can't be happening. Please tell me I'm in a bad dream. Come on, Tammy, wake up." But she didn't wake up. "I have to call Dwayne and my sisters. Oh my god and mom." Tammy had another round of hard tears. "It will devastate mom." She cried out. Her mom had told her once that she never stopped loving her father, and funnily enough, her dad had said the same thing about her mother. "God, they were just too stubborn to admit it to each other," Tammy yelled out loud. She thought of her sister, Donna, and Jenny and wondered how they would react. Things she had wished she had done raced through her mind. Shit, dad never saw his three daughters together again since he left home when I was twelve years old. That was thirty-two years ago.

Her mom's voice haunted her mind. *I only have one wish: to see all three of my girls in the same room. Is that too much to ask Tammy?* "No, it's not, mom," Tammy whispered. "I should have done something about it years ago," she said in an angered tone. Tammy spat out her next words. "I won't let you down, mom."

Tammy turned around and walked over to a photograph hanging on the wall. It was one of her and her dad at Disney World in Florida. She must have been about fourteen. It was shortly after her parents had divorced. Tammy spent the summer with her dad. She traced her dad's face with her finger. "Oh, dad. I'm going to miss you so much. Why is life so unfair?" Tammy took down the frame and kissed the picture. Tears streamed down her face. "I love you, dad." She sniffed hard to push back her tears. "I can't believe you are gone." and placed the picture on her desk where it would be close. "I need to call Dwanye."

He answered on the second ring, and Tammy's emotions took over. She cried hard into the phone, unable to speak.

"Tammy! Is that you?" Dwayne asked in a panicked state. All he heard were her sobs. "Tammy, talk to me! Are you okay?"

"My dad is dead," Tammy said between her heavy tears.

"Our dog is dead? Oh, no! Which one?" Dwayne cried.

Tammy continued to cry and choked out her next words. "No, my Dad! My dad is dead."

"Oh my god! No! What happened?"

Tammy continued to choke on her words. "He had a heart attack. He's gone, Dwayne."

"Oh, sweetheart. I'm coming home. I'll be there in an hour. I love you."

"I love you too. I gotta go."

~

Tammy didn't remember the last few days. They were a blur. She walked around in a daze, numb, and feeling the saddest she had ever felt. Unable to wrap her head around the fact that her father was gone. Tammy thought of his writing and how, just last month, they had a long conversation over the phone about his latest novel that he had been working on. He had so much more to write. And now that book will never get finished.

Tammy waited a day before calling her mom and sisters. As she had expected, her mom took it the hardest. "I need to see my girls, Tammy. This could be me tomorrow. I'm older than your dad by five years." Rose had cried down the phone.

"I know, mom. This is just as important to me as it is to you. Now, even more, since dad has passed." Tammy had replied.

Tammy sat on the grass in a lounge chair wrapped in a blanket, chilled by the night air. Two days had passed since the devastating news of her father's death, and it was all she could think about. She looked up into the night skies and watched a shooting star, smiling for the first time in days. "Hi, dad, is that you?" It bought her comfort thinking it was. Tammy turned and looked at the old house that still needed to be built and whispered, "Dad will never get to see the new house." Thoughts of her dad's house in Ireland clouded her mind. It was a place she had never visited but had every intention to one day. It was a part of her dad unknown to her. She had no idea how her dad had lived or what his office looked like. Growing up, Tammy remembered her father always had a reading chair. Did he have one in his home in Ireland? Tammy sat up straight. She needed to know these things and connect with the last part of her father's life. And the only way she could do that was to go to Ireland.

Lost in her thoughts, Tammy didn't hear Dwayne open the gate to the grass. "Hey, are you okay? It's getting cold out here," he asked before taking the seat next to her.

Tammy nodded and smiled. "I'm going to Ireland."

Dwayne's jaw dropped."What?"

"You heard me. I'm going to Ireland." Tammy rubbed his knee. "I need to do this. It just hit me. His funeral will be there, and I wasn't sure If I could go because I don't have a passport. But there's a way to get it expedited. But there's more to it. I need to connect with where dad lived before they sell the house. And not only that, Jenny and Donna can't afford to travel. One of us needs to be there for dad."

Dwayne nodded. "I get you, Tammy. Do whatever you must do. I'm behind you one hundred percent. You know I won't be able to go because of all the animals."

"Yeah, I know that, and thank you."

A week later, Tammy arrived in Dublin, Ireland. She had doubts she would make it in time for her father's funeral, which was to be held the next day. But the passport office came through and issued her an emergency passport two days ago. Tammy scanned the small airport In search of Elsa, her stepmother, who Tammy hardly knew. A woman resembling pictures Tammy had received stood away from the crowds waving her hands above her head. Tammy smiled and waved back and walked in her direction with her one suitcase in tow.

"Elsa?"

"Yes. Tammy, Hi."

Tammy freed her hands from her luggage and embraced Elsa. Tears immediately flowed. "I can't believe dad has gone."

Elsa welcomed her embrace and held her tight. "I know me too. It's a shock to all of us."

Tammy pulled away and wiped her tears. "Were you there?"

Elsa shook her head. "No, I was at the store. I found him when I returned."

Tammy gasped. "Oh, I'm so sorry."

Elsa pulled out a tissue and dried her eyes. "It's okay. I'm just happy you are here. Andrew is flying in tomorrow morning and will stay in town with his wife."

"Oh, wow! I've not seen him in over twenty years."

"I've met him a few times," Elsa replied. "Come on, let's get on the road. We have a two-hour drive ahead of us."

Tammy didn't speak much in the car. This was her first time in Ireland, and she sat in silence, taking it all in. It was beautiful and reminded her so much of England with its luscious green rolling hills and damp, dewy weather. "I can see why dad moved here," Tammy whispered to herself.

Tammy immediately saw the big red barn that her father had bragged about many times when they pulled into her father's driveway. He hadn't been joking when he told her it was huge, and he had no idea what he was going to use it for. It had become a frequent joke during their phone conversations. Tammy looked around the few acres of land that surrounded the stone farmhouse and wept. This is what her dad always wanted—a house in the country where he could write his books.

Elsa opened her door. "Are you ready to go inside?"

Tammy shook her head. "No, I need a few minutes. I'll be in a bit."

Elsa rested her hand on Tammy's shoulder. "Take your time. I know how difficult this must be."

Tammy waited until she was alone, and then the tears came heavy. Through her tears, she spotted her dad's red car parked in the barn and his wellington boots sitting outside the house's back door. Tammy didn't know if she could go into the house without losing it and screamed, "I can't do this, dad," as tears continued to gush down her face. "I want to see you." Tammy tilted her head back into the seat and let out a heart-wrenching cry. "This is so fucking hard." She sobbed and buried her head into her hands.

Tammy didn't know how long she cried for the loss of her dad. Elsa had come out once and asked if she was okay, and Tammy had nodded. Somehow, Tammy found the strength deep within to gain her composure and tried to focus on finding the door handle to the car through her swollen drenched eyes. The unbearable pounding headache that tortured her head was the worst she had ever experienced. Rubbing her temples didn't provide any relief.

The skies were now dark when she stepped out of the car. Tammy embraced herself to block out the night time chills and once again looked up to the stars. A bright star caught her attention, and she smiled. "Hi, dad. Do you see me? I'm sorry I never came to your house sooner. I would have loved for you to show me around and go into town for lunch with you." Tammy blew a kiss to the star. "I miss you." and turned to walk towards the house.

When her hand touched the doorknob, Tammy took a deep breath before turning the knob and then slowly entered her father's home and found herself standing in the kitchen. Elsa must have heard the door and came from another room off to the left. Like Tammy's, her eyes had evidence of tears. She raced to Tammy and embraced her. "I miss your father," she cried.

"I know. I do too. I feel dad here. I'm so glad I came." Tammy glanced around the cozy country-style kitchen with its wooden cupboards and pine floors.

"Do you want a cup of tea?" Elsa asked.

Tammy took a seat at the large wooden planked table. "Sure, that would be great." and scanned the counters and saw many of her dad's favorites, Gingersnap cookies, Marmite, and treacle, and then she spotted his hat hanging on the back of the door. "Oh, dad," she whispered before she left her seat and freed the hat from its hook. "I remember this hat. He's had this for ages." Tammy said as she glided her fingers across the top of it.

Elsa glanced over her shoulder. "Yes, that was his favorite. Take it home if you'd like."

"Can I?"

Elsa nodded. "Of course."

Tammy didn't return to her seat. Instead, she walked over to one of many of her dad's bookshelves and began looking through his collection. Many she recognized from when she was a child. "Wow. I can't believe dad still has some of these."

"Yes, your dad rarely got rid of his books. Those books have moved everywhere with him," Elsa smiled.

"And still no TV, right?" Tammy joked.

"That's right. He's never owned one, as I'm sure you know."

Engrossed in getting to know about her father's last chapter of life, Tammy wasn't paying attention to where each doorway led and soon found herself in a living room. A cozy brick fireplace decorated with what she recognized as her grandparent's brass ornament collection was the room's focal point. "Wow! I remember these," Tammy whispered while carefully picking one up to inspect it. Memories of her grandparents flooded her mind and the house where they lived. Pictures of her and her sisters and one of a young man who had an un-canning resemblance to her dad adorned the mantel. "That must be Andrew. Damn, he looks like dad," To the left was another picture of three young men. All looked like dad. Tammy realized they were the other two half-brothers she had never met.

Through her tears, she glanced around the room and clutched her heart when she focused on the brown armchair with a pair of slippers next to it. Draped over the back was a wool blanket. "Oh, dad." Tammy cried as she slowly walked over to the chair and took a seat. Chilled by her emotions, she pulled the blanket from the back of the chair and buried her face into the soft wool. It had the scent of her dad's cologne—Old Spice. "God, I miss you so much, dad."

Tammy stayed in the chair for some time, afraid to leave the comfort that her father's scent bought her. That was until she noticed another door off to the left.

Tammy had a feeling she knew where it led and dragged herself out of the chair and wrapped herself in her father's blanket. When she reached the door, she took in a deep breath and slowly turned the handle. Her intuition was right; it was her father's office. Frozen in the doorway, her body trembled, and her emotions were high from seeing her dad's office for the first time. Tammy gasped and bought her hand up to her mouth before releasing a heart-wrenching cry. "Oh, my god."

The room was wall to wall bookshelves, posters of his book covers, and many awards. In the middle of the room were two desks connected in an L shape; Tammy walked over to the desk and slid her hand over the mahogany wood as she pictured her dad sitting in the leather chair creating his next novel. She took a seat, leaned back, and closed her eyes as tears streamed down her face. All of her dad's dedicated work over the past thirty years had come to an end. There would be no more stories. Tammy couldn't believe it. His sudden departure from the world numbed her to the core. When she opened her eyes and glanced over his desk, the memory of how organized he had always been popped into her head. Everything on the desk had a place. To the left was a yellow legal-size notepad. Tammy picked it up and recognized her dad's neat handwriting. There seemed to be notes for the book he had been working on. To the left, next to a container of pencil, Tammy saw a trinket she had sent him a few years ago for his birthday and smiled. It was a small statue that said, *World's Greatest Dad.* She picked it up and studied it before holding it close to her chest. "He still has it."

As sad as the moment was, Tammy felt at peace sitting in her father's chair. She felt his presence and snuggled into the blanket still wrapped around her shoulders. The connection she yearned for had been made. Her trip to Ireland had filled in the blanks when it came to the last chapter of her dad's life. She had no more questions.

Tammy wanted to make her father proud, just like he had done her all his life. She couldn't have asked for a better father and was who she was today because of him. Tomorrow was going to be the hardest day of her life when she will stand before family and friends to read the eulogy at the funeral. Tammy hadn't begun to write it; she couldn't. It was just too hard. But sitting in her dad's office had given her the strength she had been missing. Through her words, the world would know what a great man he was, and that he left behind an amazing legacy. Tammy felt confident she could deliver the farewell he deserved.

On the day of the funeral, Tammy had no problem spotting her half-brother Andrew amongst the crowd of people gathered to say their final goodbyes to John. He was a younger version of their father, with short black hair, a chiseled chin, identical to her dad's, and a tall body frame. She collapsed into his arms and let her tears fall. Andrew held her tight until Tammy was able to pull herself together. "The last time I saw you, you were just a toddler. I'm sure you don't remember me," Tammy said with a half-smile. "I can't believe how much time has gone by. Dad's death has made me realize how short life really is."

"I've seen pictures of me sitting on your lap when you lived at dad's house in Lonesridge." Does that count?" Andrew laughed. "But we have the next two days to catch up and get to know each other."

Tammy gave him a caring smile and took his hand. "Yeah, I'm going to like that."

❧

By the time Tammy headed home, her heart was filled with memories of her dad's home and the funeral. She felt she did her father proud and hoped he was smiling down upon her from heaven as she read the eulogy. On the plane, heading back to America, Tammy reminisced on reconnecting with her half-brother Andrew, who reminded her so much of her dad. They compared their childhood days and laughed at how similar they were. Andrew talked of his two younger brothers, Conner and Bobby, who could not travel to Ireland. "I sure hope I get to meet them someday," Tammy said while listening to Andrew describe them. Together through tears and laughter, they toasted to the memory of their dad in the pubs, and when it was time to say goodbye, Tammy felt she had gained a lost brother.

On her long journey home with plenty of idle time to think, Tammy's thoughts turned to her mother and her one wish, to have all her three daughters together. Guilt swept through Tammy. Her mother had dreamt about a reunion for years, but Tammy had always been too busy to give it much thought. Bust as she sat on the plane, alone, deep in thought, she realized her mother was right when she had said, "Any one of us could die tomorrow." Tammy was done procrastinating and knew it was time to make it happen, but Donna struggled as a widow and didn't have the funds to travel. The only way Tammy could make it happen would be when her mom visited the states. Tammy was going to call Jenny in England and see if she could come with mom on her next trip.

CHAPTER 30

Tammy smiled when she spotted Dwayne at the airport and raced into his arms. She kissed him hard and melted into his embrace. It felt good to be held by him. It's where she belonged.

Dwayne held her tight. "Oh, I've missed you so much, Tammy." He kissed her again and studied her eyes. "How are you doing? Are you holding up okay?"

Tammy nodded and rested her head on his shoulder. "Yeah, I'm okay. I'm so tired." She looked up and gave him a loving smile. "Even though it was one of the toughest things I had to do, I'm glad I went. It gave me closure."

"I wish I could have been with you to support you," Dwayne said with pity in his eyes.

Tammy patted his chest and pulled away. "It's okay. How could you with the farm we have back home," she chuckled

Dwayne changed the subject. "Hey, if you feel up to it, Matt wants to meet us for dinner. He wants to hear all about your trip."

The thought made Tammy smile. "I would like that. I've not seen much of him since dad passed, and I have to remember he lost a grandpa too. I'll call him from the car and see where he wants to meet."

"Sound good," Dwayne said as he grabbed Tammy's luggage.

They arrived at Cocoa's restaurant shortly after five. Tammy was exhausted, but she was excited to see Matt. Tammy figured she could sleep in the car on their drive home.

Anita, Matt's girlfriend of two years, also joined them. They had met at a party and were the same age.

Tammy beamed her a smile as she took a seat at the table across from them. "I didn't know you were going to be here."

Anita laughed. "Surprise."

"You look good." Tammy always loved it when Anita wore her thick, long black hair down. It was far too pretty to hide and tie back. "Your hair looks great."

Matt raised his hand and ran it across Anita's head, pulling her hair back away from her face. "You do have pretty hair." He turned and faced Tammy. "How are you doing, mom? Are you okay?"

"Yeah, I am. It was rough, but your grandfather is smiling down upon us. I'll miss him. But going to Ireland was a good decision. It filled in so many gaps with the relationship I had with him, and even though he is no longer with us and as strange as it may sound, I feel closer to him."

Dwayne took Tammy's hand and kissed it. "It makes sense."

Matt turned to Anita and smiled, and she nodded. "Well, we were going to wait until after dinner to tell you, but I think you need cheering up," Matt said with a huge grin.

Tammy looked at him suspiciously, "Tell me what?"

"Anita is pregnant."

Tammy gasped and raised her hands to her mouth. "What!" She turned to Dwayne, who looked as shocked as she felt. "Oh my god, I'm going to be a grandma."

Matt and Anita laughed together, "Yes, you are mom," Matt laughed.

"And you are going to be a daddy." She turned to Anita and

took her hand. "And you will be a mommy." Tammy shook her head in disbelief and dabbed her eyes with a nearby paper napkin. "I can't believe it. I'm going to be a grandma. My baby boy is going to be a dad."

Dwayne reached across the table and gave Matt a firm hand-shake. "Congratulations, son.

I guess that makes me a grandpa, right? Can I have that title?" Dwayne joked.

"You're damn right, you are," Matt laughed. But his laughter was cut short when he noticed Tammy looked sad and seemed to be deep in thought. "Mom, are you okay?"

"Yes. I was just thinking about how sad it is that your grandfa-ther will not be here to meet his first great-grandson. It's strange how one great life has ended, and a new one is about to begin." Tammy said as she wiped away a tear.

"Yeah, me too," Matt replied. "I know we are not married yet, but the baby will have grandpa's last name."

Tammy sucked in some air. "Oh, that's wonderful. Your grandpa would have been so proud of you." Tammy shook her head to keep back her tears. "I still can't believe he is gone. I've been thinking a lot lately about all the stuff I want to do in life. Life is so precious. None of us know how much time we have. Look at Donna's husband, Jason. He was so young when he died." She turned to Dwayne and squeezed his hand. "We have to get our house built. I want my mom and your parents to see it." Tammy thought of the other things she had been procrastinating for years." I want mom to see all her girls together. Do you realize it's been over thirty-two years since we were all together?" She looked over at Matt. "Jenny has never met you, Matt."

"I know, and I've never met her kids either."

Tammy leaned back in the booth. "God, there's so much I want to do. I've had an idea for a book ever since I was with Steven. I'm going to think more seriously about that too."

Dwayne sat up. A look of surprise blanketed his face. "A book? You never told me you wanted to write a book."

Tammy laughed. I haven't told anyone. It's just an idea I've carried with me all these years. I'm just going to give it some more thought—anyway, enough about me. Let's order our food. I'm not sure how much longer I'll be able to stay awake," she joked.

CHAPTER 31

ammy woke the next morning anxious to call Jenny in England. She couldn't wait to tell her she was going to be a grandmother and her idea about Jenny coming to the States with their mom.

Tammy calculated in her head the years the twins had been separated and was stunned, "Wow! Thirty-five years." She glanced at the latest two pictures she had of them hanging on the wall. They no longer looked alike—Donna had long bleached blonde hair and wore a lot of make-up. Jenny was the opposite—little make-up and long dark brown hair. Tammy wondered if she would notice any physical similarities or habits in person. It was impossible to tell from a photograph.

After her usual three cups of morning coffee and seeing Dwayne off to work, Tammy settled into a patio chair outside the tiny house and dialed Jenny's number. She answered after three rings.

"Hello, Jenny, speaking."

"Hey, Jenny, it's Tammy. I'm home now."

"Oh, hello, Tammy," Jenny said in a thick English accent. "I was going to call you later today to see if you were home. How was it? I'm so sorry we couldn't make it to Ireland. We will miss Dad immensely."

"Yes, he will be missed. It was one of the hardest things I have ever done, but dad's at peace now. It was a beautiful service, and we made dad proud. Please don't feel bad about not being there. You are always there for mom when I can't be."

"Thank you, Tammy. I got the pictures you mailed from Ireland, and I'm glad you called. I wanted to talk to you about mom."

Tammy raised her tone a notch. "Is mom okay?"

"Well, I hope so. She's been acting differently lately."

Tammy creased her brow. "Different? How?"

"I'm sure it's nothing serious. She just seems to forget a lot lately, and she seems a little confused about some things."

"Like what?" Tammy asked.

"Well, the other day, she put her shoes on the wrong feet and never realized it until I said something to her. She laughed it off, but I found it strange."

"Wow, I can see why. Do you think it's just old age?"

"I don't know, Tammy. She's not that old, and her body is as fit as a fiddle. I just wanted to let you know mom has changed a bit, and I'll be visiting her more often so I can keep an eye on her."

"That's good to know, Jenny. Keep me posted on how she's doing."

"I will."

Tammy smiled when she spoke. "I do have some brighter news."

Jenny's tone switched to a lighter tone. "You do. What is it?"

"I'm going to be a grandma." Tammy squealed into the phone. "Matt and Anita are going to have a baby."

Jenny gasped. "Oh my goodness! I'm going to be an auntie. Oh, congratulations, Tammy. I'm so happy for you. It's such a shame dad will never get to meet his first great-grandchild."

"I know." Tammy hesitated for a moment and decided not to mention to Jenny her idea of coming over next year with their mom. She felt it wasn't the right time after what Jenny had told her about their mom's health.

After their conversation had ended, Tammy left to take a much-needed shower. She hadn't bathed since leaving Ireland. Standing naked, she checked the water with her hand before stepping into the shower stall and closed her eyes as the water soothed her. "Man, that feels good," she whispered and reached for the soap. After a few minutes, she paused when she felt the lump again on the underside of her right breast. "Huh. It's still there." Tammy ran her hand around the area. She had discovered it a week before her trip to Ireland. It was still that same size. Tammy assumed it was a bug bite and thought nothing of it. But today, she became concerned. "Bug bites don't last two weeks." Tammy squeezed it. It was hard and about an inch in diameter close to the surface. "I wonder what it is?" Thoughts of cancer crossed her mind, but she quickly discarded the ridiculous notion with a vigorous shake of her head. "I'm only in my forties. I'm too young to have cancer." Tammy decided if the lump were still there next week, she'd make an appointment with the doctors. For now, her mind was made up not to say anything to Dwayne or Matt.

Tammy continued to check for the lump every night, and her anxieties increased when it was still there a week later. "Fuck. What the hell could it be?" She wondered after stepping out of the shower Friday evening.

Dwayne knew her well and noticed her sad look. "Hey, are you okay?"

Now dressed in her bathrobe, Tammy took a seat next to him on the small two-seater couch. "I hope so."

Dwayne sat up from his relaxed position. "What does that mean?"

"I'm not sure. It might be nothing, but I've had this lump on my breast for over three weeks, and it's not going away."

Dwayne rested his hand on Tammy's knee. "Don't you think you should go get it checked? I'm sure it's nothing serious."

Tammy nodded. "Yeah, It's probably a swollen gland or something. I'll call the doctors on Monday and make an appointment." She replied and gave Dwayne a reassuring pat on the thigh.

Tammy was relieved when Wednesday finally arrived. She had an appointment with her doctor in the afternoon and was looking forward to having any worries of cancer be erased.

"Do you want me to leave work early and go with you?" Dwayne had asked in the morning.

Tammy shook her head. "No, I'll be fine. I'll call you as soon as I'm done."

After the doctor had examined her, Tammy waited anxiously for his prognosis. "I won't know anything until I look at the mammogram. It will be in a couple of days."

Tammy rolled her eyes. "You mean I have to wait a few more days," she whined.

"I'm afraid so. You will need to come back on Friday for the results."

After making an appointment at the front desk, Tammy stormed out of the clinic feeling frustrated. She didn't want to worry anymore. This was clouding her mind every day, and she struggled daily to be productive. Before heading home, she called Dwayne from her car.

He answered on the first ring. "Tell me it's good news," he said, sounding anxious.

"I didn't find out anything. The doctor won't know until he looks at the mammogram. I have to go back Friday." Tammy scooched down in her seat and let out a big sigh. "This sucks."

"I know it does, hon," Dwayne said. "But at least you are getting checked. I'm sure it's nothing, and this will be all behind you next week."

"Yeah, I know. But all this waiting and not knowing is driving me nuts."

"Just hang in there, babe. It's just a few days."

"I will. I love you," Tammy said in a softer tone.

"I love you too."

Friday couldn't come soon enough for Tammy. She'd had enough worrying and was ready for some answers, but the doctor had a different plan.

"What do you mean I need to see another doctor and have a biopsy?" Tammy shrieked.

"So we can take a sample and see what the lump is."

Tammy hesitated before she spoke. "Do you think it's cancer?"

"I'm not going to make any guesses, Tammy. The results from the biopsy will tell me. Until then, try not to think about it and keep yourself busy by taking your mind off it."

"Easy for you to say," Tammy snapped.

Four days after she'd had the painful biopsy, Tammy and Dwayne were hiking with their dogs when Tammy's cell phone rang. She pulled it out of her back pocket, looked at the screen, and gasped. "It's my doctor's office."

"Then answer it," Dwayne said while nudging her arm.

Tammy took a deep breath and took the call. "Hello."

She recognized the voice of the receptionist at the clinic. "Hi, is this Tammy Mellows?"

"Yes, it is," Tammy replied, unable to hide her nervousness.

"Hi. This is Sheila at doctor Shelton's office. We need to schedule an appointment for you to discuss your biopsy results with the doctor."

"Can't you just give them to me over the phone?" Tammy asked.

"No, I'm afraid not. It has to be done in person."

Tammy didn't want to wait any longer. "Can I come in today?"

"Let me put you on hold for a minute, and I'll check."

Tammy suddenly heard classical music playing in her ear.

"What is going on?" Dwayne whispered while petting Harley.

"They have the results of my test. She's checking to see if I can go in today to discuss them."

A few minutes later, Sheila came back on the line. "Can you come in at four?"

Tammy glanced at her watch. Even though her phone had a clock, she still liked to wear a watch. It was two-thirty. Yes, I'll be there."

"Great, we will see you then."

After ending the call, Dwayne took her hand. "Are you okay?"

"Yeah, just nervous. What if it's cancer? I never thought I'd be thinking of cancer at my age."

"Let's not think those thoughts. Let's wait to hear what the doctor has to say."

"It's all I've been thinking about. It's hard not to."

With his free arm, Dwayne wrapped his arm around her waist and pulled her in. "I'm sure you are fine. I want you to relax. Everything is going to be okay."

Tammy nodded and rested her head on his chest. "We should get back. I want to take a shower before we go."

CHAPTER 32

On the short drive to the doctor's office, Tammy and Dwayne were silent. Both deep in thought. Tammy rubbed her sweaty palms as she glanced out of the window, wondering how she would feel on their drive home. When they pulled into the parking lot, Tammy's anxieties peaked. From the car, she looked over at the double doors to the building entrance and was fearful of exiting the car. Was she about to begin the hardest battle of her life, or had life thrown her a curve-ball? Would she be able to continue living with no fears and put all of this behind her? She had so many unanswered questions, and they would be all answered on the other side of that door.

She felt safe in the car. Life was good, and she didn't want it to change.

Dwayne pulled her out of her concerning thoughts. He rested his hand on her knee. "Are you ready?"

"As ready as I'll ever be."

Dwayne stepped out of the car, walked around to the other side, and opened her door. Before Tammy took his extended hand, she rubbed her palms again and tried to stop her body from trembling but failed. She stood before Dwayne, where he clutched her waist. Her breathing was heavy, and her eyes looked down at the ground.

"Hey, it's going to be okay," Dwayne said in a soft voice as he rubbed her shoulders. He kissed her lightly on the lips. "Relax, okay."

Tammy couldn't speak and nodded as she took his hand and held it tight. Her feet felt like cement as she took time walking to the clinic. Her brow dripped sweat, and she wanted to turn around and run back to the car. She didn't want to know her fate. Afraid, Tammy dug her nails deep into Dwayne's hand as they approached the door. Before they entered, Tammy looked at Dwayne, unable to hide her worry.

He gave her a loving smile. "You are going to be fine," he said as he opened the door,

Tammy took a deep breath and entered the building. She scanned the waiting room, and it was quiet. After they had checked in, they took a seat and waited. Tammy didn't let go of Dwayne's hand as he held her in his arms and tried to soothe her trembling body. A few minutes later, a young blonde nurse appeared through the door that led to the examination rooms. She called Tammy's name. "Tammy Mellows," scanning the room.

Tammy slowly raised her hand. "Here."

The nurse nodded. "Follow me, please."

The nurse led them to a small room where they both took a seat next to each other. "The doctor will be right with you." She closed the door behind her.

Tammy tried to read her eyes for any clues of her fate. Did the nurse know? Tammy wondered. If she did, she wasn't giving away any clues. Were they trained to do that? Tammy thought. "Thank you," Tammy said as she took Dwayne's hand again.

After the nurse had left the room, Tammy lowered her head

onto Dwayne's chest. "What if I have cancer? I can't stop thinking about it."

Dwayne tightened his hold on her and kissed the top of her head. "Let's just wait and see what the doctor says."

After what seemed like an eternity and reading every poster on the wall, they finally heard a knock on the door.

"Come in," Dwayne called.

Tammy pulled herself away from Dwayne's chest and tried to calm her nerves. She again tried to read the doctor's eyes for any clues on what he was about to tell them, but like the nurse, he wasn't giving anything away.

"Good afternoon, Tammy. How are you feeling?"

Tammy sat up straight. "That all depends on my test results," she said with a hint of sarcasm.

Doctor Shelton took a seat across from them in front of a monitor and opened up her file. Tammy took a deep breath and waited. Dwayne squeezed her hand.

"Well, the tests came back positive, I'm afraid. You have breast cancer."

Tammy and Dwayne gasped at the same time. "No!" Tammy screamed in a panicked state. "I'm too young."

Dwayne pulled her in. "Shh, let doctor Shelton speak. What stage cancer does she have?" Dwayne asked.

"Tammy has an invasive Carcinoma, and from the mammogram images, the size looks to be between stage one and two." He released a subtle smile. "That is good. It looks like we caught it early, but we will know more after we have checked your lymph-nodes for any spreading."

"Oh my god, I can't believe this is happening. I don't want to die."

Doctor Shelton tried to calm her. "Tammy, medicine for breast cancer has come along away, and the survival rate is very high if it's caught early. But you will have to go through some rigorous treatment to ensure we remove the cancer and take preventive medicine to stop it from coming back."

"What kind of treatment?" Dwayne asked.

Tammy shook her head, sat up straight, and spoke with a stern voice. "Look, I can beat this crap. I honestly don't have time for this. Tell me what I have to do, and I'll do it."

Dwayne turned and looked at Tammy with wide eyes. Her sudden change of attitude surprised him.

"I like your attitude." Doctor Shelton said with a smile. "Well, you have a few choices. All of which will be discussed in detail with your advice counselor. She will go over everything with you and will help you make the right decision for you. The two prescribed treatments are a lumpectomy where we will remove a partial part of the breast where the cancer is, followed by radiation treatment."

"Radiation treatment." Tammy barked.

"Yes. It will destroy any lingering cells. Your other choice is a full removal of the breast or breasts, and no radiation would be required, and we would do reconstructive surgery."

Tammy lowered her head. "God, I feel like I'm in a nightmare."

Dwayne pulled Tammy into his space and cradled her in his arms. "Does she have to decide now?" He asked.

Doctor Shelton shook his head. "No. We will assign Tammy an advice counselor who will go over everything in detail with both of you, and she will make sure the right decision is made for Tammy."

Tammy's head was spinning with words she'd never heard before in her lifetime, survival, surgery, cancer, mastectomy. She was petrified. Everything she had experienced before in her life seemed so trivial compared to this. She thought back to the many battles she had conquered in the past, escaping Steven and his warped world of Heroin addiction, becoming a commercial fisher-woman when many doubted she could—overcoming alcohol addiction. If she could beat those challenges, then she knew she could and would beat cancer.

"So, what happens now?" Tammy asked.

"Your advice counselor will call you in the next day or so to set up an appointment, and once a decision has been made on what treatment you want, we can set up a date for surgery as soon as possible." Doctor Shelton put Tammy's file on his desk and folded his arms. He gave her a caring smile. "Tammy, you will have a great team behind you at the CBCC clinic where you will be treated."

Tammy nodded. "Thank you. I'm just really scared right now. You hear about others getting cancer, and you never think it's going to happen to you. I feel like I've just been thrown under a bus."

"I'll be here for you," Dwayne told her as he stroked her hair. "We'll fight this together."

Tammy gave him a loving smile. "I know you will. I couldn't do this on my own."

Doctor Shelton extended his hand to Dwayne. "She's in good hands. Take as much time as you need in here. I'm going to call the advice counselor, and we will be in touch."

"Thank you, doctor," Dwayne said.

Tammy lifted her head and sat up straight. She folded her arms and leaned back against the wall. "Thank you, doctor."

After doctor Shelton had left, Tammy let out a heavy sigh. "Wow! I never in my wildest dreams would have thought I would get cancer. Especially at my age."

"I'm in shock," Dwayne replied. "But you're going to be fine. The doctor believes it's in the early stages. I'll be there all the way with you."

Tammy shook her head. "Surgery, radiation. Bloody hell. I wasn't expecting this."

Dwayne rubbed her knee. "Are you ready to go? We can talk more at home." He paused. "Are you going to call Matt?"

Tammy raised her hand to her brow and flipped back her head.

"Oh god, I have to tell Matt. He has no idea about any of this. I didn't want to worry him and figured I'd only say something if the news were not good." She took in a deep breath. "Yes, I'll call him tonight. But I'm not telling anyone else. Definitely not my mom. She doesn't need to know. I'm not going to scare her."

"What about your sisters?" Dwayne asked.

Tammy gasped, and she raised her hand to her dropped jaw. "Yes! I need to tell them. My aunt on my dad's side died of breast cancer. It's in our genes. I don't even know if they've ever had a mammogram, but they need to get checked." Tammy raised her hand. "But that's it. I honestly don't want many people knowing. This is my battle, and once I know I'm in the clear, and I'll be okay, then I will tell others."

"I understand." He took her hand. "Come on, let's go home."

When they reached the car, the first thing Tammy saw was a pack of cigarettes sitting on the dash. She leaned forward in her seat, grabbed the pack, and crushed them in her hand before throwing them out of the car window.

"What are you doing?" Dwayne shrieked.

Tammy gave him a hard stare. "I'm done with cigarettes. I have cancer." She paused for a moment. "Wow. It feels weird saying that —no more smoking for me. And you know something. I'm okay with it. It's like a switch went on. When you face fighting cancer, quitting smoking doesn't seem so hard. Huh, I'll be damned. So many times, I've tried to quit, but I know I will succeed. I have no desire to smoke any more." Her eyes grew wide. "I'd be afraid to."

Dwayne released a slight chuckle. "Okay, then. I guess we are quitting."

Tammy placed her hand on his shoulder. "You don't have to. You don't have cancer."

"I'm not going to smoke in front of you. I told you we are in this together." He leaned in closer to her. "No more cigarettes for both of us."

Tammy nodded with approval. "Okay, then. The next thing I

have to do is call Matt, and then hopefully, my advice counselor will call tomorrow, and I can begin to kick cancer's ass."

Dwayne beamed a huge smile. "There you go. Keep that attitude."

CHAPTER 33

ammy wanted to wait a few hours before she called Matt. She was still in shock over the life-changing news that she had cancer. Dwayne joined her on the grass where she had sat since they arrived home. Their mood was somber. "Here, I made you a cup of tea."

Tammy turned her head and managed to give him a weak smile. "Thanks."

Dwayne sat in the chair next to her. "Are you okay?"

Tammy had her knees up under her chin as she cradled her body. She nodded. "Yea. I'm just stunned by all this. There's so much shit I want to do in life, and when you're told you have cancer, it puts it all into perspective." She turned to face Dwayne, "I mean, imagine if I just ignored the lump for a year. It might have been so far along that I'd be dead before the age of fifty. And even now, they don't know if it has spread to my lymph nodes. What if it has?"

Dwayne took her hand. "I know, hon. I still can't believe it myself. You are a healthy, kick-ass woman, and it's that quality about you that will help you beat this thing."

"Oh, I have every intention of beating it. I plan on being around to welcome my first grandchild, and my mom still needs to have all of her daughters together." She shook her head. "God, that's something I've been putting off for years, and I could really kick myself now. It's going to have to happen when mom comes out next year. Jenny is going to have to come too, and then we can do a road trip to Colorado."

Dwayne Chuckled. "Slow down. We have no idea how you are going to be feeling next year. You will have just gone through cancer treatment. Let's take care of you first and then think about the other stuff."

"I know, but Jenny says mom has been acting strange lately. I want to do this before it's too late. It's a promise I made to mom years ago."

Dwayne's voice became stern. He knew how stubborn Tammy could be. "And you will, once you are well enough to take on the task and travel."

Tammy rolled her eyes. She knew she wasn't going to win this debate. "Fine." She checked her watch. "I need to call Matt. Can you grab me the phone?"

"Sure, it's in the house. I'll be right back."

Tammy remembered her mom's favorite quote as she took a sip of tea for courage before calling Matt. *Never underestimate the power of a cup of tea.* Tammy took a huge sip and savored the hot liquid as it slid down her throat. "You're right, mom," Tammy said out loud as she took another large gulp. The urge for a cigarette kicked in again for the numerous time since she had thrown her pack out of the car. Tammy did what seemed to work to overcome the craving. She took a deep breath and said out loud. "You have cancer. You can't smoke anymore." The simple reminder relaxed her need for a cigarette substantially. Feeling the cravings going away, she smiled and took in another deep breath.

Dwayne returned with the phone and handed it to her. "Here you go."

After three rings, her son Matt answered the phone. "Hey buddy, it's your mom."

"Hey mom, how's it going?"

Tammy took a deep breath. "Well, I've been better."

"What's going on?" Matt asked, sounding worried.

"Well, it seems I have breast cancer."

"What?" Matt gasped.

"Now, I don't want you to worry. The doctor believes it's in the early stages, and I should be able to beat this thing." Tammy was determined to hold it together, even though she was scared to death. She gripped the phone hard as she spoke and bit her lip to hold back her tears. "I'm going to be fine."

"You better be," Matt said with a nervous laugh. "We'll come up this weekend."

"That would be great. I'll know more by then."

They talked for a few more minutes, and Tammy told Matt she would have surgery and radiation treatment, and Matt said he would be there for her.

"I love you, Matt. We'll see you this weekend."

"Love you too, mom."

After she had hung up the phone, Tammy broke down and cried for the first time since she had been told she had cancer. Telling her son made it seem all surreal. She had a lot to live for, including the birth of her first grandchild, and she'd be damned if she was going to let cancer take it all away from her. Dwayne scooched his chair closer to her and wrapped her in his arms. "We'll get through this. You've always been a fighter and a strong woman."

Tammy shook her head and straightened her back. She held her head high as she spoke. "You damn right I'm a fighter. I've got this. Okay, enough of the sappiness. After calling my sisters, I want to have a nice quiet dinner and watch a movie. I need to take my mind off this crap."

"You got it," Dwayne said with a loving smile.

CHAPTER 34

"*I* want to go with a lumpectomy." Tammy had told Wendy, her advice counselor, two days later. "A mastectomy and then reconstructive surgery scares the hell out of me," Tammy confessed.

Wendy sat across from her and nodded. "We have covered all the basics for each option, and I think you have made the right decision. You will have to go through seven weeks of radiation therapy and five years of taking the medication Tamoxifen, which is a hormone therapy drug and will help prevent the cancer from returning." She said before removing her glasses.

"I'm okay with that?" Tammy replied.

Wendy put her glasses back on and looked down at her notes. "Okay, then I will schedule you for surgery for next week, and a nurse will call you later today with all the instructions and more details." She told Tammy.

~

Since learning that she had cancer, Tammy's life had been a blur. Each day rolled into the next. Everything she had done revolved around her fight against the horrible disease. Tammy couldn't believe how her life had changed in just over a week. And now here she was lying in a hospital waiting to be taken into surgery.

Dwayne had just stepped out for a cigarette. He was finding it harder to quit, but then again, he hadn't been told he had cancer. He had cut down a lot and refused to smoke in front of her. Tammy had faith he would eventually quit altogether. They had just finished making all the necessary phone calls to Matt and a few friends to let them know she was about to go in for surgery. Tammy was anxious to have it all behind her and be waking up in the recovery room. Surgery didn't scare her. Her worry was the outcome of her lymph-nodes. Had the cancer spread? She feared it had.

Dwayne returned, looking more relaxed, but the worry in his eyes was still visible. "How are you doing, babe?" he asked with a loving smile.

"I'm good. I wish they'd take me in. I hate laying here doing nothing."

Dwayne chuckled at her remark. She never was one to sit still. "Well, you'd better get used to it. You're going to be laid up for a while."

"Not if I have anything to do with it." Tammy barked. "I won't let this shit keep me down. I may rest for a day or so, but I gotta keep busy to keep my mind off this crap; otherwise, I'll go crazy."

"I hear you. And you will do whatever you want to do and not what the doctors tell you. I already know," he laughed.

A few minutes later, they were approached by a male nurse. "How are you feeling, Tammy?" he asked.

Dwayne stepped aside so the nurse could check Tammy's vitals.

"Good," Tammy replied.

"Well, I'm here to take you into surgery, and when you wake up, your husband will be in the recovery room waiting for you." He looked over at Dwayne and gave him a nod.

It suddenly felt so surreal for Tammy, and she choked back her tears. She wasn't going to cry.

Dwayne took her hand. "I'll be right here. I love you."

Tammy saw the tears pooling in his eyes and felt tears trickle down her cheeks. "I love you too."

Dwayne walked alongside the bed she was being pushed in, holding her hand tight until they came to the double doors where he wasn't allowed to enter. He kissed her hard on the lips. "You're going to be fine." She watched as the doors swung closed behind her. All he could do now was wait.

～

"Tammy, can you hear me? Tammy, it's Dwayne."
Tammy blinked a few times. She heard his voice, but her eyes felt so heavy. She strained to open them.

"Tammy? It's Dwayne. It's over. You're in the recovery room."

Tammy tried to open her eyes again and managed for a few seconds.

She felt him take her hand. "Hey sweetie, can you hear me?"

She remembered everything and opened her eyes once more. She had just had surgery. She looked up and saw Dwayne's beautiful blue eyes and his gorgeous smile looking down on her. "Hi," she whispered.

"Hey, beautiful. You're awake."

"Am I?" She was now semi-conscious and scanned the room with just the movement of her eyes. "Where am I?"

"You're in the recovery room. They bought you about an hour ago. The doctor will be here shortly."

Tammy closed her eyes for a second. The last thing she remembered was when she tried to count back from ten. She remembered only getting to seven. She suddenly remembered why she had surgery. The fear swept through her. "Did they say anything about the cancer? Did they get it all?"

"The doctor will tell us when he gets here."

Tammy tried to scooch herself up and felt the tight bandages around her chest. "Ouch. That wasn't a good idea."

"Easy. You have stitches. What are you trying to do?" Dwayne asked, surprised by her sudden movements.

"I want to sit up. My neck hurts."

"Oh, you're going to be a hard one to keep still. Come on, let me help you."

A few minutes after Dwayne had helped Tammy get comfortable, they were greeted by Tammy's surgeon. He extended his hand to Dwayne. "I'm doctor Peterson." He turned and smiled at Tammy. "How are you feeling, Tammy?"

"Sore and thirsty." Tammy didn't want any small talk. She wanted to hear about the cancer. "Did you get it all? How big was it, and how were my lymph-nodes?"

Dwayne took her hand and listened intently as the doctor spoke.

"The surgery went really well. We managed to get all the cancer, which was about the size of a grape, and I'm happy to say we removed nine lymph nodes, and they were all clean, which means it has not spread."

Tammy and Dwayne released a huge sigh of relief at the same time and smiled at each other with tears in their eyes. "Oh my god. That's so good to hear. Thank you, doctor." Dwayne said.

"It's all good news, Tammy. We caught the cancer early. You'll be following up with radiation therapy in a few months after you have healed." He smiled. "It looks like you are going to be fine."

Tammy rested her head back in the softness of the pillows and let her tears roll down her cheeks. She believed the worst was behind her. The cancer was gone. After radiation, she should be able to get her life back on track, but she knew the worry of it returning would haunt her for the rest of her life. She never believed she would ever get cancer and now her number one concern was, would it come back?

Not only had her life been transformed, but her outlook on life had changed. Death had come knocking at her door with a small warning and a reminder that she will not be on this earth forever, and she should make the most of it while she has the privilege of being here. Tammy thought about Jason, whose life was cut too short by cancer at the young age of thirty-nine and her father's recent death. Once she was well, she would start doing the things she had been putting off for years.

She looked over at Dwayne and smiled. She was so lucky to have him by her side. They had built a life together, and now he was here for her when she had been knocked down. He leaned in and kissed her forehead while he held her hand. "How are you doing?"

"I'm good. When can I go home?"

Dwayne chuckled. "You just had surgery, woman. I'm sure it won't be for at least a few hours." He watched as Tammy strained to keep her eyes open, and within a few minutes, she was asleep. He gently brushed her bangs to the side and released his hold on her hand. "I'll be back in a few minutes. I'm going to go call Matt," he whispered.

CHAPTER 35

ammy was making the hour drive from her radiation therapy to home. It was one of the days she made the trip alone. Dwayne went with her when he didn't have to work. Her treatments were going well, to her surprise, and she wasn't experiencing any side effects. She was in week five and had two more weeks to go. She couldn't wait until she didn't have to make the two-hour round trip five days a week at the crack of dawn to get her daily dose of radiation. What a way to start your day—she had said to her friend Mandy, who drove with her three times a week. They had become close since meeting at a neighbor's barbecue a few years ago and, like Dwayne, had been there for her during her fight with cancer. "Who needs coffee? Radiation will get you going." Tammy had laughed while riding with Mandy one morning.

Along with the radiation treatment, Tammy took Tamoxifen and showed her displeasure when she was told that she would have to take it for the next five years.

Tammy was anxious to get home. After healing from her surgery and before the radiation treatments had begun, she and

Dwayne didn't want to put off building the house any longer and dove right in. They tore down the old house with the help of many friends and Matt. They drew plans up, and in their spare time, they began the build.

For Tammy, it couldn't come at a better time. It was excellent therapy for her. It helped take her mind off the brutal treatment she was still going through and instead dream about the future she and Dwayne would have in their new home. After she had attended to her work tasks, she planned to spend the rest of the day digging dirt for the foundation of the new house with some neighbors' help.

By week seven—her last week of radiation, Tammy was struggling. Her breast area where she was receiving the treatment was severely blistered, and the lotion that the doctors had prescribed wasn't helping. Fatigue was an issue every day, and her mind was a constant blur. She couldn't focus or think straight, and her entire body ached. There was no working on the house during the last week of treatment. She slept, and on her last day of radiation, it surprised her at how emotional she became. She hugged the technician, Brenda, who had become a familiar face every morning for the past seven weeks. "This may sound weird, but I'm going to miss you," Tammy cried.

"I'm going to miss you too, Tammy. You stay strong, okay."

Tammy nodded and gave her another hug. "I will."

Life returned to what Tammy now called her new normal, slowly. She no longer took life for granted. Those days of thinking she was immortal were long gone. Life was a precious gem, and she needed to make every day count. She and Dwayne continued to chip away at the new house. Her father, John, may never see the house built, but Dwayne and Tammy were determined that his parents, Cathy and Charlie, and her mother Rose would see it before their health declined. Sadly, Charlie had been diagnosed with early signs of Alzheimer's, which crushed them.

"God, I hope my dad gets to see the house built before he gets too sick," Dwayne said when he first found out two months before Tammy was diagnosed with cancer. And Tammy had concerns about her mother's health, too.

Dwayne and Tammy took daily hikes with the dogs, which helped rebuild Tammy's strength after radiation, and three weeks after completing her radiation treatment, she was feeling pretty good. Her blisters had healed, and her skin had returned to its normal color. She was excited about the days ahead and getting her life back on track. But she became concerned when she suddenly had a shortness of breath on a hike she did daily with no issues. She stopped in the middle of the trail, bent over, and heaved her chest.

Dwayne stood beside with a look of worry. "Are you okay?"

Tammy continued to suck in oxygen. "I can't breathe," She gasped.

"Do you want to take a break?" Dwayne asked.

Tammy remained bent over at the waist. Her hands gripped her knees. "Just for a minute." She took a few more deep breaths before straightening her back. "Why am I out of breath? I hike this trail all the time."

Dwayne shrugged his shoulders. "Maybe you're just having an off day. We spent all day yesterday working on the house. You may have overdone it. You are supposed to be still taking it easy, and you worked your butt off yesterday. Do you want to keep going or turnaround?"

Dwayne wasn't surprised by her reply. "No, I'm not quitting. Let's keep going." But fifty yards later, she had to stop again and catch her breath. "God, this sucks. I can't breathe," she said as her heart raced beneath her chest. She raised her hands and turned around. "I'm done. Let's go back to the car." She said as she leaned on Dwayne's arm for support.

"Are you sure you're okay?" Dwayne asked. "I can take you to the hospital if you'd like?"

"I'm not going to the hospital; I'm just out of breath. I'll be fine," Tammy snared.

The next day Tammy had forgotten all about the incident until she went to a friend's house to water their house plants because they were out of town. She was surprised at how out of breath she was after climbing the flight of stairs. She sat at the top and gasped for air. "God. I have no energy." She panted. Tammy wondered if her body was still recuperating from radiation or if it was some of the side effects of the Tamoxifen.

At her appointment with her oncologist the next day, Tammy mentioned it to him.

"How are you feeling, Tammy? Any abnormalities or changes?" her doctor asked.

Tammy hesitated for a minute—wondering if she was overreacting. "Well, I've been out of breath a lot lately." Tammy tried to shake off her concerns with her hand. "But it's probably no big deal."

But it seemed Doctor Baton wasn't so sure. "Okay. Tell me more."

"Well, my husband and I went on a hike the other day, and I had to stop a few times to catch my breath. I've never had to do that before, and yesterday I barely made it up a flight of stairs."

"Tammy, I'm going to schedule you for an ultrasound. But I want it done today. Can you stick around while I get it set up? Obviously, something is going on, and I don't want you to have to come back. You live an hour away."

"Sure, that fine," Tammy said. Puzzled by his urgency. "What do you think it is?"

"I can't say for sure until you have the ultrasound."

Tammy returned to the waiting room and called Dwayne. "Hey. I'm going to be here a little longer."

"Everything okay?"

"I hope so. I told Doctor Baton about my shortness of breath, and now he wants to do an ultrasound."

"Well, that's good, Tammy. At least he's not ignoring it. You're in good hands. I'm sure you're fine. He's being precautionary."

"Yeah, I guess you're right. He said I could go home after the ultrasound, and they will call me with the results as soon as they have them."

"Okay, sound good. Call me when you are on your way home."

"I will. Love you."

"Love you too."

For the rest of the day, Tammy tried not to worry about the ultrasound. She believed Dwayne was right, that they were just cautious and that she had nothing to worry about, even though her shortness of breath was still present. She tried to keep her mind off of it by keeping busy with her work and doing projects in the new house. As more hours passed, she became more relaxed, and her fear that something could be wrong had subsided.

"Any news from the doctor?" Dwayne asked before he headed off to work the next morning.

"No, nothing yet. I'll call you if I hear anything."

Dwayne smiled and gave her a light kiss on the cheek. "Sounds good. In the meantime, take it easy, and don't be doing too much."

Tammy laughed. She loved how he always watched out for her. "I have some work to do on the computer, and I want to do some yard work."

"Tammy, yard work is not taking it easy."

"I won't do too much. I promise."

Dwayne shook his head. "You're impossible," he joked.

Tammy was pleased when she had all of her work done for her online business completed by eleven. She could now catch up on some weeding that had been neglected because most of their spare time had been spent working on the house. It was a crisp May morning with scattered clouds in the sky and a comfortable sixty-eight degrees. It was perfect weather for gardening and for the dogs to watch from under a shade tree.

Like always, when she was alone, her thoughts drifted to the day when she first learned she had cancer. She couldn't believe that was seven months ago. She remembered how scared she was when she first found out, and the fear was still present that it might return. Her doctors had told her that the first five years were the most critical. After that, the odds of the cancer returning, even though it would still be a concern, will drop substantially. It would require her to see her oncologists every three months for the first two years, then every six months after that.

The ringtone of her cell phone interrupted her thoughts. Tammy rose from her knees and raced to the phone, sitting on the bench. "Hello."

"Tammy, it's doctor Baton. I have the results of your ultrasound."

Tammy felt a lump rise in her throat. "Is everything okay?"

There was an urgency to doctor Baton's voice when he spoke. "Actually, no. I need you to listen to me carefully and do exactly what I ask."

Fear swept through Tammy, and her brow dripped with sweat. "Okay."

"I want you to stop whatever you are doing. Do not make any sudden movements and get yourself to the nearest emergency room as soon as you can. Do not drive yourself."

"Why? And if I go to the ER, they will have me wait for hours."

Doctor Baton raised his voice and spoke with a sharp tone. "Tammy, you have four blood clots on your lungs—also known as Pulmonary embolisms. You have three on the right lung and one on the left. This is nothing to mess around with. If they travel to your brain, it could mean instant death."

"What?" Tammy shrieked. "I've never heard of this."

"It's pretty serious and explains your shortness of breath. Now listen to me. When you get to the ER, you tell them you have four PE's on your lungs, and trust me; they will take you right away."

Tammy was shocked, "Really? But I feel fine today."

Doctor Baton expressed his frustration with her questions.

"Tammy, don't put this off because you are feeling okay. Get yourself to the hospital now! The ER will contact me once they have admitted you."

Tammy cowered from his raised voice. "Okay, I will."

After ending the call, Tammy wasted no time calling Dwayne. "Hey, I just got off the phone with my doctor, and he told me to go to the emergency room. I could call Mandy to take me because he told me not to drive."

Dwayne sounded alarmed. "The emergency room? Why?"

"He says I have blood clots on my lungs."

Dwayne gasped. "Shit! I'm coming home. I'll be there within the hour. I'll take you to the hospital. Don't do anything until I get there. Go have a cup of tea or something," he said, unable to hide the panic in his voice.

CHAPTER 36

*D*wayne made it home in record time. He wasn't sure how many driving laws he broke, but he was thankful he didn't get caught. He found Tammy sitting on the grass, sipping hot tea with their two dogs at her feet. "Hey, how are you feeling?" he asked with a look of worry.

She turned and smiled. "I feel fine. I did, even before the doctor had called me. I'm not sure why I have to race to the emergency room?" she confessed.

"I know why. I called some friends on the way home and talked to them about Pulmonary embolisms. They are serious and can be deadly."

"That's what my doctor told me. He told me not to make any sudden moves."

"A guy at work told me his wife had cancer like you and went through the same treatment. She had a blood clot, and she died in her sleep."

Tammy gasped. "What! Oh shit. Now I'm terrified. This is worse than the damn cancer."

Dwayne hated how badly it scared her, but she needs to realize the urgency. "I'm just trying to put it in perspective for you. I'm not trying to scare you. Let me put the birds away, and then we are heading straight for the hospital."

Tammy nodded. "Okay. Do you want me to do anything?" she asked.

"Yes, sit still. I know it's hard," he chuckled.

Tammy stuck out her tongue. "Oh, stop. I listen when I want to."

"Exactly. Only if you want to," he laughed. "I'll be right back."

An hour and a half later, Dwayne hooked Tammy's arm with his and walked her slowly through the doors of the emergency entrance. Tammy scanned the waiting room. It was busy. "Wow, this place is packed. They won't see me right away. Look at that guy over there. The towel wrapped around his hand is covered in blood," she whispered. "He needs a doctor more than me."

Dwayne led her over to the receptionist. The middle-aged woman wearing glasses looked up from her computer monitor and gave him a half-smile. "Can I help you?" she asked,

Dwayne unhooked his arm from Tammy's and rested it on the counter. "Yes. My wife has four PE's on her lungs, and her doctor told her to come straight to emergency."

Tammy waved her hand and gave the nurse a faint smile.

The nurse looked surprised. "Okay, I'm going to call for a wheelchair for your wife and get her admitted to the trauma unit right away." The nurse said as she quickly picked up a telephone and made a call.

"Wheelchair? Trauma unit?" Tammy said with a creased brow. "I can walk. I don't need a wheelchair."

The nurse hung up the phone and gave Tammy a stern look. "In your condition, anything can happen. The wheelchair will be here soon."

Tammy and Dwayne didn't have to wait long. Within a minute, a hospital porter approached Tammy pushing a wheelchair. "I want you to ease down into the chair slowly," he instructed her.

Tammy did as she was told, and Dwayne followed close behind as they wheeled her into the trauma unit. She was greeted by three doctors who helped her up onto the bed, immediately hooked her up to an IV, and took her vitals. Fear swept through Tammy. This was serious, and she watched with concerns as she was being probed, poked, and pricked.

"We've talked to your oncologist, and he is sending your records over." A nurse told her as she put another needle in her arm.

"What's that for?" Tammy asked.

"It is a blood thinner. You are a fortunate lady. It's bad enough to have one blood clot, but you have four. It only takes one of those to break loose and travel up to your brain."

"Is she going to be okay?" Dwayne asked.

"We are going to monitor her real closely and continue to give her the blood thinner through IV until she has another scan. More than likely, she will have scans done on her legs tomorrow because that is where blood clots begin—especially behind the knee. So we will want to check for that."

"Tomorrow?" Dwayne questioned. "You mean she's being admitted?"

"Oh yes, she's not going anywhere until those clots have gone."

"How long will that take?" Tammy asked.

"It all depends on how your body reacts to the blood thinner. It may take anywhere from one to five days."

"Five days," Tammy hissed.

The nurse gave her a stern look, just like the nurse at the front desk. Tammy was getting used to them. "Now you just lay still. You don't need to be fidgeting around." The nurse told her.

"I can't stay here for five days," Tammy protested.

This time it was Dwayne that gave her a stern look.

"Oh, yes, you will," he barked. "Now I'm going to step outside and call Matt. I love you. I'll be back soon."

Tammy showed her bottom lip more than she needed to "Love you too."

After four hours of being monitored in the trauma unit, Tammy was relieved when they finally moved her to a different ward. Even though she wasn't allowed to get out of bed or walk around, she appreciated the window and a view of the outside world. The doctors had told her she would have a scan on her legs tomorrow to see if she had any more clots. Until then, she was to take it easy and only get up to use the bathroom, which she soon found out was a chore because she was still hooked up to an IV and had to drag the apparatus with her.

"Hey, as much as I want to stay with you all night, I need to get home. I have to feed the falcons and the dogs," Dwayne said from her bedside as the sun went down.

Tammy took his hand. "Yeah, I know. Call me in the morning, okay. And plan on going to work. There's nothing you can do here but sit around. Why lose money? I'm in good hands."

"Are you sure?" Dwayne asked with a creased brow.

Tammy nodded. "Yes, I'm sure. Matt is coming up tomorrow for a while. I'll be fine. You bought me plenty of reading material and puzzle books."

Dwayne leaned over and kissed her softly on the lips. "I'll be here tomorrow afternoon. I'll feed all the animals before I leave."

"Okay, I'll see you then."

Tammy drifted off to sleep soon after Dwayne had left and didn't wake until she heard one of the nurses' voices.

"Rise and shine, Tammy. Breakfast will be here in a few minutes, and then I'm taking you down for your scans."

Tammy rubbed her eyes and turned her head away from the bright sun beaming through the window. "Can you close the blinds, please?" Tammy asked as she pulled herself up to a sitting position. Tammy scanned the walls and saw no clock. "What time is it?"

"Almost seven," the nurse replied as she placed a tray of food in front of her. "I'll be back in thirty minutes. Make sure you are finished with your breakfast by then."

By lunchtime, Tammy was back in her room after having the scans and was waiting for the doctor to tell her their findings. He showed up just before two.

"Hello, Tammy. How are you doing today?" he asked.

Tammy smiled. "Good, thanks."

"That good. Well, we found three more clots behind your right knee."

Tammy was shocked. "Really? Why am I getting these clots? This is scary. Especially since I hear they can travel to your brain and kill you."

"Yes, they can, which is why we are keeping you here until all the clots have dissolved."

"But what if I get more after I leave? Do you know why I'm getting them?" She asked again.

"I believe it's because of the Tamoxifen you've been taking, and I don't want you to take them anymore."

"But that's for my cancer?" Tammy said, sounding concerned.

"It is. But I think you will be better off taking nothing at all. We will monitor you closely and have you come in more frequently over the next five years, which is the critical time frame when the cancer is at high risk of returning."

Dwayne entered the room while they were talking. Tammy threw him a big smile. "Hey, I wasn't expecting to see you for a few more hours."

Dwayne shook the doctor's hand. "I left early so I could come here. So what's going on?" Dwayne asked as he stood next to the bed and held Tammy's hand.

"I was just telling Tammy that we found three more clots behind her knee and that it's probably a side effect from the Tamoxifen. It's rare, but it has been known to happen."

"Oh, no," Dwayne gasped.

"As long as we monitor her blood and keep her on blood thinners, she should be okay. For the first week after she goes home, Tammy will need to take Lovenox, which is injected into her abdomen twice a day."

Tammy's eyes turned wide. "Whoa. Wait a minute. I have to do it myself. Stick a needle in my stomach." Tammy shook her head. "Hell no. I can't do that."

"I'll do it," Dwayne called out with no hesitations.

"You will?" Tammy said, shocked by his words.

"Of course, I will," Dwayne spoke to the doctor. "Twice a day?"

"Yes, twice a day, and then she will be on Warfarin until her blood returns to normal and is not at a danger level of coagulating."

Tammy was confused. "How will you know? I'll be at home."

"You will have to come here once a week and have your blood checked."

"Once a week? For how long?" Tammy questioned.

"For as long as it takes to get your blood back to normal. Your blood will be checked, and your medicine doses adjusted accordingly."

Tammy laid back against the pillow and sighed. "I recently got done driving here every day for radiation, and now I have to come here every week for this. I used to be so damn healthy. What the hell happened?"

"And you will be again," Dwayne told her.

"So, how long will I be here?" Tammy asked.

"You should be able to go home tomorrow. The clots are shrinking. The nurses will go over everything in detail with you before we release you."

CHAPTER 37

ammy had been making the weekly two-hour round trips to have her blood checked for the last six months. She was hoping this would be her last time. Now that she had a three-month-old grandson, she was eager to put all her health scares behind her and begin making memories with her grandson. She was thankful that her mother wanted to skip coming out this year and get well herself. It would give her and Dwayne a chance to finish the house and take care of her health. Her mom promised she would be there the following year.

The nurses had hinted that her blood was looking good, and if the results were good today, she wouldn't have to be checked anymore. But her emotions were split. Yes, she was excited to have the ball and chain released and no longer have to make the long drive every week. But the visits put her mind at rest when she was told things looked good. The test told her she had no blood clots. If the visits stopped, she would no longer have that peace of mind. She would have to rely on signs from her body that something was wrong, just like when she was out of breath on a simple hike that she had done daily. But Tammy had also heard that people who had died from blood clots had no prior symptoms in many cases. The thought terrified her. Not only did she have to fear cancer returning, but also blood clots.

As she drove on the desolate five freeways surrounded by miles of farmland, she thought again how precious life was. She was still young and wanted to be around to see the house completed that she and Dwayne had been working so hard on. She thought again of her dad, who would never get to see it, and then her mother, who she feared would never see it either. Tammy still had not told her mom or her sisters about her health scare and probably wouldn't until they convinced Tammy she was out of danger. She didn't want anyone to worry. When her mother would visit in September, which was just five months away, Tammy thought that would be a good time to tell her.

Tammy thought of Dwayne's parents, Charlie and Cathy, who were now in their late seventies and moved into assisted living because of Charlie's Alzheimer's progress. It saddened Tammy and Dwayne that neither one of them would see their house finished either. If only they had started the house sooner, Dwayne and Tammy had often said.

With Matt's help on the weekends whenever he could and some good friends, they made substantial progress on the house, but it would still be a year before they could even think about moving in.

Tammy wiped her sweaty palms on her jeans as she entered the blood and cancer clinic. A place she had gotten to know well since she had been diagnosed with cancer over a year ago. She received all her radiation treatments here, and now she had her blood tested weekly. She knew the girls at the front desk on a first name basis and always spent a few minutes having a friendly chat with them before heading to the blood clinic. Tammy was going to miss them if her results were good.

When she entered the blood clinic, Molly's friendly smile, the phlebotomist nurse who did the test every week, greeted her.

"Hey, Tammy. I'm all ready for you. Have a seat."

"Hi, Molly." Tammy said as she took her usual place and waited for Molly to prick her finger."

"So this might be the big day where I may tell you I don't want to see you anymore." Molly laughed.

"I know," Tammy said with a nervous smile.

The test only took a few minutes, and Tammy waited anxiously for Molly to read the results.

Molly looked up and smiled. "They are good, Tammy. You don't need to come back, and you no longer need to take the blood thinners."

"Really? That's awesome." Tammy said, but she couldn't help feeling a little sad and concerned. "If I stop taking the blood thinners, isn't there a danger I may get the blood clots again?"

The nurse gave Tammy a reassuring smile. "The clots were caused by the drug Tamoxifen which you haven't taken in over six months. Your blood work has been good for the last month. You're as good as new, Tammy."

Tammy laughed. "Okay, then. I guess I'm a free woman."

After saying goodbye to the girls at the front desk and telling them the good news, Tammy pulled out of the parking lot and called Dwayne on her cell phone to tell him the good news. "I'm all done. No more blood work. They said my blood is fine, and I can stop taking the blood thinners." Tammy beamed.

"Yes! That's fantastic. I'm taking you out for dinner tonight to celebrate," Dwayne said, sounding elated.

"Sounds good. I am kind of worried, though, that my blood won't be getting checked every week. It gave me peace of mind knowing my blood was okay."

Dwayne tried to reassure her. "I'm sure they wouldn't tell you to stop coming or not take the meds if they weren't one hundred percent certain you would be okay. Now stop worrying. You're healthy. Life is getting back to normal again. You're a grandmother, and we are building a house together."

Tammy smiled at his words. Like always, he knew just what to say. "Your right. I feel great. My strength is back, and I want to hustle on the house before mom gets here in September."

But their dreams were soon crushed when Tammy received a call from her sister, Jenny, in England a few months later.

She sounded somber when she spoke. "Hi, Tammy I'm calling about mom."

Tammy's heart sank, and she sat on the edge of the bed where she was folding laundry. "Is she okay?" Tammy asked, matching her sister's somber tone.

"Not really. She's been diagnosed with dementia. I'm afraid she won't be able to travel to America anymore."

Instantly tears pooled in Tammy's eyes. "Oh my god. How bad is she? Does she recognize you?" Tammy asked. The only thing she had heard about dementia was that the victims of the disease soon stop recognizing people—even their spouses and children. The thought terrified Tammy.

"Yes, she does, but we are not sure for how long. She is very confused. She hallucinates a lot. Just last week, she said there were thousands of ants crawling on her wall. Of course, there wasn't, but to her, it was real. She was petrified. I didn't know what to do. It was horrible to watch."

"Oh, Jenny, I'm so sorry I'm not there to help you. I feel awful."

"No, don't feel bad. You took care of dad's place when he passed. I can take care of our mom. But it's so heartbreaking, Tammy. The sparkle has gone from her eyes. She looks like a lost soul."

Tammy suddenly realized that it was now too late to fulfill her mother's one wish-*I just want to see my girls all in the same room one more time.* She had waited too long. Donna's status was still in limbo, she couldn't go to England, and now her mom would never set foot on American soil again. Tammy let the tears trickle down her cheeks. It crushed her to know she had let her mom down. She took a deep breath before she spoke. "Jenny. I'm going to talk to Dwayne. I think I am going to come to England."

Tammy heard the surprise in her sister's voice. "You are?"

"Yes, and I'm not going to put this off like I've done with so many things in the past. I don't want to wait until mom no longer knows who I am. I couldn't bear the thought of being in the same room with her, and I am a stranger to her. A child she gave birth to and raised. I don't think I would be able to handle it."

"I understand, Tammy."

Tammy wasn't finished talking. "From what I understand, little by little, we will lose the mom we know until only an empty shell remains. I want to see her before that happens." Tammy paused and choked back her tears. "I guess in my own way I'll be saying goodbye to mom while she still knows me. It might even be the last time I see her. If I go, it will be my first time there in over thirty years. I don't know if I'd be able to make it over again."

"I know, Tammy. We have missed out on so much as sisters—all three of us. I last saw you at my wedding, and as for Donna, I was fifteen when I last saw her. We are twins, and yet we don't know each other at all. It's unfortunate."

Tammy tried to hide her tears, but Jenny was crying too, which didn't help. "I'll call tomorrow after I've talked to Dwayne. But knowing Dwayne, he will probably tell me to go after I tell him about mom's declining health. He is going through the same sadness with his dad."

Tammy didn't waste any time talking to Dwayne. As soon as he walked through the door, she patted the empty cushion on the couch where she sat. "Hey, I want to talk to you. Have a seat."

"Am I in trouble?" Dwayne joked. He made himself comfortable next to her and put his arm around her shoulder. "What's up?"

Tammy rubbed his knee as she spoke. "I talked to my sister Jenny today, and my mom is not doing good."

Dwayne pulled her in and hugged her. "I'm so sorry. Are you okay?"

"I am, but I think I should go to England while my mom will still be able to recognize me. She won't be coming to the states anymore."

Dwayne spoke in a somber tone. "None of our parents will see our house finished."

"I know. God, I wish we had started it sooner."

"Me too, but we didn't have the cash flow."

"Yeah, I know. And mom will never see her daughters together again. I feel like I let her down. My sisters and I should have done something." Tammy leaned back in the cushions of the couch and released a heavy sigh. "We've been so wrapped up in our own lives and then Donna with her status in limbo. It just never happened, and now it never will."

"Hey, don't be so hard on yourself. You've had a lot to deal with over the past few years with your father's passing and then the cancer and the blood clots. We don't plan any of this shit, but yes, go to England. Be with your mom and Jenny. At least she will have two of you, which is more than she had in a long time." Dwayne furrowed his brow. "How many years has it been?"

"Over thirty years," Tammy replied. "It will be so good to see Jenny again, too. Sisters should not go this long without seeing each other." Tammy raised her hands. "How did we become so estranged? God, we have years of catching up to do. So that's settled. I'm going to England?" She smiled.

Dwayne grinned. "Yes, you are going to England."

Tammy returned a huge smile. "I'll call Jenny in the morning." She tilted her head slightly, "Next week is not too soon, is it?" she asked.

Dwayne chuckled. "Didn't we just talk about how we procrastinate so much over the past few years? Next week is fine."

"Great, I'll book my ticket after I've talked to Jenny. Wow! I'm going to England. I wish you could go with me."

"I wish I could too, but who's going to watch all the birds and animals?"

"Yeah, I know. I'll miss you," Tammy said as she folded into his arms.

Dwayne gave her a tight squeeze. "I'm going to miss you too."

CHAPTER 38

*F*or the first time in over thirty years, Tammy stepped onto British soil. It was going to be her home for the next two weeks. Memories of her teen years immediately flooded her mind. She stood in Heathrow Airport, waiting for her baggage. The last time she was here was with her father when she moved to America at seventeen. She was forty-eight, a wife, a mother, and now a grandmother or as she likes to call herself, Nana. She had spent two-thirds of her life in America, and yet she felt like she was returning home to tie up loose ends that had been haunting her for years.

After claiming her baggage and going through the customs' daunting task, she stepped outside of the airport and burst into laughter. "Oh my god, wouldn't you know it? It's bloody raining. Just like it was on my last night in England." She let go of the hold she had on the trolley that held her luggage and held her face up to the cloudy skies. She opened her mouth and allowed the raindrops to tickle her tongue. "Hello, England. I'm back," she said and laughed again.

She looked across the road and saw the long line of bright red double-decker buses. "Gosh, I haven't seen one of those in years," she giggled. She then notices everyone was driving on the other side of the road. "And to think at one time in my life that would seem normal. I'm glad I won't be driving over here." The rain came down heavier, and Tammy pulled her trolley under the airport's entranceway. She looked at her watch and saw she had four hours to kill before she was to take a two-hundred-mile coach ride up to Leeds, where Jenny would meet her at the bus station. The coach ride would take seven hours because of the many stops it would make, and she wouldn't arrive until two in the morning. Tammy was planning on sleeping most of the way. She had gained eight hours from the time difference and was already feeling the effects.

Tammy knew she had to call Dwayne and Jenny to let them know she had arrived. Tammy smiled—she couldn't wait to hear Dwayne's voice. She couldn't believe how much she was missing him already. He had been so worried at the airport, knowing that she would be six-thousand miles away in a strange country.

"It's my homeland. It's not strange to me," she laughed. I'll be with family," she reminded him.

"I'm still going to worry about you, just like I did when you went to Ireland."

Tammy soon found a phone booth. After spending a good five minutes figuring out how to make an international call with a credit card, she finally heard the familiar American ringtone. Dwayne answered the house phone on the second ring.

"Hey, babe. I made it," Tammy squealed into the phone.

"Tammy! I miss you," Dwayne hollered back.

"I miss you too. I miss my cell phone. It doesn't work here,' she laughed. "It feels so weird to be back here, but at the same time, it's bittersweet. I have so many memories. I wish you were here with me to share them with me."

"I do too. We will go together someday. I promise."

Tammy thought of all the places she would like to show

Dwayne— where she grew up, her old school, and the Tridale moors. "I would like that."

Tammy filled him on her flight and her upcoming scheduled coach ride to Leeds. "I'm nervous about seeing Jenny," she confessed. "Why is that?" she asked herself out loud. "She's my sister."

"Well, you haven't seen her in decades. This is huge, Tammy." Dwayne told her. "You can't just pick up where you left off. Of course, you are nervous. You have to get to know her all over again. And the same goes for her. I'm sure she is feeling the same way."

"I know. It just seems wrong to feel this way about a sister."

"It's not wrong, Tammy. If anything, it's sad that it's taken this long for you two to be together again. Make the most of it. Embrace and send me lots of pictures," he said with a laugh.

"Oh, I already have a bunch, and I'm still at the airport," she joked. "At least I can use my phone to take pictures."

"I can't wait to see them. I'll call Matt after we hang up and tell him you arrived safely."

"Thanks. I'll call him on my sister's or my mom's phone tomorrow. I'm going to call Jenny next."

They remained on the phone for a few more minutes, and after proclaiming their love for each other many times, Tammy finally hung up and called Jenny.

She heard the familiar thick accent of her sister. "Hello, Jenny, speaking."

"Hey, Jenny, it's Tammy. I'm here in bloody England." She laughed with tears streaming down her face.

"Oh my gosh, I cannot believe it." Jenny cried. "Tommy and Kate can't wait to meet you."

"I can't wait to meet them either. How old are they now?" Tammy asked.

"Tommy is twenty-one, and Kate is twenty."

Tammy thought about all the time she had missed out on

getting to know her niece and nephew. "It's so sad that they are that old, and this is the first time I will meet them. It's the same with Matt. He is twenty-seven, and you've never met him."

Jenny released a heavy sigh. "I know. And he's a new daddy too. How is that little grandson of yours? I love the pictures you sent. He is adorable."

"Oh, Jenny, he stole my heart the day he was born, just like Matt did." Tammy released a heavy sigh. "It's so sad that mom will never get to meet her great-grandson."

"I know, and now Kate is pregnant. So Stuart and I are going to be grandparents. She's due at the end of the year."

Tammy gasped. "That's fantastic! You never told me."

" I was going to last week when I called you about mom, but when you told me you might come over, I figured I would wait to tell you then."

"I can't believe we are going to see each other in less than twelve hours," Tammy confessed. She sniffed back her tears.

"Me neither. We have so much catching up to do. Kate will give me a ride to the bus station because Stuart has to leave for work at five."

"You never learned to drive then?" Tammy asked.

"No. We have great public transportation here in England. There's no need for a car like there is in America. And besides, Stuart drives. We don't need two cars."

"Makes sense to me. America is so spread out. You can't get anywhere without a car." Tammy changed the subject and realized she was paying for this call with her credit card. "Anyway, we have the next two weeks to chat. My coach gets in at two in the morning at Leeds bus station. If there are any delays, I will call you at one of the stops."

"We will be there. Can't wait to see you, sis."

"Me neither. Love you."

"I love you too, Tammy."

Tammy's hand trembled as she hung up the phone. She was

overcome with emotions. Tears streamed down her face. God, how she wished Donna was with her. The best she could do for her mom was to have two of her daughters together. Tammy checked her watch. She still had three hours before she needed to be at the bus terminal. She hadn't eaten since breakfast on the plane and went in search of a restaurant.

After a delicious fish, chips, and mushy peas lunch, Tammy was now convinced there was no comparison when it came to English fish and chips. They truly were the best. On her way to the bus terminal, she stopped at a shop inside the airport and loaded up on English candy she had not had in years for the coach ride. She suddenly felt like a little kid in a candy store. All her favorites from her childhood days were still around, Barratt fruit salad chews, Black Jacks, Cadbury's Flake Chocolate, Wine Gums, Crunchie, and Quality Street all-sorted chocolates. "God, I'm going to get sick." Tammy laughed to herself as she stuffed the candy in her bag. But it was all so good, and she couldn't resist.

She arrived at the bus terminal thirty minutes early. Fatigue and jet lag were certainly beginning to kick in. Her eyes were heavy, and her body ached. Tammy was sure she'd be able to sleep most of the way.

After handing her luggage to the driver who stored it on the bus, Tammy found a seat near the back and was pleased when the bus left the station that her row remained empty. She had it all to herself. She spent the first hour looking out of the window and taking it all in and reading every road sign, admiring the small English shops and quaint English homes. The further they got out of London, the less traffic there was, and Tammy was in awe of the rich green rolling hills. Living in California, she'd forgotten how green England was. It was beautiful and lush. As the sun began to set and she strained to see anything in the evening shadows, Tammy nestled her body into a comfy position and soon drifted off to sleep.

She wasn't sure how long she had slept, but the slowing down of the bus woke her. Tammy looked out the window. It was pitch black except for the lights of the station up ahead and a few surrounding buildings. She scanned the bus and saw there were a few new passengers. At the precise moment that Tammy wondered where they were, the bus driver announced it over the intercom. "We are now pulling into Wakefield." He repeated for the second time. "All remaining passengers that are going to Leeds. This will be a fifteen-minute stop."

Tammy remembered Wakefield. They were about ten miles from Leeds. She couldn't believe that she would see Jenny in less than half-hour if the bus didn't make any more stops. Tammy left the bus stretching her legs, and took a much-needed bathroom break. She wasn't too keen on using the one on the bus.

"We'll be leaving in ten minutes." The bus driver hollered as she stepped off the bus."

Tammy turned and smiled. "Thanks. Hey, is the next stop Leeds?" She asked.

"Yes, ma'am. Should be there in about twenty-five minutes."

Tammy nodded and made a quick dash for the bathrooms.

When she returned to her seat, the bus pulled out of the station a few minutes later. Tammy rooted through her purse for her hair-brush and cosmetics and spent the last leg of the trip freshening up. Her nerves peeked, and beads of sweat surfaced on her palms. City lights outside the window caught her attention. The sight was familiar. They were driving through Leeds. A place she knew well and the last-placed she lived in England. She scanned the old buildings and recognized them all. The Queens Hotel was still there. A place she had spent many nights drinking with co-work-ers. Across the road was the hotel she used to work at. Tammy saw the bus driver had turned down the street where the train station was. It was still there, and a block further down, she saw the bus depot.

Her twenty-four-hour journey was ending. It was almost two o'clock in the morning, but she wasn't tired. She had slept for most of the bus ride. She was too excited to sleep. There were very few cars on the road, and the streets were practically empty. Tammy peered out of the window as they pulled into the bus depot and saw Jenny immediately standing inside, pointing at the bus she was on. Tammy gasped. "Oh my god, there she is, and that must be her daughter." They were the only ones inside. Tammy saw Jenny wipe a tear from her eye. She wasn't sure if she had spotted her on the bus.

When the bus came to a stop, Tammy took a deep breath and wiped away a few of her own tears. She couldn't believe she was finally going to be holding her sister after thirty-plus years.

CHAPTER 39

ammy was one of only three passengers left on the bus by the time they reached Leeds. It didn't take the bus driver long to get their luggage, and he had it lined up on the curb when Tammy stepped off the bus. She thanked the driver and turned to look at the window where Jenny was standing. Jenny smiled and waved and raced towards the double exit doors with her daughter following closely behind. Tammy grabbed her luggage and walked as fast as she could to meet her, and within seconds she entered the building. She saw Jenny holding out her arms, racing towards her with tears gushing down her cheeks. Tammy let go of her luggage and ran over to her sister.

"Jenny! Oh my god. I can't believe I am here." Tammy squealed as she tried to see through her teary eyes. She wiped them with her sleeve and wrapped her arms around Jenny.

Jenny embraced Tammy and held her tight "Oh, Tammy; I've missed you so much."

Overcome with emotions, Tammy's body trembled to the core. She cupped Jenny's face in her palms and released a nervous laugh, "You still look like the Jenny I remember. You haven't changed a bit, and you look great." Her hair was longer and darker. It was now straight. Tammy remembered it being shorter and wavy when she was younger.

Jenny smiled through her tears and kissed Tammy on the cheek. "You still look the same too. Skinny as ever I see. And you still have that red hair."

Tammy laughed and smiled at her pregnant niece. "This must be your daughter, Kate."

Jenny released her hold on Tammy and embraced her daughter. "Yes, it is."

Kate smiled and walked over to Tammy's open arms.

"It's great to finally meet you," Tammy said with tears still rolling down her cheeks. You are beautiful."

Kate blushed. "Thanks."

"Where is your son?" Tammy asked.

"He lives with his girlfriend. They will be popping in tomorrow." Jenny replied and then took Tammy's hand. Well, come on then. Let's get home. You must be bloody knackered."

"I don't feel that bad. I slept on the bus for most of the way."

Jenny chuckled. "Well, I am. I don't remember the last time I stayed up until two o'clock in the morning." She hugged Tammy again. "Gosh, where has the time gone, Tammy. We have our whole lives to catch up on in just two weeks."

It was a short twenty-minute drive to Jenny's house. Tammy and Jenny had talked for the entire ride, but the mood had turned somber.

"So, how is mom doing? Tammy asked. "I missed her coming out last year."

Jenny turned to face her from the front passenger seat. "Not good. Don't be surprised when you see her tomorrow. She has aged a lot since you saw her last."

Tammy waved her hand. "Oh, come on. She can't have aged that much." Tammy said with a nervous chuckle.

"She's not the same mom Tammy. I just want to warn you, so

you won't be too shocked when you see her. We are going over there tomorrow when Stuart gets home from work."

Tammy wondered if Jenny was exaggerating their mother's health, and if she wasn't, Tammy feared her reaction. She had to hold it together for her mother's sake.

When they pulled up in front of Jenny's house, Tammy stood outside in the fenced front yard and admired the surroundings. Her sister lived on a quiet cul-de-sac street in a semi-detached house. She thought back to the many times she had wondered what her sister's house looked like. It was quaint, and when they walked inside, it sparkled. The house was spotless from top to bottom, and everything had its place. Tammy trod lightly through the living room to look at a collage of pictures hanging on the wall. She whispered when she spoke carefully not to wake her husband, Stuart. She looked at the photos and saw it had her, Donna, mom and dad, and Jenny's two children. "I love this," Tammy said softly.

"It's a way to keep the family together," Jenny replied in a whisper. "Do you want some tea?" she asked.

Tammy shook her head. "No, I better not. I'm going to try and get some sleep. Otherwise, I'll be no good tomorrow."

Jenny approached her and hugged her. "I'm so happy you are here."

"Me too."

The next morning after her daughter and Stuart had left for work, Tammy and Jenny spent the morning having coffee and sharing stories of their separate lives over the past thirty years. Jenny pulled out tons of photo albums, and together, they sat on the couch, and Tammy listened as Jenny told her the stories behind the pictures. They laughed, they cried, and they embraced each other as the gaps were filled in about one another's lives.

"Oh, Jenny, you have a beautiful family, and it looks like you've had a wonderful life so far. I'm sorry I have not been a part of it except for the occasional letter and picture."

Jenny took Tammy's hand. "I'm sorry too. Now that the kids

have grown up, Stuart and I can do more." She gave Tammy a large grin. "In fact, I may have a little surprise for you before you leave. But I'm still talking to Stuart about it."

"Well, what is it? I hate surprises," Tammy laughed.

"I can't tell you yet."

Stuart arrived home shortly before three. Tammy remembered him well. When she had last seen him, his beard was black. Now it was a silvery grey. Tammy thought it looked better grey. After he had changed, they left to go to their mother's flat. Tammy knew the route well from her school days. Every landmark they passed sparked a memory waiting to be revisited. When they pulled into the grounds of where their mom now lived, Tammy scanned the neighborhood. "I know this area well. My old flat was just across the road." Tammy pointed with her hand in the direction of her old flat. "And down there is the pub I used to hang out at. I wonder if it's still there?"

"Yes, it is," Jenny replied.

"Wow. It's like time has stood still. I'm going to have to take a walk later and check out my old flat."

Jenny had told Tammy earlier in the year that their mother lived in assisted living. She still had her own one-bedroom flat, but there were trained caregivers on the premises around the clock. It had gotten to the point that Jenny and Stuart didn't feel comfortable leaving mom alone without any help if she needed it. Tammy agreed.

Tammy stepped out of the car and liked what she saw. Rose bushes and luscious green grass surrounded the grounds. It was quiet and had a peaceful atmosphere to it. You would never know behind the row of oak trees that there was a busy main road. "This is beautiful," Tammy said.

"The people here are very nice. Mom lives up there on the second floor flat."

Tammy looked to where she was pointing. "How many flats per building?"

"Four. Two upstairs and two downstairs."

Tammy saw they were about a dozen buildings. "They look to be a good size," Tammy said as she scanned the area.

"They are, and the staff checks on everyone every day. They serve meals or mum can cook; she has a kitchen. They have events like bingo, movie night, and stuff."

"Bingo. I can't see mom playing bingo," Tammy laughed.

Jenny chuckled. "Believe it or not, mom loves bingo. I told you she has aged. Now prepare yourself."

Tammy took a deep breath. "Okay. Let's go. I'll follow you."

Jenny rummaged for her key to their mom's flat and finally retrieved it from the bottom of her purse. "Ahh, here it is. Are you ready?" she said as she took Stuart's hand and led the way up the stairs.

Tammy followed closely behind, unsure of what to expect.

After unlocking the door to their mother's flat, Jenny stood at the bottom of the dark narrow stairs and hollered. "Mother, it's Jenny; someone is here to see you."

There was no answer. Stuart led the way up the stairs with Jenny close behind. "Hello, mom," Jenny called again.

Tammy suddenly heard the faint voice of her mom coming from upstairs. "Is that you, Jenny?"

"Yes, mom. We are coming up the stairs. There's someone here to see you."

"I'm in the kitchen," her mother called back.

Jenny turned and smiled at Tammy and waited for her at the top of the steps with Stuart. "Are you okay?" Jenny asked Tammy.

Tammy nodded. "Yeah, I just can't believe I'm here in mom's flat."

"Me neither. Come on. Mom's going to be so shocked to see you. I had told her that you were coming, but I think she's forgotten already."

It alarmed Tammy that her mother would forget that her daughter would be visiting from America. "Is she that bad?" Tammy whispered.

"She's not the same, Tammy. I had warned you." Jenny took Tammy's hand and led her to the galley kitchen. They found their mother stooped over the counter, spooning sugar into a cup. Tammy's heart sank. It was worse than she had imagined. She didn't recognize the frail lady with grey hair and wearing a long nightie. Tammy watched as her mom put four teaspoons of sugar into her cup. Jenny walked over and took the spoon from her hand. "I think you have enough sugar, mom." She wrapped her arm over her shoulder and guided her to face Tammy. "Look who is here, mom."

Tammy looked into her mother's eyes and cried. Her mother's eyes that had always smiled back at her and believed in her were lifeless. Jenny was right; the sparkle had gone. Tammy knew the mother she once knew was slowly disappearing. "Hello, mom," Tammy said as she sniffed back her tears.

Her mom gave her a sweet smile. "Tammy! Oh, my goodness. You came all the way from America to see me?"

Tammy approached her mom and embraced her. "I did, mom. I figured it was my turn to come to see you."

Rose looked over Tammy's shoulder. "Is Donna with you?"

Tammy felt a lump rise in her throat. Her mom was still clinging on to her one wish. "No, mom, I'm afraid not."

Her mom nodded. "Well, I have two daughters here. I never thought I'd see the day." She freed herself from Tammy's hold and gave her another smile. "Do you want some tea?"

"I would love that, mom. Thank you. I'll help you fix it." Tammy turned to Jenny and spoke in a soft voice. "She remembers that I live in America, but yet she forgot that I was coming over to visit?" she questioned.

Jenny nodded. "Yes, her long distant memory is sharp. She

remembers a lot. It's her short term memory that is bad. You can tell her something, and a minute later, she will have forgotten."

Tammy nodded. "Oh, I see."

Rose released a nervous giggle, which soon turned into tears. Jenny pulled her into her arms. "Mom, what the matter?"

"I can't believe my Tammy is here from America in my flat and having tea."

Tammy's body shook. Her heart was heavy, and her hands trembled. "Oh, mom, don't cry. Come on, let's fix tea together. You can show me where everything is. Okay."

Her mom nodded and wiped her tears. "The cups are in the top cupboard. Jenny, can you put the kettle on."

"Sure, mom. Then I'll go join Stuart on the sofa and let you two finish making the tea."

Tammy stayed in the kitchen with her mom but remained quiet as she helped her. She was still trying to wrap her head around the vast changes in her mom. It was the first time she had ever seen her mom with uncombed grey hair, no make-up, or nail polish. Something her mother had always been adamant about.

Her mother snapped her out of her depressing thoughts. "Do you want some biscuits with your tea?" She asked.

Tammy had to think for a minute. Biscuits? And then she suddenly remembered biscuits were cookies in England. "Sure, mom, I'd love some. Where are they? I'll put some on a plate."

"I have your favorite. They are in the cupboard next to the cups. "Chocolate digestives. You used to love them when you were a kid. You would never save any for anyone else." Her mom laughed. "I always had to hide some otherwise, you'd eat them all."

"Ooh, yummy. I still love them. I've not had one in years."

"Come on, Tammy, I want to show you my flat," her mom said after setting down the plate of cookies on the coffee table.

"But what about the tea, Mom?" Tammy said as she put the tray down.

Her mom took her hand. "In a minute." She said and led her to the other side of the room to a large picture window. Tammy looked out onto the grounds below. Green grass and rose bushes just like the ones in the front of the building adorned the grounds below. Tammy noticed a small wooden bench and horses in the field beyond. "You have a nice view, mom."

"I love sitting here and watching the horses. They come by every day and stand by the fence, wagging their tails. There are two of them. I think they come to see me."

"I'm sure they do, mom," Tammy replied and then noticed the shelf of photo frames. Tammy walked over to the shelf and picked one up. "It was a picture of Jenny and Stuart at their wedding. "You have a lot of pictures, mom."

"Well, I never see anyone, so these make me feel close to you all."

Tammy picked up a picture of her, Dwayne, and Matt on the *Baywitch II*. Tammy remembered sending her the picture many years ago. It looked like mom had not forgotten anyone. There were pictures of Donna, her dad, and even some old photo of mom from the sixties wearing miniskirts. "Look at you, mom," Tammy said, admiring how beautiful her mom looked in the picture.

"That's when I first met your dad. I used to be a knockout."

Tammy laughed. "Yes, you were."

Her mom's apartment was small, with one bedroom, a bathroom, kitchen, and living room. Her bedroom was decorated in her favorite color, purple, with more family pictures on the white dresser.

"We are going to the shops for you, mom. What do you need?" Jenny asked when they returned to the front room.

"Chocolate," Rose replied.

Jenny laughed. "You always say that. You have loads of chocolate, mom. I'll go take a look in the fridge and write a list."

"Are you ready?" Jenny asked Stuart, who was still sitting on the couch, letting the three women have their space.

"Yep. Let's go."

Tammy was surprised they were all leaving. "Is mom going to be okay by herself? Does she want to go with us?" Tammy asked.

Jenny shook her head. "No, she doesn't like crowds. She panics. She hasn't been to the store in months. Stuart and I go for her three times a week."

Tammy gasped. "You never told me that."

"Oh, Tammy. So much has changed. She feels the safest here in her flat. We come by four to five times a week, and there are plenty of people and staff that are constantly checking in on her" Jenny hooked arms with Tammy. "Come on, let's go. We'll talk more in the car and while we are shopping."

Tammy walked over to her mom, who was now sitting in a recliner, drinking her tea. "Do you want the TV on, mom? We'll be back in a bit."

"Oh yes, my favorite show is on." She looked over at Jenny. "What is it called?"

"East Eden, mom," Jenny replied.

Stuart used the remote on the coffee table and found her mom's show before heading over to the stairs to follow Jenny and Tammy out to the car.

Tammy sat in the back, and Jenny sat next to Stuart in the front while he drove. She turned her neck to talk to Tammy. "How are you doing, sis?" she asked.

"Okay, I guess. I just can't believe how much mom has changed. She's like a different person, and it's happened so fast. I can see why she can't come to America." Tammy left out a heavy sigh. "And she never will again." Tammy thought of all the things her mom will never see. The house they were working so hard to build, her son Matt and her new great-grandchild.

Unless Donna made it to England, Tammy doubted, her mom would never see her other daughter again. The thought horrified Tammy. There was so much she should have done sooner and instead procrastinated. A quote popped into her head, *Don't put off until tomorrow what you can do today.* A quote she had heard for years suddenly meant something to her and made a lot of sense. Why hadn't she lived by that years ago? she wondered

"No, I'm afraid she won't be able to travel anymore," Jenny said, pulling Tammy out of her upsetting thoughts. "In fact, Stuart and I are looking into putting her into a home. I'm not sure how much longer she will be able to live by herself. I worry about her constantly when I'm not with her." Jenny confessed. "I have to work."

"I can see why," Tammy replied. "I think you are doing the right thing." Tammy paused for a moment and chose her words carefully, not wanting to offend Jenny. "In fact, do you mind if I stay with mom while I'm here? I can sleep on her couch."

Jenny smiled, which put Tammy at ease. "Of course, I don't mind. Why would I?"

"Well, I've not seen you in ages either. But I'm not sure when or if I will ever see mom again. And if I do make it out here again, the odds are that she won't recognize me. I want to spend as much time as I can with her." Tears pooled in Tammy's eyes. "I guess, in a way, this is my goodbye to mom."

"Oh, Tammy. Make those memories with mom. Do what you have to do. I understand. We'll be by every day after work, and we'll spend some time together. In fact, Stuart and I have been talking, and we are thinking about going to America next year."

Tammy's eyes lit up. "You are? What about mom?"

"If we find her a good home, she will be taken care of. Stuart and I need to do things for us too. Our kids are adults now, and I don't want to wait another thirty years before seeing you again. I'll be dead," she laughed.

Tammy matched her laugh. "You have a point there."

"I hate to say this, Tammy, but since dad died and mom's health has taken a turn for the worst, you and Donna are all I have left. We have to stick together."

"You're right" Tammy looked at Jenny and gave her a big smile.

"You know there is something I would like to do if you do come to America."

"What's that?" Jenny asked with a furrowed brow.

"I'd like to take a road trip in honor of mom to Colorado."

Jenny's eyes became bright. "You mean to Donna's?"

Tammy nodded. "Yes. You have not seen your twin since you were fifteen and mom's only wish was to have all her daughters in the same room. If the three of us are all we have, then we need to reunite our sisterhood and have a steak dinner together where we will raise our glasses to mom."

"Oh, Tammy, I think that's a brilliant idea. I would love to see Donna. Gosh, I often wondered if we still look alike."

"Well, you know from the pictures she has sent you, you can see her hair is blonde but put that aside, and yes, you guys still look alike. Not as much as you did when you were younger."

"Really?" Jenny questioned.

"Yes. I mean, you have both lived in different cultures, so of course, you aren't identical, but you both have the same smile. Your eyes are identical, and you both play with your hands too much," Tammy laughed.

Jenny looked down and saw she was rubbing her fingers into her palms and quickly stopped. "No, I do not." She protested and then laughed. "Oh, Tammy, I'm getting teary-eyed just thinking about it. Thirty-five years later, we are finally going to be together. What a reunion this is going to be.

CHAPTER 40

*W*hen they returned from the store, they found their mom still sat in the chair glued to the TV. Tammy wanted to cook her mom a special meal and remembered her favorite was Shepherd's Pie.

"Hey, mom, Jenny, and I are going to cook dinner. Do you want to help?" she asked. "It will be fun to all cook together. Don't you think?"

Stuart had finished putting the groceries away and took a seat on the couch. "Go on, Rose. When was the last time you cooked a meal with two of your daughters?"

Rose beamed a cute smile. "I would love that. What are we making?"

Tammy took her mom's hand and helped her out of the chair. "It's your favorite, Shepherd's Pie."

"Oh, I love Shepherd's Pie," Rose said as she followed Tammy into the kitchen where Jenny was already peeling the potatoes. She turned to her mom. "Do you want to help mom?" Jenny asked and pulled a chair out from the small bistro table that sat in front of the window. "Why don't you sit here and break up the mincemeat into a bowl or, as Tammy calls it, the hamburger." She laughed.

For a brief moment, while she laughed, joked, and cooked dinner with her sister and mom, Tammy felt reconnected with her family. How she wished Donna could have been with them. So much time had been lost between all of them. A simple thing like cooking dinner that most families do every night and take for granted was a memory Tammy would carry with her for the rest of her life. She knew it would never happen again once she returned to America. The thought that the three of them would not be in the same room also saddened her. And if it were to happen, Tammy knew her mother's health and declining memory would not allow her to realize it.

Tammy tried not to cry as her mom reminisced on the times she could remember. She talked a lot about their father, and Tammy wasn't sure if she remembered that he had passed away. She spoke as if he was still alive. "When was the last time you saw your dad?" she asked.

Tammy didn't know what would happen if she reminded her he was dead and instead gave a simple answer. "It's been a while, mom."

Over dinner, Tammy told her mom about the house she and Dwayne were building and showed her some pictures she had brought with her, but her mother was confused. "You're building a house? Why?"

"So we can live it in, mom. We live in a tiny house right now. We want to live in a bigger house."

"But I thought you lived on a boat," she said.

"That was years ago, mom. I don't fish anymore. We moved to the mountains." She looked over at Jenny with a blank stare and then tried to jog her mom's memory some more. "You've been to the house, mom. You always stay in the hotel by the freeway because there is no room in the tiny house."

Tammy continued to tell her about her changed life, but as

Jenny had told her, any recent news, she will forget about a few minutes later. Her mom still believed that Tammy was fishing and lived on a boat. For her time had stood still.

After dinner, Jenny and Tammy did the dishes while Stuart kept Rose company in the living room. Before they left to go home, Jenny showed Tammy their mom's routine. "Here are her night pills," Jenny said as she handed them to her. "When no one is here, a nurse comes every morning and around dinner time to give them to her. But I already called them and told them you would be staying here."

Tammy nodded and put the pills on the kitchen counter. "Can I take her for a walk in the morning? Do you think it would be okay?"

"Yes, she loves going for walks around the grounds; just don't take her to any crowded places."

"Where I used to live is just across the road. I would love to see it. Do you think she'd be okay walking over there?"

"Yes, as long as you hold her hand while walking across the main road." Jenny glanced around the clean kitchen. "Okay, then. Well, everything is put away in here. Mom will probably watch TV for another hour, and then she'll be ready for bed. Stuart and I will be here tomorrow afternoon, and we will bring your luggage."

Tammy smiled and hugged her sister. "It feels so good to be here. I guess I'm living in these clothes until I see you," she laughed.

Jenny walked to the stairs where Stuart was waiting. "Call me if you have any problems."

"Will do. Love you, sis."

"Love you too. We'll see you tomorrow."

An hour later, just like Jenny had said, her mom was ready for bed, and after tucking her in, Tammy kissed her good night and closed her bedroom door.

Still exhausted from her travels, Tammy called it an early night, made her bed on the couch, and soon drifted off to sleep. She wasn't sure how long she had been sleeping, but the sound of her mom talking from her bedroom woke her. Confused, Tammy sat up and pinned her ears.

"I will not leave. You leave," she heard her mother say.

Tammy knew there was no one in the room with her mom, but her mom was having a full-blown imaginary conversation with someone.

"You come here every night and tell me to leave. I won't. Do you hear me?" Her mom said in a louder and harsher tone.

Tammy wondered what she should do. Should she go in there? What if her mother has forgotten she was visiting, and she scares her? Suddenly she heard her mom scream.

"Get out!"

"Shit," Tammy whispered under her breath. "What the hell should I do?" Tammy tip-toed across the living room in the dark, feeling her way with her hands until she reached the opening of the kitchen doorway, where she turned on the light. Her mom shouted again.

"I told you to get out!"

Tammy looked at the clock hanging on the wall. It was two in the morning. "Shit, I can't call Jenny at this hour. She has to go to work in the morning."

Tammy left the lights off in the living room and tip-toed over to the door of her mother's room, using the glare from the kitchen lights to find her way. She pinned her ear to the door and held her breath. There was silence on the other side. Tammy remained quiet and continued to hold her breath as she listened hard for any sounds coming from the room. Her heart soon relaxed when she heard the faint snoring sound coming from the other side of the door. Tammy realized her mom was sleeping and released a huge sigh of relief before quietly returning to the couch.

The sound of a kettle whistle from the kitchen woke Tammy. She stirred, wiped her eyes, and sat up. "Mom, is that you?"

Rose hollered from the kitchen. "Of course, it's me. Who else would it be?" she snapped.

"Sorry, mom. Just checking," Tammy replied. Surprised by her mom's mean spirit. "Are you making coffee?" she asked standing up from the couch.

"No. I'm pissing in the sink," her mother barked. "What's with all the stupid questions?"

Her mom's demeanor shocked Tammy. Last night she was sweet and loving, and together they shared so many fond memories, and this morning, she was acting like the wicked witch from the east.

Tammy walked to the doorway of the kitchen, where she found her mom pacing. She slammed the cupboard door shut after grabbing a cup and snarled at Tammy. "What are you looking at?"

"I wonder if you need any help."

"I don't need your help. Why are you here?"

"I'm here visiting with you. I want to spend some time with you." Tammy said in a soft tone attempting to calm down her mom.

"I don't like visitors. I like to be alone. Why don't you go back to America and leave me alone?"

Her mom's words crushed Tammy. Surely she didn't mean what she had just said. Did her mother even know what she was saying? Tammy wondered. Tammy stared at the woman that she no longer knew. That was not her mother standing before her. Her mom would never talk to her in such a spiteful way, with words that were only meant to hurt. It was the disease talking, just like last night when she heard her in the bedroom. Tammy believed that subconsciously her mother was yelling at the disease to go away. Tammy folded her arms and sobbed as she watched the awful disease of dementia possess her mom. She wanted to hold her tight and protect her from the sickness that was invading her mind and stripping her of all the goodness she once owned.

Her mother stood in the kitchen and narrowed her eyes at her. "Why are you crying? Stop being a baby."

Tammy shook her head. She wasn't going to talk back and try to reason with her. She read about the mood swings of dementia and knew this would pass. She just didn't know how long it would last. "I'm going to take a bath. I'll make my coffee when I get out."

"Fine," her mom said without looking at her.

When Tammy returned thirty minutes later, she knew her mom's mood had flipped. She was still in the kitchen, sitting at the table. She was looking out of the window and hadn't heard Tammy enter.

"Hi, Mom," Tammy whispered, unsure how her mother would react.

Her mom turned and beamed her big smile. "Tammy. You're awake. I made some coffee."

Tammy smiled back, feeling relieved, and poured herself a cup of coffee. She sat across from her mom and took her hand. "How are you feeling? Did you sleep okay?"

"I slept like a baby all night long," she replied with a smile.

Her answer told Tammy that her mom had no recollection of her screaming last night.

Tammy nodded. "I'm glad you slept well. I thought we'd go for a walk this morning. Would you like that?"

Her mother smiled again. "Yes, I would like that. But I don't want to go to any shops."

"Don't worry; we won't go to any shops. I used to have a flat close to here. I thought we'd take a walk over there and look at it."

"I remember that. Yes, you did."

"Okay, then. Let's get you dressed and find you a coat, and we'll take a nice morning stroll together."

When they stepped outside into the damp morning air, Tammy took a deep breath and filled her lungs. She'd forgotten how chilled the mornings were in England. She looked down the pathway and saw the haze. Dewdrops blanketed the grass, and the air smelt clean. She locked arms with her mom, and they walked. The first thing Tammy noticed was how slowly her mother walked. And it wasn't because of her age. It was because every few minutes, she had to stop and look at something and ask so many questions. She had stopped at the edge of the grass and stared down at it, "Why is grass green?" she asked.

Tammy didn't have an answer. "I don't know, mom."

Further down the path, her mom stopped again, picked up a twig, and then looked up at the surrounding trees. "I wonder which tree this fell off?"

Tammy waited patiently while her mom continued to investigate the twig. "I don't know, mom. There are lots of twigs on the ground. It could be from any of these trees."

Tammy watched as her mom bent down and picked up a leaf. "Do you think this twig and leaf fell off the same tree?"

Tammy shrugged her shoulders. "Maybe."

When they reached the main road, Tammy saw the fear in her mom's eyes. "I can't cross the road, Tammy. The cars are going too fast."

Tammy took her hand. "Mom. There is a crosswalk. The cars will stop for us."

Her mom took Tammy's hand and squeezed it tight. Tammy winced from the pain of her grip. "How do you know they will stop?" her mom asked with fear.

Tammy led her to the curb. "Because there is a traffic light and when it turns red, they have to stop. It's the law." Tammy pushed the button at the crosswalk. "Now, when our light turns green, it means we can walk."

Her mom looked at the crosswalk light. "It's red."

"It will change in a minute," Tammy replied. When the light turned green, and the cars had stopped, her mom stepped back from the curb. "I can't do this, Tammy."

"It's okay, mom. You're with me. I won't let anything happen to you." She said as she squeezed her hand tighter.

Rose hesitated and then slowly took Tammy's lead. Tammy quickened her pace, fearing her mom may freak out in the middle of the road. But she did not. When they reached the other side, Tammy praised her like she would a child. "Good job, mom! You did it."

Tammy knew the area well. She spent her last few years in England in this neighborhood. She turned onto the familiar road, Manor terrace, and immediately spotted her old flat. Emotions and memories raced through her. She stood in front of the red brick terrace house and looked at the door that was once her entranceway to the ground flat where she used to live. Ironically, it still looked the same except for the fresh white paint job on the window frames.

Her mom stood by her side. "Is that your old place?" she asked.

"Yep, it sure is." Tammy looked at the window off to the left of the door and remembered the room as if it were yesterday. It was the main room to the flat where she had her bed. She pictured the small kitchenette and chuckled when she remembered she shared the bathroom with her neighbors.

She thought back to her last night in England. She had gotten drunk at her surprise, leaving the party, and had come home and called her boyfriend, Ian, from this flat. For the first time, she had told him she was leaving him and going to live in America. Tammy realized how wrong that was of her leaving Ian in the dark until the night before she was to leave. She wondered where he was now. Did he ever marry or have kids? "So many memories," Tammy whispered to herself. She turned to her mom and saw she was shivering. "Come on, mom. Let's get you home. You're cold. I'll make you a nice hot cup of tea."

When Jenny and Stuart arrived later in the afternoon, Rose was taking a nap in her bedroom. Tammy had used the time to call Dwayne and Matt and give them the sad news about her mom's health. "Did you know mom has severe mood swings?" Tammy asked Jenny.

"Oh, yes. I should have told you about those. She can be quite nasty at times."

"I'll say," Tammy said. "This morning, she was awful. She told me to go back to America."

"Well, I see you didn't listen." Jenny laughed. "You're still here."

Tammy stuck out her tongue. "Ha. Ha. Very funny. I just ignored her and took a bath. By the time I got out, she was fine."

"Yep, that's all you can do. Don't argue with her. That will just make it worse and agitate her more."

"After I have gone for a walk with mom, I think tomorrow I'm going to jump on a bus and visit Tridale. I guess I want to take a trip down memory lane. This morning mom and I went and saw my old flat. It brought back so many memories. Now I want to see Tridale and see the house we grew up in. I also want to take a walk on the moors."

"That's a great idea, Tammy. Do as much as you can while you are here. It's only a twenty-minute bus ride. I'll be at Mom's place by noon tomorrow. So take as long as you need."

Tammy patted her knee. "Thanks."

CHAPTER 41

The next morning, Tammy was pleased to find her mom in a pleasant mood, and after going for their morning stroll, she left for her much-anticipated trip to Tridale. By ten, she was sitting on the upper level of a double-decker, traveling down the familiar roads that she had done so many times as a child. Every street held a memory. She recognized many of the old stone buildings, and even some familiar pubs were still around, which surprised her.

When she stepped off the bus in the heart of Tridale, it was pouring rain. She laughed. Memories of her last night in Leeds popped into her head again. She knew every part of the town, and it all came back to her as though she had never left. It seemed time had stood still in the quaint little town she once called home. She looked up to the sky and stuck out her tongue. She giggled when the cold raindrops splashed on her tongue. The rain was coming down hard, but Tammy didn't care. In fact, she loved it. The English rainfall felt good.

She looked up at the steep road that led to the moors and headed up that way first. Every step took her deeper into her memory vault. She had friends that used to live on this street. She stopped and looked at the house they used to live in and reminisced back to the days when they played outside in the yard. She could see as clear as day herself as a child playing hopscotch with her schoolmate on the sidewalk.

When she reached the edge of the moors, the rain was beating hard against her face. She had no umbrella or hat, and her hair was drenched. Her sweater stuck to her arms, and the wool sagged around her wrist. Tammy squeezed them to wring out the excess water. Her jeans were tight against her skin from being soaked and squeaked against her thighs as she walked. But it didn't faze or upset Tammy. She was back on the moors after being away for so long, and it felt bloody fantastic.

She knew her way around the moors like the back of her hand; it was her after school playground as a child. She headed for the wading pool first, wondering if it was still there. She smiled when she saw it still was and was surprised to see it overflowing from the downpour of rain. She spent so many summer days at the pool with her sisters and friends from school. Her mom would bring them with a packed lunch, and they would spend entire days there. When she grew older, Tammy ventured on her own with her sisters or school mates.

Tammy looked up into the distance and saw the trail that led to the tarn and walked that route next. On either side of the trail stood tall bracken and fenced yards to the houses that backed up to the edge of the moors. The trail still looked the same, and Tammy wondered how many times she had walked and ran up and down it in her younger years. She had spent most of her childhood years on the moors, hiding in the bracken, chasing foxes, and searching for hedgehogs.

It took her roughly ten minutes to reach the tarn. The rain continued to pour and splashed when it hit the surface of the water. Tammy stood before the tarn and smiled. She pictured herself as a much younger Tammy, wearing wellington boots and wading in the water, looking for frogspawn and leaping through the water trying to catch tap-poles. Many times she'd trip, lose her balance, and fall in. But those were the times when she would laugh the hardest. Her times on the moors were happy times—filled with laughter that she shared with childhood friends and her sisters. Tammy wondered whatever became of those friends. When they had all left school, they had all gone their separate ways and never kept in touch.

Tammy spent the next few hours on the moors hiking the familiar trails that she knew so well. She was revisiting her childhood and wasn't ready to leave. She wanted to ignite as many memories as she could—some that she had long forgotten. When she was ready to go, she was surprised the gate at the back of a hotel was still there and still unlocked. As a child, it had been her passage to the moors from the house she had grown up in when her family was still together.

Tammy pushed on the gate and walked down the long driveway that would take her to the narrow dirt path at the top of her old street. As she walked down the street, she took a minute to remember all the people who lived in each house when she was growing up. The houses hadn't changed much except for paint jobs, new windows, and spruced up yards. Tammy was surprised that she could remember most names of her old neighbors. Children she used to play with and their parents. The grumpy old guy Stan would yell at them for playing outside his house and making too much noise. And then she saw it.

Tammy gasped, and tears pooled in her eyes. There it was. Her old house. The house where she was once part of a family, where they all sat down and ate dinners. They played board games at night; it was a house with two parents and three children. Tammy cried when she looked up and saw her old bedroom window, and next to it was the window to her mom and dad's room. She cried harder when she saw the wooden gate across the driveway. It was now red. It used to be green. It warmed her heart to see it was still there because she had watched her father build it in the garage and had helped him hang it on the hinges. He was so proud when he had stood back and admired his work. "It's still here, dad," Tammy whispered through her tears.

Tammy stood there for some time. She was picturing the layout and every room in the house. But when the memory of her mom crying as she held her daughters and told them that their father had moved out crept into her head, Tammy knew it was time to leave, and she did.

After her emotions had subsided, Tammy walked through the town and saw the grammar school was still there, and some more fond memories of her school days returned. She stopped and had a scone and tea in a café, and afterward, she jumped on a bus back to her mom's flat—by which time the rain had stopped.

She found her mom and Jenny sitting outside on a wooden bench underneath a shade tree. Stuart was inside changing some burned-out light bulbs and doing some other small tasks.

"My God, look at your hair. Your clothes are soaked," Jenny said.

Tammy giggled. "Well, it rained most of the day for my walk through Tridale and the moors. Of course, it stopped when I got on the bus to come back here."

"Sounds like typical English weather," Jenny joked. "Hey Stuart, and I want to take you out for dinner tonight. Mom will be fine with the TV on."

"Sounds good. It would be nice to spend some time with you guys." Tammy looked down at her wardrobe. "I guess I should go take a bath and change."

Jenny nodded and laughed. "Good Idea."

～

T ammy couldn't believe how fast her time in England went by. When it was time to leave two weeks later, she wasn't ready. She felt like she was finally getting to know her sister again and her family. Her children were no longer just names in a letter and faces in a photo. They were real people she had grown to love.

The hardest part was saying goodbye to her mom. Tammy knew deep in her heart that this would be the last time she would look into her mother's eyes, and her mother would recognize her as her daughter. Tammy's heart was in pieces. She didn't want her mom to forget her, but she knew it was inevitable. For Tammy, this was a final goodbye, whether or not she made it back to England. Over time, Tammy would become a stranger to her mother. It had already begun. The handwritten letters that her mom used to write to her had stopped arriving a few months ago. There were no more phone calls, and soon her mother's lips would stop calling her name. Tammy couldn't wrap her head around the thought that there will come a day that her mom will forget she has three daughters. The pain was unbearable, and Tammy sobbed as she held her mom for what might be the last time as mother and daughter as Tammy knew it. This would be one of the last memories she would have of her mother before dementia strips her of her soul and mind. What a cruel disease, Tammy thought. "I'm going to miss you, mom," Tammy cried.

Her mom cried too. "Why do you have to go, Tammy?" she asked between her tears.

"Because I live in America, mom. My home, my husband, and my son are there. And I have a grandson now too." Tammy mentioned her grandson to her a few times during her visit, but her mother soon forgot an hour or so later.

"Can you come back tomorrow?" her mom asked.

Tammy shook her head and sniffed back her tears. "No, mom, I'm afraid I can't. I live too far away."

Her mother's mood suddenly changed. She glared at Tammy

and narrowed her lips. "Fine then." She released herself from Tammy's embrace. "I'm going to go make some tea. I'll see you later."

Tammy watched with disbelief as her mom marched off to the kitchen. She turned to Jenny, who was wiping the last of her tears away. "Now what? I just go?" Tammy whispered.

Jenny nodded. "I'm afraid so. She won't remember any of this by tonight."

It was hard not to feel hurt by her mother's actions, but Tammy had to remember her mother was not herself anymore. She picked up her flight back, and Stuart grabbed her suitcase. "Okay, then. Bye, mom," Tammy called from the front room and walked over to the doorway of the kitchen. Her mother had her back to her and was putting a tea-bag in a cup. She didn't turn to look at her and said, "bye."

"Oh, Jenny, I feel awful leaving you here to take care of mom. It won't be easy." Tammy said from the back seat of the car.

"It's okay, Tammy. I'll manage like I said before. You took care of dad and went to Ireland. It's my turn now. I'll keep you updated on what's going on."

Tammy reached over and squeezed Jenny's shoulder. "Thank you."

"You don't have to thank me. She's my mom, too. Stuart has been a lot of help. We'll get through it." Jenny said while giving Stuart a loving smile.

By the time they reached the airport, Tammy's tears were flowing again. "Oh, I hate all these goodbyes." She sobbed after checking in her baggage, holding Jenny tight. She and Stuart could go no further with her at the airport. The departing gate that led to the flight's lounge was just a hundred yards away. It was time to say goodbye once more.

Jenny was also crying. "I know me too."

"I'm so glad I came. I needed this. I need to reconnect with my roots and you. I love you, sis," Tammy said as she wiped her eyes.

"I love you too. We will do our best to come to America next year. Let's see how mom does, and I'll let you know."

Tammy nodded and then hugged Stuart. "Thank you for taking care of Jenny. You are a good man."

Stuart smiled. "Thanks, she's my world."

Tammy took a deep breath and hugged her sister one more time. "Well, then, I guess this is it. Bye, sis."

"Bye, Tammy. We'll see you soon, I promise."

Tammy couldn't hold back the stream of tears that gushed down her cheeks and cried hard as she spoke. "I know. I'll call you when I'm home. Bye." She stepped back, reluctantly walked toward the gates. Every few steps, she turned her head and saw her sister and Stuart standing arm in arm, waving their arms high. Tammy waved back until she walked through the gates, and she could no longer see them.

It was still daylight when the plane finally took off two hours later. Tammy had a window seat and leaned as far forward as she could and watched her native land fade off into the distance as the plane climbed up into the skies. "Bye, England," Tammy whispered and then closed her eyes and dreamt of her mom when she was of mind and body.

CHAPTER 42

*W*hen Jenny called a month later to tell Tammy they had booked their tickets for America; Tammy almost dropped the phone. "You're kidding. When will you be here?"

"September of next year." Jenny squealed down the phone.

Tammy counted the months in her head. "That's in just over a year. Wow! I can't believe it. You're coming to America. What about mom?" Tammy asked. "How is she doing?"

Jenny released a heavy sigh. "Oh, Tammy, she is much worse since you saw her. She forgets everything. She left the gas on the cooker once and the bathtub running. Thank god the nurses check on her regularly when I'm not there. But it's not safe to leave her alone. We've found her a nice home, and this weekend she moved in."

Tammy spoke with a somber tone. "You're doing the right thing, Jenny."

"Thanks. It's just hard. We'll go there every weekend to visit her and whenever we can go after work. But at least we have peace of mind, and we know she will be safe." Jenny released another heavy sigh. "Just last week, one of the staff where she lives now found her walking at night in the pouring rain in her nightie and bathrobe. She had no idea where she was. It's time, Tammy."

"Oh, my goodness. That's terrible—poor mom. I agree, Jenny. It's time." After saying her goodbyes and hanging up the phone. Tammy raced out to the yard to find Dwayne. He was inside the new house taking measurements. She raced over to him, unable to hide her excitement. "Dwayne! Dwayne."

He looked up startled and stood up from his knees. "Hey, what's up? Are you okay?"

Tammy came to a sudden stop and heaved to catch her breath. "Jenny and Stuart are coming to America. They've booked their tickets."

Dwayne's eyes grew wide. "What? When?"

"Next September. In thirteen months."

Dwayne glanced around their unfinished house. The framework was completed. It had a roof and windows. The wiring and light needed to be installed, which Matt planned on doing with the company he worked for. The plumbing would be done in a month. Wow! We have just over a year to finish this house and be moved in so they can stay in the tiny house."

Tammy looked around the shell of the house. "Yep. Think we can do it?"

"I guess we will find out." Dwayne laughed. We have lots of work ahead of us. Cabinets have to be installed—drywall and installation. We need to install the floors and carpeting and paint all the walls. Oh, and let's not forget all the tongue and groove for the high vaulted ceilings. The planks will have to be stained and nailed up by hand."

"We got this." Tammy said with a ray of confidence." We are also going to have to fix up the tiny house. It's going to need a paint job and new carpeting, I'm sure."

.   .   .

They worked hard over the next year in a race to move into the new house before Jenny and Stuart arrived. But they had another reason to expedite the completion of the house. Now that their grandson was older, Tammy was eager to have him spend weekends with them. There was no room in the tiny house.

They spent many late nights after working all day staining, painting, or installing cabinets. But the excitement of Jenny visiting and spending more time with their grandson kept them going, and they pushed through the fatigue and sore muscles. They got only a few hours of sleep every night, and a week before Jenny and Stuart's arrival Tammy was sitting on the couch in their new home beaming a huge smile. "I can't believe we did it." She said to Dwayne, who was positioning the recliner beneath the window.

"Me neither. I've always said we make a great team."

"We still have a tiny house to do. It will need a good cleaning before pulling out the old carpet and putting in the new. And I want to paint the walls too."

"We have a week. I think we can do it," Dwayne said.

Tammy glanced around the house they built. It was beautiful with a rustic charm and lots of natural wood. A wood-burning stove sat in the corner of the main room, surrounded by slate tiles and a majestic log mantel made from a fallen tree off their mountain. Another log stood tall in the center of the room, also from the mountain. It supported the loft that looked down over where she sat on the couch. One day I will write my book up there, she thought to herself.

Tammy felt a twinge of sadness, knowing that none of their parents would see their labor of love. They would have been so proud of them both. How she wished they had started the house sooner before their parents' health had failed them.

The week flew by, and Tammy raced to get the tiny house completed with Dwayne's aid when he wasn't working and her good friend Mandy. She couldn't believe with just a day to spare before she would have to pick up Jenny and Stuart from the airport, the tiny house was finished. She sat outside on the patio and wiped her brow. Dwayne handed her a tall glass of ice tea. "I can't believe we did it. Everything looks fantastic," Dwayne said with pride.

Tammy smiled. "It sure does. And I even planned a road trip. Everything is booked. We leave in four days."

"We need to find someone to watch the animals sometime so that I can go with you on one of these trips," Dwayne said in a somber tone.

"I know, but you can't just ask anyone to take care of the falcons. And you would worry the whole time we were gone. They need special handling. Very few people know how to take care of a falcon. Let alone six?"

"Yeah, I know, but I'm still going to figure something out eventually." Dwayne changed the subject. "Are you excited?" Dwayne asked.

"I am, but I'm also really nervous. The three of us have not been together in decades. It's going to be emotional, but also strange. I wonder how Jenny feels about it? She hasn't seen her twin since she was fifteen. I still can't believe it's been that long." Tammy leaned back and gave her head a shake. "God, where has the time gone?"

"Well, it's going to be a memorable trip, that's for sure."

"It is. We are going to stop in Vegas on the way and the Grand Canyon on the way back. I also want to take them to Laughlin and the small town of Williams. We have missed out on so much that I want to make memories with my sisters again. It's what mom would have wanted. This road trip is not only for us but for her too."

Dwayne took the day off from work the next day. He couldn't go to Colorado with Tammy, so he wanted to make sure he would be there with her at the airport to pick up Jenny and Stuart.

The flight arrived on time, and after waiting a few hours in the arrival terminal while they cleared customs, Tammy finally spotted them walking up the ramp. She waved her hands high above her head and screamed. "Jenny!"

Jenny heard her and scanned the terminal until she spotted Tammy and beamed at her with a huge smile. Stuart waved, and Dwayne waved back. "They are here." Tammy cried as she leaned into Dwayne and hugged him.

"Yes, they are. I'm looking forward to meeting them both for the first time."

"I know you and Stuart will get along. You guys have a lot of the same interests."

"Oh, I plan on taking him shooting, fishing, and hunting when you guys get back from Colorado."

"He'll love it." Tammy laughed while walking towards her sister. "There's not much of that in England."

Within minutes Tammy was in the arms of Jenny with her eyes full of tears. "Oh, I can't believe you are here."

"Me neither. I shouldn't have waited so long." Jenny wiped her eyes and hugged Tammy again. "But we are here now, and it will be the first of many trips."

"Oh, I hope so. You are welcome anytime. You know that, right?"

Jenny laughed and then smiled at Dwayne. "Hello, you must be Dwayne."

Tammy left her sister's arms, wrapped her arms around Dwayne, and gave him a loving smile. "Yes, this is my man."

Dwayne squeezed Tammy and then leaned in and gave her a lingering kiss before letting go to give Jenny a friendly hug.

Stuart approached him and smiled. "And I'm Stuart. Good to finally meet you, mate." He said in a thick English accent.

"You too. Core blimey. I'll be talking like you English folks by the time you go home." Dwayne joked while trying to imitate an English accent

Stuart laughed. "I dunno about that. Might take a bit of work," he laughed.

Tammy and Jenny laughed out loud at their husbands, making fun of each other. "Oh, this is going to be an interesting visit with these too, "Tammy laughed. She took Jenny's hand. "Come on, sis. Through those doors is America, and I want to show you a piece."

The sisters locked arms and together skipped out of the airport into the glorious California sunshine while the guys continued to make jokes while lagging behind them.

"So does Donna know we are coming?" Jenny asked from the back seat of the car. Dwayne was driving, and Tammy sat in the front passenger seat. Stuart sat next to Jenny.

Tammy turned her head to face her. "Yes, she knows. I called her a couple of months ago. I thought about surprising her, but what if she had plans or something? It would suck if we drove all the way out there, and she was out of town."

"So how did she seem? Is she excited?" Jenny asked.

Tammy nodded and then giggled. "Oh my god, yes. She's been asking all kinds of questions about you since I saw you last year. I sent her pictures, and she still can't believe that we will all be together in a few days," Tammy laughed again. "I can't either."

"When was the last time you saw her?" Jenny asked.

"Oh gosh, it's been a long time. It was when Jason died. God, that was so sad. He was way too young. It's a shame you never met him. He was a nice guy and did so much for Donna." Tammy paused. "She's remarried now. He sounds nice, and Donna seems happy, which is the most important part, but I think a piece of her heart will always be with Jason."

"Yeah, I know. I'm sorry I didn't either. Gosh, Tammy, there's so much I wish I had done. We missed so much growing up."

"I know we did. I hope we can all make up for the lost time and make this the beginning of our newborn sisterhood. Not just for us, but for mom too."

Jenny smiled. "I agree. Before we left, I told her we were finally getting together and about the road to Colorado, but there was no recognition from her. Just a blank stare. It's so heartbreaking."

"I know. I would like to think she knows, and somewhere inside of her, she is smiling with joy, knowing her three daughters will be together again. I was crushed when you called me a few months ago and told me she can no longer speak and is now bedridden. Got what a horrible disease. It just rips the victim of everything."

"I won't lie, Tammy. It's been hard watching mom slowly disappear from us. I no longer know what she understands or even hears when I talk to her. I try not to cry when I visit her, and I talk to her just like I've always done. Like she understands everything I'm saying. What helps is having Stuart with me. He is with me every time."

Tammy looked over at Stuart, smiled at him, and then took her sister's hand and gave it a gentle squeeze. "Thank you for being there for mom."

Jenny shook her head to fight her tears. "Okay. I'm going to cry. Let's talk more about the trip. As much as I can't wait to see Donna, I'm also excited about going to Vegas. We are really going to Vegas?" Jenny squealed.

Tammy chuckled at her excitement. She wanted this trip to be memorable and had planned their trip and booking the rooms in Vegas. They would stay at the Lexor on the strip, and she had booked two rooms at a hotel near Donna's house. She had left the return trip wide open and figured they would find a hotel in Williams for the night after spending some time at the Grand Canyon and Monument Valley. Laughlin would be their last stop, and from there, they would head home. "Yes, we are going to Vegas. You will love it. We'll spend one night there. Play the slots and walk the strip and head out in the morning."

Three days later, Stuart and Dwayne put the last of the luggage in the car, and Dwayne shook Stuart's hand. "Now you take care of these two girls, okay, and I'll see you all when you get back."

"I won't let anything happen to them," Stuart replied with a nod.

Dwayne turned to Tammy, who was rooting through her purse next to the car for her keys. She smiled and pulled them out of her purse. "Found them," she yelled in triumph.

Dwayne pulled her into his arms and kissed her hard on the lips. "I'm going to miss you. Call me every chance you can and be careful out there. I'm going to be worried about you."

Tammy patted him on his chest." I'll be fine. Don't worry, okay. I'm going to miss you too. I wish you were going with us."

"I do too." He kissed her again. "Now go on, get in, and I'll get the gate."

"Bye. I love you," she said before stepping into the car and starting the engine.

Dwayne watched from the driveway and waved as then descended the road. Tammy looked in her rearview mirror until she could no longer see him and then looked at Jenny sitting in the back seat. "The road trip has begun. Fasten your seat belts; you are in for a long ride." She laughed.

Stuart, who was sitting in the front, laughed. "What have I gotten myself into—you three girls together. This is going to be interesting."

"**M**y God, I've never seen anything like it," Jenny said as they walked the Vegas strip later that evening. "It's after nine, and it's still bloody hot out," she laughed. "And with all these lights, you'd never know it was nighttime unless you looked up at the sky."

Tammy laughed at her sister, who looked like a kid at Disneyland. Her eyes were wide, and her smile was big. "And there are no clocks in Vegas," Tammy added.

Jenny creased her brow. "There aren't. Why?"

"Because they want you to lose all track of time and just keep gambling."

"Really! Wow, those crafty buggers. Well, they are not getting any more of my money." Jenny announced. "I couldn't believe all those people sitting at the slot machines, and they just kept feeding the machines with money. How much were they spending?" Jenny asked.

"A lot," Tammy chuckled.

"Well, I spent $10.00. That's enough for me," Jenny said adamantly.

"Yes, and you won $10.00, so you broke even."

"Yes, I did," Jenny said with pride as she continued to look in awe at all the bright lights and everything Vegas offered. "I can't believe all these people. It's crowded."

"Yep. It's the city that never sleeps." Tammy glanced at her watch, "But I'm ready to call it a night. I want to be on the road early tomorrow."

"Sounds good to me," Stuart said. "This place is wearing me out."

After a hearty breakfast and a few last plays on the slots, they were back on the road by seven but soon made a detour when they came upon the Valley of Fire National State Park. "Oh, I've always wanted to see that place." Tammy squealed as she hit the brakes and skidded off to the side of the road with a dust trail on her tail.

"Hey, steady on their lass," Stuart said from the back seat.

Tammy laughed. "Do you guys want to go check it out?"

"I'd love to," Jenny said.

"Great. This is what road trips are all about—exploring. This place is supposed to be amazing. We'll spend half a day here. What do you say?"

The detour was just what they needed after the hustle and bustle of Vegas. It was peaceful, refreshing, and beautiful. The views and rock formations were spectacular. "God, I'm so glad we stopped here," Tammy said while taking one last look at the breathtaking views of the valley. "I want to bring Dwayne here. I don't think he has ever been here."

It was after ten in the evening when Tammy had to pull into a gas station to refuel. They were about two hours away from where Donna lived, and Tammy called her to give her an update. "Hey, Donna, we are almost there. But we took a detour and won't arrive until around midnight. So I figured we'd check into the hotel and come see you in the morning."

"Wow. You are almost here. Yes, that would be fine. I don't think I can stay awake for another two hours," she laughed. "Hey, Tammy, why am I so nervous about seeing you guys? I've been a nervous wreck all day."

"I think we all are. Jenny was saying the same thing. It's been over thirty-five years since we've all seen each other. God, I wish mom could have been with us."

Donna released a heavy sigh. "Me too. It breaks my heart when I see the pictures Jenny sends me. She used to be so full of life. I miss her, Tammy."

"We all do, Donna. It's one of the reasons why we are doing this. For mom. Jenny is going to take home a picture of all three of us together and put it next to mom's bed."

"Okay, well, I'm about to cry now. I can't wait to see you and hug you both. I'll see you in the morning. Love you."

"Love you too. Bye."

Tammy hung up the phone and choked back her tears. In less than twenty-hours, she and her sisters would be reunited after thirty-five years. She couldn't wrap her head around it. For years she had been thinking about this moment, and now it was finally about to happen. She smiled at the thought and returned to her car.

"So, are you ready?" Tammy asked Jenny over their breakfast in the hotel.

"As ready as I'll ever be," Jenny replied before taking a sip of her coffee. "I can't believe I'm going to see her. I never thought I would." She said as she tried to steady her trembling hand. "Look at me. I can't stop shaking."

Tammy rested her hand on Jenny's. "I know me neither. I have butterflies in my stomach, and it's churning so much from my nerves. I feel like I'm going to throw up."

"Jenny had a hard time sleeping last night," Stuart said. "She worried that she and Donna wouldn't get along."

Tammy looked surprised. "Why would you think that?"

Jenny shrugged her shoulders. "I don't know. I guess I'm being silly. But you remember how we always used to fight when we were kids."

Tammy laughed. "Jenny, that was a long time ago, and like you just said, you were kids. You're a grown woman now. I don't think Donna is going to chase after you and pull out chunks of your hair like she used to."

Jenny laughed. "I guess you're right. But still, She's a stranger to me. I just hope I like her."

Tammy chugged down the last of her coffee. "Well, there's only one way to find out. Are you ready?"

Jenny and Stuart finished their drinks while Tammy made a quick call to Donna. "Hey, Donna, we're on our way. We'll be there in ten minutes."

"Wow, I can't believe it. I'm so nervous."

"We all are. See you soon."

When Tammy turned onto Donna's street, she felt the tears pool in her eyes. She strained to see the road ahead. Her sweaty palms slipped on the steering wheel so much that she had to wipe them on her jeans. She took short, deep breaths to calm her racing heart that beat beneath her chest, but it was no use. She heard Jenny whisper to Stuart in the back seat where they sat together holding hands. "How do I look?" she asked him.

"You look beautiful," he replied.

Tammy took a deep breath and swallowed hard to remove the

lump wedged in her throat. "How are you doing, Jenny?" she asked as she looked at her through the rearview mirror.

"I'm not sure. I'm shaking all over. I hope I can get out of the car."

Tammy had to search for Donna's house. She had moved since her last visit when Jason was sick. She slowed down to read the numbers of the houses and soon spotted it on the left. Tears streamed down her face. She laid into the horn and wound down her window.

"What are you doing?" Jenny yelled while covering her ears with her hands.

"I'm letting Donna know we are here. It's been a hell of a long time, and I want to make a bloody entrance." Tammy laughed and hollered out the window as she turned into her driveway. "Donna! Donna!" she screamed with tears gushing down her face.

Within seconds the front door opened, and Donna came running out with her husband that Tammy had yet to meet, following close behind. "Oh my god! I can't believe it! You are here." She screamed with her arms wide open as she raced towards the car.

Tammy was the first to exit the car and raced over to Donna and hugged her hard. "We made it. I can't believe it either." She turned and looked towards the car and watched Jenny step out. "And look, here is Jenny."

Jenny wiped her eyes and laughed hard. "Hello, Donna."

Tammy stepped aside and watched as her two sisters raced into each other's arms and embraced. They wrapped their arms tight around each other with tears flowing down their cheeks. "Thirty-five frigging years. I can't believe you are here." Donna cried and squeezed her tighter.

"Me neither. Oh, Donna, I've thought about this moment for so many years. Wondering if it would ever happen." Jenny said between her many tears.

Tammy looked on and smiled, unable to keep up with the

continuous flood of her own tears. Finally, they were all together —the three sisters separated by divorce and an ocean so many years ago. Tammy walked over to her sisters, and each one opened their arms to let the other one in. For the next few minutes, they held each other tight and cried while the two husbands looked on with tears in their eyes too. Together they whispered. "We did it, mom. We are together. Just like you had wished for."

After the emotional reunion, Donna led them into her home, and the first thing Jenny saw was a picture of mom sitting on the mantel. She walked over and picked it up. "I remember this day. It was Christmas dinner at my house about five years ago. Look how beautiful she looked."

Tammy and Donna approached her and stood on either side and stared at the picture of the mom they knew and had now lost. "How I wished we had done this sooner," Tammy said in a somber voice.

"I would like to think mom knows we are together. I told her before we left, and when I go home, I'm going to share everything with her and show her the pictures."

"I believe she does," Tammy agreed.

"Me too," Donna said with a nod.

Tammy pulled away from her sisters. You know, all my life, I've procrastinated on stuff that I've regretted later, like Dwayne and I building our house. None of our parents got to see it. We finally reunited, but mom is not here to witness it. I waited to visit dad's house in Ireland until after his death. I'm done procrastinating. I've thought about writing a book for years, but I've been too afraid to start it because I don't think it will be good enough for the literary world. I have so much that I want to share. I want to give others hope, and I want to tell people to chase their dreams and never give up, and then there is the price to pay if you procrastinate.

Jenny and Donna looked on with wide eyes as Tammy took a

stand and told them about a dream she'd had been keeping to herself.

"When I get home, I'm going to start writing it. There will be no more procrastinating in my life, and I'm going to call it Reckless Beginnings. And I will dedicate it to mom and dad."

A LETTER FROM THE AUTHOR

When I first had the idea to write Reckless Beginnings over thirty years ago, I intended to write one book. I had a strong message of HOPE for others that might find themselves caught up in the web of an addict. As you can see, I had a lot more to say after Reckless Beginnings was published.

I also received many emails from readers asking what happened to Tammy after her life with Steven. Soon after, Better Endings was born, a story about chasing dreams and never giving up—another strong message. It was a fun story to write. It bought back some wonderful memories of my fishing days, and I am thrilled that it won the Readers' Favorite gold medal award for Best Fiction Adventure 2020.

Prior to these two books being published, a magical event happened in my life, which you read about in this book, The Reunions—my sisters and I were finally reunited after thirty-five years but not without sacrifices and regrets. The regrets of procrastination weigh heavy on me regarding this special reunion and many other things that I finally got around to doing but waited too long to do.

Writing the final book in the series made me realize just how precious our lives are and that we should make every day count. Live it to the fullest and enjoy every moment. Don't sweat about the small stuff, and be thankful for another glorious day.

Where I am today:

I never in my wildest dreams would have thought that my debut novel Reckless Beginnings would take me on such an incredible journey. The Reunions will be my sixth book since Reckless Beginnings was launched in 2018. It's been an amazing ride, and I can't wait to bring you more stories.

The Reunions is the final book in the Tammy Mellows series, which, as many of you know, is based on my life. Maybe in another ten years, I will have a few more chapters to write. But in the meantime, I thought I would bring you up to date.

I'm happy to say I have been cancer-free for ten years and continue to get checked every year—(Ladies, get your mammograms). My husband and I still live in the mountains in the house we built from the ground up, and hubby is still a falconer. We are now proud grandparents of two wonderful grandsons. My son is still a fishing fool and fishes every chance he gets.

Sadly my mother passed away in October 2019 from dementia. She is at peace now, and I know she is watching over her daughters with pride.

To My Readers:

I would not be where I am today without my readers. It is because of you and your continued support that I enjoy creating stories. I get excited when I write them, and I'm anxious to bring them to you. You are an amazing group of people that makes this author feel good about her work. So thank you to those I am mentioning and the many others that have read my work. I'm sorry I couldn't mention all of you:

Pamela Grant Provence (the best sister-in-law), Jennifer Dobos-Bubno (my awesome niece) Pat Shupinski Fayo, Jennifer Bryan-Vawser, Pam Shear Vogt, Ruth Benson, Agnes Shapiro, Darlene Johnson, Gloria Marchegiano Seevers, Bambi Rathman, Janet Weisbred, Virgie Lane, Christina Mages, Cathy Friedland Yahiaoui, Lori Chasko, Bea Followhill, Gloria Youngbauer, Sylvia Dominick, Heather Oman, Rachel Blackburn, Susan Campton, Teresa Moyer, Laura Mclendon, Jazmine FA, Nancy Gorman Schadd, Dainelle Williams, Tammy Powell, Nancy Reed Legowsky, Donna Land Dobbs, Tina Myers, Christine Davis, Michele Ann Wate, Christine Close, Lecha Haney, Reena Agarwal Gilja, Dyana Hulgan, Debbie Felkner Carney, Barbara L. Waloven, Kay Enderline, Dana Duplantis, Amy Weaver, Lisa Murray, Denise Burt, Pauline Grime, Peggy Patterson, Karen Wright.

The author and book community is an amazing group of people I am proud to be a part of. I am thankful for the great friendships I have with not only readers but also many authors. Many, I consider close friends. We support each other, and I think in a way, we all know that if need be, we will listen when times are hard or not going our way. They will encourage us, read our work, and give us valuable feedback. We are not in a competition; we are a family. Thank you for your friendship to those I have mentioned below and to all the others whose paths I have crossed with. I highly suggest you check out these author's books:

Sharon Gloger Friedman, Erina Bridget Ring, C. M. Santoro, G.C Allen, Beth Worsdell, Carol Koris, Anne Perreault, Susan Schild,

Annette Glahn, Maria Henriksen, Carmina Levergne, Barbara Josselsohn, Jill Hannah Anderson, Kerry Anne King, Marcie Keithley,

I hope you enjoyed the final book in the Tammy Mellows series and will continue to read my future books.

Until next time: happy reading.

Love

Tina

xoxo

ABOUT THE AUTHOR

ABOUT THE AUTHOR

Tina Hogan Grant loves to write stories with strong female characters that know what they want and aren't afraid to chase their dreams. She loves to write sexy and sometimes steamy romances with happy ever after endings.

She is living life to the fullest in a small mountain community in Southern California with her husband and two dogs. When she is not writing she is probably riding her ATV, kayaking or hiking with her best friend – her husband of twenty-five years.

www.tinahogangrant.com